Luana Xavier Pinto Coelho / Lorena Melgaço Silva Marques /
Regina Orvañanos Murguía (eds.)
Mundus Urbano: (Re)thinking urban development

Luana Xavier Pinto Coelho / Lorena Melgaço Silva Marques /
Regina Orvañanos Murguía (eds.)

Mundus Urbano: (Re)thinking urban development

Editorial Coordination:
Luana Xavier Pinto Coelho
Lorena Melgaço Silva Marques
Regina Orvañanos Murguía

Reviewers and Language Editors:
Kari Smith
Lorena Melgaço Silva Marques
Alexander White
Carolina Guimaraes

Layout:
Regina Orvañanos Murguía
Greta Sanches Correa
Ana Eugenia Ureña Chaves

Cover image:
Jose Luis Chong

ISBN 978-3-86596-532-5

© Frank & Timme GmbH Verlag für wissenschaftliche Literatur
Berlin 2013. Alle Rechte vorbehalten.

No part of this publication may be reproduced or transmitted in any form or by any means, electronic, or mechanical, including photocopy, recording or any information storage and retrieval system without permission in writing to the publisher.

Das Werk einschließlich aller Teile ist urheberrechtlich geschützt. Jede Verwertung außerhalb der engen Grenzen des Urheberrechtsgesetzes ist ohne Zustimmung des Verlags unzulässig und strafbar. Das gilt insbesondere für Vervielfältigungen, Übersetzungen, Mikroverfilmungen und die Einspeicherung und Verarbeitung in elektronischen Systemen.

Herstellung durch das atelier eilenberger, Taucha bei Leipzig.
Printed in Germany.
Gedruckt auf säurefreiem, alterungsbeständigem Papier.

www.frank-timme.de

CONTENTS

(Re)thinking urban development: Preface
Ugur, Lauren — VII

CHAPTER I

Socio-cultural production and urban space: Introduction
Prof. Dr. Rapoport, Amos — 3

Heritage forgetting-remember dynamics in Liberia's historic centre
Ureña Chaves, Ana Eugenia — 9

The role of architectural cultural heritage in postwar recovery. Case study: Bosnia and Herzegovina
Varatanovic-Guso, Alma — 21

Using information and communication technologies to foster social encounters
Melgaço Silva Marques, Lorena — 31

Appraisal of the effects of non-performing policies. Housing development in a new planned city, Naya Raipur, India
Rajasekharan, Rajesh — 43

CHAPTER II

Urban governance and social challenges in planning. Old themes for new realities: Introduction
Prof. Britto Pólvora, Jacqueline — 57

Social media: a new tool for public organisations
Guimaraes, Carolina — 63

Participatory budgeting in South America and Europe: a social inclusion perspective
Xavier Pinto Coelho, Luana — 73

An eternal spring for the "Jasmine" revolution? Governance and corruption in Tunisia and the democratic revolution in Middle East and North Africa (MENA)
Lim, Hui Ling — 85

The wall, the door, and the key: resilience, education and planning in segregated urban communities
Smith, Kari — 95

CHAPTER III

Contemporary planning and cooperating in the south: Introduction
Prof. Yang, Guiqing — 107

A tool for bridging the formal-informal divide in São Paulo
Sanches Correa, Greta — 111

Understanding the needs of urban poor: case study of vp singh camp, a slum settlement in Delhi, India
Saharan, Tara — 123

Disappearing cities: the case of the refugee settlements
Orvañanos Murguía, Regina — 133

The political economy and strategies of international development cooperation. A case of agricultural sector in Bangladesh
Rahman, AKM Fazlur — 145

CHAPTER IV

Sustainable urban infrastructure and disaster risk reduction: Introduction
Prof. Dijkgraaf, Cor — 157

Urban planning approach to urban flooding. The Ho Chi Minh City case study
Huynh, Le Hai Chau — 159

Approach towards sustainable management of watershed areas in dry climatic conditions. Lima, Peru
Poblet Alegre, Rossana — 173

Strategic approach to prevent future disasters in risk prone areas. Case study: Lima's hillsides
Chong Chong, José Luis — 187

Infrastructure for development: urban infrastructure, *shari'ah*-compliant investments and development bank membership
White, Alexander — 199

(RE)THINKING URBAN DEVELOPMENT: PREFACE

Ugur, Lauren

Global urbanisation is one of the most dynamic and challenging processes being faced by the contemporary world, as more and more people join the ranks as urban citizens each day. We increasingly live, work and interact within our rapidly changing urban environments, boasting as much challenge as they do potential. It is the unpredictability of the modern urban milieu, which fascinates us most and forces us to recognise opportunity in developing innovative, practical and of course sustainable development solutions for the future of our professional playground – the city.

(Re)thinking Urban Development is a publication developed in the spirit of innovation, originality and advancement, as the perspectives of interdisciplinary, multi-national students are drawn together to produce a new look at some of the most current issues testing our urban experiences.

The requirement to re-think implies inadequacy and this is exactly what our young, internationally experienced graduates aim to address. The identification of what previously went wrong, what may have worked well and what might work better in the future is what the process of re-thinking involves and the challenges with which we, as urban development planners, are being faced provides the physical reality that new and innovative approaches to urban development are crucial in order to create and develop cities in which we all can and want to live.

The ever prominent and increasing challenges facing cities throughout the world calls not just for a process of re-thinking but also for a re-structuring and re-education on how these forceful challenges can be approached within very diverse urban settings, across the so-called developed and "developing" world. A re-thinking of urban development and the ways in which we approach planning obstacles is only possible through pioneering the education of young professionals from a diverse range of backgrounds resulting in a far broader range of views and ideas that contribute to developing more workable solutions than ever before. It is when these differing and sometimes opposing concepts and experiences come together that highly innovative solutions to incredibly complicated urban puzzles can be realised in order to ensure, not just workable, but innovative and sustainable solutions.

Ours is no longer a world in which it suffices to blindly replicate previously successful examples of urban development. Dynamic, contextual shifts, constantly being driven by various global forces are ubiquitous and need to be both understood in contextual isolation as well as part of the global "bigger picture" so to say. Through publications such as this, our alumni work towards bridging the gap between an interdisciplinary education and the variety of practical challenges existent in urban contexts. This book encompasses such topics and addresses such challenges in a variety of urban settings as their academic research aims to present viable conclusions, drawing on real and very current urban challenges.

(Re)thinking Urban Development is a starting point for the process of experienced graduates to explore, express and implement their ideas aimed towards addressing urban challenges with a new perspective and creativity. Some solutions will be outrageously successful while others will need to once again be re-thought and re-moulded but it is this kind of publication that forms the basis and sews the seeds from which the future of urban development and planning as a profession will evolve.

On a personal note, I am honoured to have been a part of this publication process, not just because I believe that re-thinking what we do is a fundamental part in developing our purpose but because I have had the experience of being able to work closely over the past couple of years with such an inspirational and motivated group of international professionals whom have brought with them a diverse wealth of knowledge that I would not have been able to benefit from in any other setting.

As the 2009-2011 Mundus Urbano group moves forward I wish each and every one of them only the best for successful, productive careers. Whatever path you choose, keep in mind that, as Gandhi once said, you must *be the change* you wish to see in the world.

Mundus Urbano: (re) thinking urban development

INTRODUCTION

(re) penser le développment urbain . (ri) pensare lo sviluppo urbano . (re) thinking urban development . (re) pensando el desarrollo urbano . Stadtentwicklung (um) denken . (re) pensando o desenvolvimento urbano . penilaian semula pembangunan bandar

CHAPTER I

SOCIO-CULTURAL PRODUCTION AND URBAN SPACE

Prof. Dr. Amos Rapoport
Ana Eugenia Ureña Chaves
Alma Varatanovic-Guso
Lorena Melgaço Silva Marques
Rajesh Rajasekharan

SOCIO-CULTURAL PRODUCTION AND URBAN SPACE: INTRODUCTION

Prof. Dr. Rapoport, Amos[1]

The growth and development of any field depends on continuity. The future of Environment-Behaviour Studies (EBS) generally and culture-environment relations specifically depends on whether and how students will carry on the work of the past 40 years. It is therefore encouraging and gratifying that the students of the Erasmus Mundus Master course have undertaken the present project. I am delighted to have been asked to write this introduction on culture and urban space.

I begin with a few important general points I have made previously. First, 'culture' as such is too abstract and general to be used – it is not possible to relate it to the environment. To make is usable, to operationalise it, it needs to be dismantled into specific expressions and components. Note that dismantling is a general process and that 'environment' (among other concepts) also needs to be dismantled.

In the use of 'culture,' a major dismantling dealing with its excessive abstractness considers social variables separately as a set of less abstract, more concrete and potentially observable social expressions. It follows that the term 'socio-cultural' may not be helpful. The social expressions of culture such as kinship, status, identity, institutions, etc., unlike culture, can be considered separately and related to specific aspects of environment (also dismantled, e.g. as the organisation of space, time, meaning and communication; systems of settings; cultural landscapes consisting of fixed, semi-fixed and non-fixed features; etc.).

In response to the excessive breadth and generality of culture, it needs to be dismantled into ever more specific components such as world views, values, ideals, images, schemata, meanings, norms, standards, rules, expectations and especially lifestyles and activity systems which can relatively easily be related to aspects of the environment.

---

1 Distinguished Professor in the School of Architecture and Urban Planning at University of Wisconsin–Milwaukee, USA. Author of many books and articles, among them the book House, Form & Culture. One of the founders of the field of Environment-Behaviour Studies (EBS).

These steps are, I believe, essential in order to make 'culture' usable, i.e. in making it operational.

It should be noted that most of the literature on culture-environment relations (including my earlier work) has been concerned primarily with arguing for the importance of culture, trying to demonstrate it through examples, mainly cross-cultural comparisons of differences among groups and environments and trying to explain this variability, e.g. by dismantling activities and emphasizing the importance of their latent aspects (i.e. meaning) as very important functions.

As a result, culture may sometimes have been overemphasised and the impression created that it was the only (or the most important) variable. This was never the intention, this being as unlikely as the view that culture has no impact and can, therefore, be ignored.

At that point this was reasonable because culture was neglected in EBS, as was also the case in other fields (e.g. economics, business, medicine, psychiatry, the military, etc.). These fields have also become aware of the relevance of culture.

Clearly, its importance is somewhere between these two extremes, its importance generally or, in my given case, is an empirical question. It may (and probably does) vary with type of environment, scale, for different groups, different situations, in different contexts, etc.

This needs further research and I therefore turn to some suggestions about the nature of such future research emphasizing aspects that have been neglected.

This research needs to fill a major gap, not only in culture-environment relations but EBS generally – the lack of synthesis, conceptual frameworks and theory. Without these the wheel is constantly being reinvented, there is no progress and the mass of scattered empirical work is difficult if not impossible to use and may actually become counterproductive. With their development much material can be compressed and become manageable. In doing such research it is imperative not only to synthesise existing work but constantly be aware of, refer to and use new material and developments not only in EBS but in many (new) disciplines/fields, which become relevant at some level of abstraction, which conceptual frameworks and theory both make possible and demand.

I pointed out earlier that work on culture and environment emphasised differences and variability. It is important to realise that this variability may not be as extreme as it seems, which also makes culture more useable. There is much recent work in a number of fields that suggests that there are human universals, there is human nature and that even apparently variable aspects may be the expression of constants. If that is indeed the case, and I believe it is, it reduces the "search space," makes it easier to study and apply culture and needs to be incorporated into any research programme.

Related to this and the empirical study of the role of culture is the need to consider the relative importance of culture and other variables in EBS. This, in turn, implies a new kind of comparative work (which remains essential) moving from cross-cultural studies to studies of how all variables interact, making culture-environment relations an integral part of EBS.

In other words, there is a need for research that examines the joint effects of culture and other variables (economics, technology, politics, perception, cognition and way-finding, climate, resources, etc.) and their relative importance. It is encouraging that, in a way (albeit implicitly and not jointly), this book is aware of this. There is a need to begin to build more comprehensive, realistic, multi-variable models emphasizing the joint effects of all relevant variables.

In reviewing the literature on culture and environment, it is striking that almost all the work deals with housing, the residential environment. This was reasonable as a starting point because housing is the most responsive to culture and it is useful to begin with clear-cut examples. It is, however, important to begin to study the non-residential environment. The few attempts of which I am aware (a systematic review would be useful) to relate culture to office buildings, universities, airports, hospitals, etc., mainly in terms of cultural identity, have not been successful. This is partly because they are new types of settings responding to new activities and requirements which by their nature are less variable.

It may, however be partly a matter of scale. Whereas office buildings may neither need nor be able to respond to cultural variables, there is evidence that culture may be important in how offices and other settings are organised. This also seems to be the case with settings within, e.g. consular offices and hospitals. In the latter, for example, patient rooms may be strongly related to culture whereas operating rooms, laboratories, etc. are not.

Note that housing, if properly defined for cross-cultural work as a system of settings within which certain systems of activities take place, begins to overlap with the urban environment. What I call the house-settlement system inevitably includes what may be considered the non-residential environment – neighbourhoods and settings within them, urban spaces, etc. This makes the study of urban environments a useful starting point as it 'straddles' the boundary between the residential and non-residential environments.

Scale may also play a role in the study of culture and the urban environment. It seems to be the case that, considered globally, cities seem to be becoming more alike as they seem to respond to images of modernity, economics, politics, technology (e.g. transportation), etc. This, however, is occurring at large scales. The urban landscape is a particular type of cultural landscape and can be understood in terms of frameworks and infill. It can be suggested that the former are similar or the same with no (or little) cultural impact. This also is an empirical question but, since people live in these smaller units, these may respond to culture.

It also seems that even in the case of housing there is increasing uniformity. In many countries, with development and increasing affluence (i.e. starting with elites) housing becomes more similar, with the suburban image dominating. This may be partly due to constraints more than wants. There are also cultural reversals as groups try to maintain or recapture their cultural identity. While the role of the urban environment in this needs research, I have hypothesised that the infill, the smaller urban units, can be variable, more traditional and respond to lifestyles, activities, etc. of inhabitants – of the many (and increasing) number of different groups that live in cities. It can further be suggested that, in this connection, the semi-fixed features of the environment (e.g. signs, neons, 'furnishing') play a major role. This demands open-endedness which is critical not only in the framework/infill at large scales but also in the infill itself. This then allows for modernisation in place in response to changing standards, cultural supportiveness as culture (or populations) change, the expressions of cultural identity, etc. Moreover, even as all these change, they will retain their variable local character. This view of the city also increases perceptual and experiential richness and complexity as one moves among these different smaller units.

This, combined with constancy, human universals, etc. makes possible learning (not copying) from traditional and spontaneous settlements. Learning from the full range of environments about which we know or can learn is essential. These are an invaluable resource, a record of how humans have created and used environments, why and how, their successes and failures, the nature and reasons for differences and similarities. This resource has been neglected and could teach us much. It offers a most important area for research.

References

Rapoport, A. (2008) 'Some further thoughts on culture and environments' *International Journal of Architectural Research*, Vol 2, Issue 1, March, pp. 16-39, [Online], Available: http://archnet.org [15 Mar 2012].

_____ (2005) *Culture, Architecture and Design*, Chicago, Lock Science.

_____ (1997) 'The nature and role of neighborhoods' *Urban Design Studies*, Vol 3, pp. 93-118, London, School of Architecture and Landscape, University of Greenwich.

_____ (1984) 'Culture and the urban order', in J. Agnew, J. Mercer and D. Sopher (eds) *The City in Cultural Context*, Boston, Allen and Unwin, p 50-75.

_____ (2000) 'Theory, housing and culture', Housing, Theory and Society, Vol 17, No 4, pp. 145-165.

_____ (1986) 'The use and design of open spaces in urban neighborhoods', in D. Frick (Ed) *The Quality of Urban Life*, Berlin, Walter de Gruyter, pp. 159-175.

_____ (1990) History and Precedent in *Environmental Design*, New York, Plenum Press.

_____ (2002) 'The role of neighborhoods in the success of cities' *Ekistics*, Vol 69, No 415-417, July-Dec, pp. 145-151.

_____ (2006) 'Local environments in a global context' *Ekistics*, Vol 73, No 436-441, Jan-Dec, pp. 122-131.

HERITAGE FORGETTING-REMEMBER DYNAMICS IN LIBERIA'S HISTORIC CENTRE

Ureña Chaves, Ana Eugenia[1]

Abstract

This article reflects upon the socio-cultural meanings of urban heritage for the community of Liberia, Costa Rica in the context of a debate about the *Puente Real*'s conservation or demolition and replacement. The concept of heritage is discussed as a social construction, place-making process and identity building phenomenon, but also as an urban development matter that depends on political decisions.

The potential of inclusive heritage management of Liberia's Historic Centre through local participation is explored in workshops with local teenagers. This methodology is analysed and recommended as a complement to a value-centred approach.

Keywords: Urban Heritage, Liberia, Place, Teenagers, Participation, Social Construction, Urban Development

---

1 M.Sc. International Cooperation and Urban Development; Technische Universität Darmstadt. Germany. Architecture and Urbanism, Instituto Tecnológico de Costa Rica, San José, Costa Rica

Introduction

Liberia's late colonial 49 block Historic Centre in Guanacaste, Costa Rica presents a controversial situation regarding Urban Heritage Management. While the local government proposes to replace the *Puente Real* (a historic 1907 bridge in the city of Liberia); the *Comandancia* (old military headquarters) is being restored and rehabilitated to become Guanacaste's Museum and Cultural Centre. In reaction to the Municipality's decision, some community members and cultural organisations have protested in opposition to the demolition of the bridge. Consequently, between 2009 and 2011 the *Puente Real* has been a topic of discussion in Costa Rican newspapers.

Contrasting bibliographic research (Landscape Urbanism, 2011) with site visits one can observe that the rapid economic growth the region has experienced for the last 10 to 20 years is expressed in the local culture and built environment. Some sites and monuments have been destroyed, many modified. Liberia's scenario leads one to question: does Urban Heritage in Liberia's Historic Centre still have a relevant meaning for the local community? Does the *Puente Real* have a meaning for the citizens of Liberia? Is it disappearing from the citizen's memory? If it is, why shouldn't it be replaced? Why does the development of a cultural centre at the *Comandancia* have population acceptance and government support while the *Puente Real* doesn't? Are these buildings relevant for the further urban development of Liberia?

Without disregarding professional and technical inputs to urban heritage management, this paper contrasts the meaning of urban heritage for Liberia's community with the local government's approach; in which the values and potential of urban heritage as raw material to construct local, regional and global identity is being overlooked. A critical discussion on the Historic Centre's management is complemented with the results of a consultation exercise to a specific segment of the citizens, a group of teenagers.

Understanding urban heritage

The multidisciplinary nature of heritage produces a wide range of definitions. Heritage in this paper is understood as a social construction (Prats, 1997). As a process instead of an object, a result of the continuous social attribution of symbolic meanings to an artistic, ethnologic, architectonic or intangible object from the past. Heritage exists in the present, it is not a memory, but rather the contemporary identities assigned to a memory by today's social groups (Dormaels, 2010). However, heritage is also understood as a market product selected by demand criteria. Ashworth and Larkham (1994) define heritage as a commodified product that selects resources of the past to construct contemporary products that satisfy the socioeconomic demands of the population. This process of transforming selected resources into "products" is the *making of* heritage or *heritagisation*.

Both definitions view heritage as a contemporary social creation strongly determined by the present context and with the potential of acquiring and giving different meanings in the future. The monument, space or practice in the collective memory being interpreted as heritage or as a symbol of identity is simply the object that receives relevant meaning from the individuals. Whether heritage is a commodified product or an identity symbol depends on how and by whom it is interpreted.

Heritage, as a product of practices and processes of negotiation, shapes local identities while attributing meanings to an object or practice. Even though, a heritage process depends on political power, it is also on social demand. In today's society, *heritagisation* is a deliberate way in which culture is shaped (Prats, 2005; R. Mason, 2006).

Parallel to art in public spaces, heritage is now playing a more dynamic and interactive role in the urban scenarios. Conservation of towns and neighbourhoods over individual buildings becomes an urban planning matter and the treatment of historic places depends on land use priorities and decisions as well as the planning capacities of each community and its government.

In the particular case of urban landscapes, the inhabitants and visitors determine and are simultaneously influenced by the public spaces and buildings framing them. Heritage, just as art, cannot be interpreted without context, and context is always changing. Objects' meanings are defined all together by place, time, author or beholder (Bourdieu, 1979). As Vinken (2011, p.4) points out: "*Urban spaces are not merely the products of architectonic processes, of mutable social actions and attribution. Rather, they inform the social actions performed on and with them*".

Public space is the context where individuals attribute meanings through everyday experiences to objects and practices, a community influences the object and the object meanings are influenced simultaneously by the community. Tying this phenomenon with Setha Low's definition of place, as a space with cultural meaning that provides a scenario for social interaction and cultural processes to happen (Low, 1994); it can be affirm that *heritagisation* is actually a place making process where public spaces become meaningful heritage places.

Even though urban heritage is a public concern, its management is not always carried out by the community. Heritage is usually selected and activated by those with technical, administrative and political power. Therefore, a disconnection appears between those officially qualified to manage heritage and the protagonists of the space, those who attribute meanings to objects and practices. This gap is precisely what is generating conflict in Liberia.

Theories in both heritage and place propose that through participation and a value-centred approach the local needs and wants can become part of the selection and interpretation processes of heritage (Manzo & Perkins, 2006). Including these approaches into the heritage management practice would not only guide the urban planning process but it would also nurture community identity and therefore multiply the local engagement with the general urban development.

Selection and activation of Liberia's heritage

Having set a theoretical base, one is now able to tackle the questions triggered by Liberia's controversies in order to answer the introductory inquiries. There is no doubt of the presence, in quality and quantity, of meaningful objects and practices in the central neighbourhoods of Liberia; however, it has not been fully valued by the local authorities nor by some of the property owners.

The 2001 official inventory (Centro de investigación y conservación del patrimonio cultural, 2001) identifies those constructions with certain values in Liberia. The inventory recognises only some of the values existing in the historic centre: architectonic, historic and environmental while disregarding citizen's usage of the space. By doing so, once again a gap is opened between the past and the present; the Cultural Heritage Research and Conservation Centre is only evaluating preceding characteristics of an object in opposition to contemporary values. With time the original intentions and lectures of an object dilute and transform. Buildings, sites and traditional practices contain several symbolic meanings for the community that go beyond the historic or aesthetic values identified by the research centre. Also in the official inventory, the evaluation of the heritage worth considers that the level of transformations influences the cultural meaning of an object. This means for example, that if a building has been modified through time, it loses its cultural relevance. This object-centred consideration contradicts the view of heritage as a process. Physical transformations also have meanings; they are the material expression of a cultural, economic or technical change in a society. The Heritage Research and Conservation Centre must incorporate contemporary uses of the historic object into their interpretation of heritage if they aim to share a legacy from the past with future generations. If present values are not taking into consideration for a heritage assessment, any conservation or redevelopment efforts won't effectively strengthen the community's identities. If Urban Heritage is disappearing from the memory of the people of Liberia, here one cause is found. The local government doesn't perceive historic buildings as *"storehouses of collective memory"* (Vinken 2011); they are managed just as properties, as disconnected empty objects without any significant cultural added value. But still, the community claims its right to remember.

Citizen perspective; workshops with teenagers

In order to evaluate and debate the authority's heritage selection in contrast with the community's perception; the author conducted a series of consultation activities with a group of local teenagers. In opposition with the Heritage Research and Conservation Centre inventory, the most significant information regarding Liberia's Historic Centre's contemporary reality was discovered through two workshops carried out with a group of the community: 40 students between 12 – 13 years on April 2011. The methodology employed was based on Rosibel Víquez's (2006) methodology for working on teenagers' perceptions of public spaces.

The workshop as an instrument for studying citizen perception on heritage has great potential for both research and educational purposes. In this particular case, working with teenagers presented two interesting insights: (1) the unique perspectives teenager's may offer in these spaces, given that they socialise on daily bases in this context and (2) the researcher's interest in tapping into the new generation's view on heritage. It is important to note here that the findings of the workshops represent the perception of just one of the many social groups living in Liberia. Further research in this context and topic should also consider other collectives – elderly, migrants, women, etc.

First, the participants were asked to form groups, to graphically represent the Historic Centre and to identify certain distinctive features in it. The Mario Cañas Ruiz park (town's central park) and the contemporary church in front of it occupy a predominant position in the plans; they were the starting point of most of the drawings and by far the most detailed one, including the surrounding urban furniture. Also, even though the students were not requested to draw the park next to the late colonial chapel, in most of the cases they represented it and even with more detail than the chapel. The maintenance conditions of both parks are not ideal; however they are often visited (experienced) by the teenagers. In a questionnaire answered individually by the students after the drawing exercise, the Mario Cañas Ruiz park also was mentioned by 9 students as a place they consider valuable and interesting. Vinken states that the power of a monument lies on its ability to attract new meanings over its authenticity (Víquez, 2011). The park, previously a *plaza* is for the teenagers a monument. In other words for this group of Liberian teenagers, the park is the public space where they spend more time and it is for them the most valuable place in the Historic Centre. From this place in particular they get to know the rest of the Historic Centre.

In the individual questionnaire, eight features between practices, monuments and places were described (name and picture). The students answered whether the selected features presented were recognisable – meaning they remember them – and valuable to themselves. They also had to identify one or more values for each of the features and express how each feature could be better used or preserved.

Those elements recognised the most (*Marimba, Tope* and *Ermita de la Agonía*) were also identified by the majority as the most valuable. For example, the *Ermita de la Agonía* (late colonial chapel) was recognised by 92% of the participants and 87% of them attributed value to it. In general, the level of recognition and value of all features were related. Thus, the evidence suggests there to be a direct relationship between the image legibility, experience and memory of objects with the attribution of value to them.

Another interesting finding is that recognition and value do not differentiate between tangible and intangible objects; the *Ermita de la Agonía* being a building, the *marimba* an instrument and the *tope* an event. Certainly it is these elements' own unique characteristics which distinguish them from one another and might explain why they were the most recognised. For example, the *Ermita de la Agonía* is located at the end of, and perpendicular to, one of the most important commercial streets and it has a clear easy-to-read shape and colour.

The *marimba* is Costa Rica's national music instrument; this means that it is at least mentioned during the students' primary education career. Also, the *marimba* is often played in commemorative school celebrations, local civic festivities and private activities. The *tope* consists of a horse parade where cattle transport by horseback riders is represented. It is held every day of the local festivities week at noon. Music and people in traditional costumes join the parade and the vehicular accesses to the central streets of the city core are closed. It can be said that the whole city centre paralyses for a week.

But which characteristics do these elements share? What common characteristics are there between these elements? What makes them legible, remembered and valuable? They have all certainly been experienced by the participants on several occasions. The majority of the students walk to or at least through the historic centre on regular basis. Even if they live in the outskirts of the city or in neighbouring settlements, they have to go to the centre in order to commute, shop and socialise. In these travels they must have viewed the Ermita and experienced the tope and the *marimba*. Objects are remembered and acquire value through constant experience; spaces become places when people are able to develop social interactions in them; this is precisely why heritage is a social construction.

It is also interesting to highlight, that the *Calle Real* and the *Redondel* (where the bullfighting takes place during the civic festivities, located outside the historic core) were qualified among the less valuable features.

Distinctive Features

1. Agonía Chapel - Ermita
2. Guanacaste Museum
3. Kiosk and Park Mario Cañas Ruiz
4. Royal bridge - Puente Real
5. Royal Street and Barrio Condega
6. Asención Esquivel School
7. Sun gates/doors - Puertas del Sol
8. Horchata Ajiaco and Corn Rice
9. Chigüa leaf
10. Tope, La burra, Las Diansa
11. Marimba

Figure 1: Liberia's Historic Centre.

Considering the large crowds that attend the bullfighting and that part of the *tope* is celebrated in the *Calle Real*, the outcome of the consult was at first surprising for the researcher. These are two relatively well known public spaces at least according to the interviews, conversations with locals and observations during site visits. Nevertheless they have no relevant value for the consulted teenagers.

There are several probable causes for this outcome, looking into the written comments the results can be explained. Even though not many of the participants commented on the *Redondel*, there were 5 remarks on the place's hygiene conditions: meaning it is *"dirty"* and should be *"taken care of"*; this might explain the low value. On the other hand, 5 students expressed that the *Calle Real* should just remain as it is, while 11 of them noted that it should be changed or improved in a way. *Pavement, reconstruction, event, prettier, safer* are some of the improvement related concepts the participants expressed. A portion of the comments associate negative attributes to the *Redondel* and the *Calle Real:* dirty, not in use, dangerous, deteriorated. So even if the teenagers have been in these eventful places, the poor maintenance conditions reduce the possibilities of people's appropriation and influence in the memory of a space and its symbolic value.

The *Puente Real* was one of the less recognised and had lower values. The comments of the students were divided and indicate that some participants perceive the bridge as a singular unit independent from the surroundings while another group as an element of one of two compounds: the river or the *Calle Real* street. Six students expressed a need for the bridge to be fixed, to be used again as a connecting path. Seven students associated the bridge with a new activity: have fun, play, enjoy and swim for example. Even inside a homogeneous group the bridge does not have a singular clear value.

The workshops results did not point out the bridge as a significant component; this could be attributed to two reasons: (1) the poor maintenance of the bridge plus surroundings and (2) the fact the access to the bridge was closed. The first brings the reader back to the students' comments on the *Calle Real* and the *Redondel*, bad maintenance conditions influence on the memory of a place and its values, diminishing the possibilities of place appropriation and attribution of meaning. The second can be explained with the common characteristic found in the best ranked heritage features: objects are remembered and acquire value through constant experience, if the bridge remains close, it will be forgotten, even if it has a historic, architectonic value and it is a key piece to delimit the Historic Centre. If the bridge and the public space around it are not used, they will eventually vanish from the collective memory.

Conclusion

The Cultural Heritage Research and Conservation Centre inventory together with the author's site visits to Liberia identified valuable historic places and practices. But it was through the interviews with local experts and the workshops with teenage students that the existence of urban heritage as a product of a social construction was confirmed and that the meaning of the historic elements as part of contemporary identities of the community was revealed. The official declaration of the historic centre as an urban heritage site would be the first step to nurture the community's sense of place and to guide the Historic Centre's further development.

Urban heritage management is not about maintaining monuments as units in the city; it is about conserving an ensemble, about activating values in towns or neighbourhoods in opposition to singular buildings. Consequently as a part and scenario of two meaningful features: *Calle Real* and el *tope*, the *Puente Real* has a significant meaning.

The same reasons why the *Puente Real* is being forgotten are arguments that explain why the old military headquarters, also known as *Comandancia*, was present in the memory of those interviewed and of the students. For a heritage development of Liberia's Historic Centre, basic maintenance of public spaces and heritage objects as well as animation of heritage places with everyday occupation and special events are two basic actions that must be incentivised by local leaders. The community's selection of valuable practices, places or objects, and the government's urban management must feed each other in order to consolidate a historic site as urban heritage.

In the international context, a couple of controversial cases regarding the social construction of identity through heritage can be taken by the local government and organisations of Liberia as lessons for further steps. An abandoned industrial railway became an attractive and entertaining public space in the case of the High Line Park in New York thanks to the community engagement and governments' support. On the other hand, in the Stuttgart 21 case, public opinion was not synchronised with the design process of the project and the public's attachment to the construction site brought the community together to claim their desire for a less aggressive intervention to the city's main train station and park. The more the population protested, the stronger the symbolism of the train station and the park became (Friends of the High Line, 2011; Slackman, 2010).

The conservation of the *Puente Real* has to be incorporated into Liberia's development plan for both its historic and contemporary potential meanings for the Historic Centre as an ensemble and its capacity to become an access landmark to the heritage site. The municipality should use the value-activation of the bridge to set precedent for an inclusive heritage management development of the city. In addition, those organisations and citizens concerned with the conservation of the Historic Centre as a heritage site may take the conflict generated around the bridge as an occasion to come together and claim their desires to the local government. In opposition to being demolished and 'forgotten', the bridge has the opportunity to evolve from a meaningful element for some citizens to a relevant heritage component for the community while strengthening the local sense of identity. These actions would not only contribute in the consolidation of the Historic Centre, but they would also promote the appropriation of other meaningful places as well as the integration of the community in other participatory initiatives.

Historically, urban heritage has been determined through the attribution of meaning to sites by experts, often outsiders from the local community's life. However, local acceptance is increasingly seen as indispensable for sustainable monument conservation (Vinken, 2011:2). Paying attention to the local significance of heritage contributes to the success of heritage management.

References

Ashworth, GJ & Larkham PJ (eds.) (1994) *Building a new heritage: tourism, culture and identity in the new Europe*, Routledge, London.

Ashworth, GJ. Graham B. (2005) *Sense of Place, Senses of Time*. Ashgate Publishing Limited, Aldershot.

Ashworth, G. (2011) Do, can and should urban pasts be used to create urban presents and shape urban futures?', *International conference. The distinctiveness of cities. Modes of reproduction*, 15-17 June 2011, Eigenlogik der Städte, Darmstadt.

Bourdieu, P. (1984) *Distinction: a social critique of the judgement of taste*, Harvard College, Boston.

Brüdelin, M. (2004) *ArchiSculpture: Dialogues between Architecture and Sculpture from the 18th Century to present day*. Fondation Beyeler, Basel.

Centro de investigación y conservación del patrimonio cultural (2001) *Inventario Arquitectónico de la Ciudad de Liberia*. [Online], Available: http://www.mcj.go.cr/temas_artes/patrimonio/cicpc/investigaciones/investigaciones_inventario_arquitec_liberia.aspx [26 Jul 2011].

Dormaels, M. (2010) 'Patrimonio, patrimonialización e identidad. Hacia una hermenéutica del patrimonio', *1er congreso iberoamericano sobre patrimonio cultural*, 6-10 December 2010, Universidad de Costa Rica, San José.

Friends of the High Line, (n.d.) [Online], Available: http://www.thehighline.org/ [26 July 2011].

Landscape Urbanism (n.d.) Indexing Liberia, [Online], Available: http://landscapeurbanismcr.wordpress.com/ [26 Jul 2011].

Low, SM, (1994) Cultural Conservation of a place in m Hufford (ed.), *Conserving Culture: a new discourse on heritage*, Board of Trustees of the University of Illinois, Illinois.

Manzo L. & Perkins D. (2006) 'Finding Common Ground: The Importance of Place Attachment to Community Participation and Planning', *Journal of Planning Literature*, May Sage Publications Vol. 20, No. 4, pp. 340-350.

Mason, R. (2006) 'Theoretical and Practical Arguments for Values-Centreed Preservation', *CRM Journal*, Vol. 3, No. 2 Summer, pp. 21-47.

Prats, L. (2005) 'Concepto y gestión del patrimonio local'. *Cuaderno de Antropología Social*, No. 21, pp 17-35.

Prats, L. (1997) *Antropología y Patrimonio*, Editorial Ariel, Barcelona.

Slackman, M. (2010) 'Germany Halts Demolition of Train Station'. *The New York Times*, 5 October, [Online], Available: http://www.nytimes.com/2010/10/06/world/europe/06germany.html?scp=2&sq=%22stuttgart+21%22&st=nyt, [4 Jul 2011].

Vinken, G. (2011) 'Reproducing the city? Heritage and Eigenlogik', *International conference. The distinctiveness of cities. Modes of reproduction*, 15-17 June, Eigenlogik der Städte, Darmstadt.

Víquez R. (2006) *Los espacios públicos abiertos y los adolescentes: algunas consideraciones para el diseño urbano*. Urban Design postgrad thesis, Universidad de Costa Rica. San José.

THE ROLE OF ARCHITECTURAL CULTURAL HERITAGE IN POSTWAR RECOVERY. CASE STUDY: BOSNIA AND HERZEGOVINA

Varatanovic-Guso, Alma[1]

Abstract

During the war in Bosnia and Herzegovina, between 1992 and 1996, the targeting of cultural heritage and the destruction of cities violated all the regulations of the Convention on Protection of Cultural Heritage in the Case of War Conflicts, known as the Hague Convention. During that period, about 1500 religious and other monuments were damaged or destroyed. This paper tackles the issue of aggression on Bosnia and Herzegovina, the assault on the civilian population, their culture and their urban environment. Much has been written about the deliberate repression of groups' cultures - more specifically about language, literature, art and customs - but little about the repression of their architecture. This paper is distinct in that and it looks at the way that cultural heritage is perceived more than simply about heritage itself. It examines the fate of buildings as the targets of genocide and ethnic cleansing and the deliberate destruction of buildings in campaigns of terror and conquest.

Keywords: Cultural Heritage, Cities, Identity, Memory, Deliberate Destruction, Symbolic Targeting, Urban Destruction

---

[1] M.Sc. International Cooperation and Urban Development; specialisation in Sustainable Emergency Architecture. Technische Universität Darmstadt, Germany/ Universitat Internacional de Catalunya, Barcelona, Spain. Architecture, Sarajevo University School of Architecture, Sarajevo, Bosnia and Serjegovina. email: varialma@gmail.com

Introduction

The destruction of the cultural heritage and cities between 1992 and 1996 in Bosnia and Herzegovina, period of a recent war, was characterised with an intentional and systematic destruction of identities. It could be defined as a cultural catastrophe that happened in the heart of Europe.

Needless to say, a complete list of war-related damages to the cultural heritage in Bosnia and Herzegovina still does not exist. For example, according to the data from the Institute for the Protection of the Cultural, Natural and Historical Heritage of Bosnia and Herzegovina, approximately 1454 cultural monuments were destroyed or damaged, out of which 1284 were the Islamic sacred, 237 the Catholic sacred and other objects, and 30 the Serbian Orthodox sacred and other objects (Bublin, 1999:243). It is not difficult to draw a conclusion from these facts – that the destruction of the Islamic and Catholic cultural and religious heritage sites was done with intention and systematic planning.

To understand the significance of heritage in Bosnia and Herzegovina, it is important to mention some facts that led to its diverse elements of heritage. Bosnia and Herzegovina was a main trade route from the East, leading across Asia towards Venice at the top of the Adriatic, which was Europe's gateway to the Orient. This has had direct influence on country and cultural heritage, which have been a complex mixture of Mediterranean, Byzantine, Ottoman and Central European influences. Cultural heritage in Bosnia reflected a multicultural, urbane and sophisticated society, which apparently crossed symbolic boundaries relatively unproblematically. This does not suggest that society in Bosnia and Herzegovina was totally harmonious, but rather that the cultural heritage does suggest the existence of a certain amount of cohesion (De Condappa, 2006:8).

But why is cultural heritage important, especially in postwar situations? During times of death and destruction it is very understandable that people come first. Indeed, it is well known that after conflicts, during the start of the recovery process, the immediate human needs such as shelter, food and health have priority (Price, 2005:1). Naturally, the concerns for cultural heritage at such times appear to be secondary or even tertiary on the list of priorities. The importance of both human needs and cultural heritage should not be denied. It is true that people have to come first, and they do, but the survival of cultural heritage, more precisely architecture and urban life, are also important to the survival of people. Without cultural heritage as a main source, it is impossible to express and realise an identity as a group or person. That is why its role has recently increased in importance for the social evolution of nations, regions and local communities.

Nevertheless, in many postwar situations, the importance of cultural heritage quickly becomes evident during restoration and while repairing damaged heritage and immediately reviving traditions that before the war had become obsolescent. In this context, this rapidity of restoring heritage is closely connected to a strong psychosocial need to re-establish the familiar and to continue with normal life. The meaning of 'continue with normal life' in this situation evokes the concept of the 'thread of continuity' in which people try to find where the rhythm of everyday life has been changed (Price, 2005:1).

In other words, in postwar recovery processes, the role of cultural heritage needs to be recognised in its earlier stages; doing so can produce a positive outcome, both for social reconstruction and for eventual reconciliation.

Heritage and cities

Warfare in cities and against them is as old as cities themselves. Through the centuries, witnessing many wars, cities have been vulnerable to attacks as frequent military targets and objectives of conquerors. The reason was not just the role of cities as supply and communication junctions and concentrations of power, economies and people, but also because they often serve as symbols of specific territories, peoples, states and ideas (Makas, 2007:27). The cities in Bosnia and Herzegovina have always been a reflection of cosmopolitanism, cultural intersection and heterogeneity and, for these very reasons, they have had the long-standing reputation of being sites of inter-cultural tension (Turner, 1996).

However, one new characteristic of the recent war in Bosnia and Herzegovina was the systematic destruction of cities and cultural heritage. It can be said that this was a war against architecture, where the destruction of the architectural cultural heritage of another people or nation used as means of dominating and terrorizing. Furthermore, this destruction of architectural objects represents the erasing of memories, history and identity attached to this architectural objects, at the end, it become not just a consequence of war - but a goal in itself.

Cultural heritage, memory and identity

"The killing of a person destroys an individual memory. The destruction of cultural heritage erases the memory of a people. It is as if they were never there" (András Riedlmayer, 20002)

Here we start with a brief introduction to the general concepts of heritage and its connection with collective memory and identities.

In recent times, many historical theorists have argued about new theories of cultural heritage and its deeper connection with collective identities and memories. For example, Millar (1989:3) defines heritage as:

Part of the fabric of people's lives, consciously or unconsciously accommodating aspirations and providing symbols of continuity, icons of identity and places of pleasure...In its raw state heritage is simply the natural, cultural and built environment of an area.

Furthermore, Dr. Rodney Harrison (2009), a lecturer in heritage studies at the Open University, BBC, stated that

heritage has very little to do with the past, but is actually more about how we conceptualise the future. Objects of heritage are the things we pay attention to because they're still meaningful to us, not always because they tell great stories about the past but because we use them to tell stories about ourselves. Practices of heritage are customs and habits which, although intangible, also inform who we are as groups, and help to create our shared social memory.

Putting together objects of heritage and its practices gives us a complete idea about who we are as a group and as the individual persons.

Therefore, heritage should be considered as a set of tangible collective memories and as material proof of the past, physically representing the shared values and histories of a community. The importance of such places increases when efforts to destroy them reminds communities of its values. If the touchstones of identity are no longer there to be touched, memories become weaker and in the end they disappear. Out of sight can become, literally, out of mind both for those whose patrimony has been destroyed and for the destroyers (Bevan, 2006:16). Protection and rebuilding of architectural heritage helps people to remain within their historical dimensions despite the determined efforts of their persecutors and destroyers.

Nevertheless, heritage as touchstones of collective memory, here considered as a bundle of individual memories, illustrates a need to construct or solidify collective identities. Heritage legitimises and validates identity by suggesting a sense of continuity and lineage between the past and the present and by creating a sense of belonging to a specific place. Therefore, the destruction of heritage and the subsequent destruction of one's familiar environment can mean a disorientating exile from the memories they have invoked. This threatens the loss of one's collective identity and the secure continuity of those identities (Bevan, 2006).

In addition, collective identity plays an important role in the processes of differentiation and distinction between different groups; one group's heritage must be separated from that of other identity groups. It is well known, especially in recent wars, that heritage has been an integral component in the violent and destructive process of defining the boundaries of various nations, playing a central role in discourses of inclusion and exclusion of both the group and its territory.

Moreover, heritage was among the reasons for concurrence, severe conflicts and destruction between different ethnic groups. No place epitomises this more than the city of Mostar in Bosnia and Herzegovina. It is a place where, during and after the conflict, the old architecture and different historical periods have been variously recognised by the different religious communities that inhabit and share the city today. For example, the meaning of the Old Bridge and its surroundings reveals contested memories and competing ideas about what that place should represent.

Deliberated destruction as symbolic targeting

In situations of armed conflict, cities and their heritage are sometimes the target of deliberated attacks. In this case, architecture takes on a totemic quality; for example, a mosque is no longer simply a mosque, but it represents to its enemies the target for destruction. A library or museum is a warehouse of historical memory, evidence that a given community presence extends into the past, legitimizing it in the present and into the future. This deliberate destruction of heritage started on Kristallnacht in 1938 with the Nazi destruction of German synagogues and could still be noticed fifty-five years later with Bosnian and Herzegovinians' architectural heritage, with the same goal of denying a people its past as well as its future (Bevan, 2006).

While trying to understand this ideology of destruction, more specifically the destruction of the Old Bridge in Mostar, Croatian writer Slavenka Drakulic asked the question: "Why do we feel more pain looking at the image of the destroyed bridge than the image of massacred people?" (Bevan, 2006:26)

> *Perhaps because we see our own mortality in the collapse of the bridge. We expect people to die; we count on our own lives to end. The destruction of a monument to civilisation is something else. The bridge in all its beauty and grace was built to outlive us; it was an attempt to grasp eternity. It transcends our individual destiny. A dead woman is one of us, but the bridge is all of us forever* (Bevan, 2006:26).

According to Andras Riedlmayer, a Harvard academic who has been a vigorous campaigner against the destruction of heritage in the Balkans, this ideology of destruction is explained with the words of historian Eric Hobsbawm:

> *History is the new material for nationalist, or ethnic or fundamentalist ideologies, as poppies are the raw material for heroin addiction...If there is no suitable past it can always be invented. The past legitimises. The past gives a more glorious background to a present that doesn't have much to show for itself (Bevan, 2006:12).*

Furthermore, there is a need to understand which sites are selected for destruction and how. Because symbolic destruction is not vandalism, motivations are rational and can be explained in terms of the destroyer's ideology, where this particular ideology limits and clarifies their choice of targets and legitimises their selections and attacks from their perspective. It is necessary to know the historical and architectural background as well as the self-perceptions and ideologies of both the attackers and attacked in order to begin interpreting why certain sites are selected as targets.

There is very little evidence that the deliberate targeting and destruction of cultural heritage has succeeded in its aim of diminishing enemy morale. In fact, it has had the opposite effect (Price, 2005:5). This is the case with many cities in Bosnia and Herzegovina, where destruction happened with enormous consequences but where the cities and their people did survive.

Effect of war on Bosnian and Herzegovinian cities

The aggression on Bosnia and Herzegovina and its cities is a clear example of the deliberate targeting and destruction of cultural, religious and historic landmarks. Targets included both sacred and non-sacred objects such as: the National Library at Sarajevo, Sarajevo's Oriental Institute, the Regional Archives in Mostar, the Old Bridge in Mostar, local and national museums, the Music Academy, the National Gallery and entire historic districts. This cultural heritage (both buildings and documents) which has been targeted and erased, speaks eloquently of centuries of pluralism and tolerance in Bosnia. It represents the evidence of a successfully shared past that the nationalists sought to destroy (Riedlmayer, 1995).

For example, on 25 August 1992, the National Library at Sarajevo was bombarded and set ablaze. According to eyewitnesses, the shells came from seven different Bosnian Serb army positions. Only the library was hit and adjacent building remained unscathed. Once the library had been set alight the shelling stopped, but when firemen and volunteers tried to save books from the building they came under direct gunfire. Before the fire, the library held 1.5 million volumes including 155,000 rare books and manuscripts, 100 years of Bosnian newspapers and periodicals and the collections of the University of Sarajevo. About 90% of the library's collection went up in flames in this attack, the largest single incident of book burning in modern history (Riedlmayer, 1995:2). In this case, not just written heritage was destroyed but also the building itself which was one of the finest examples from the Austro-Hungarian architectural period as the former city hall was built in an eclectic neo-Moorish style redolent with nineteenth century Romanticism. Today Sarajevo's former National and University library is a shell.

Unfortunately, in many cases in Bosnia and Herzegovina, cultural destruction was equal to a cultural cleanse of a particular territory. Good examples are the destruction of mosques from the 15th Century in its cities. In occupied territory under the control of the nationalist army, far away from the battlefront, most mosques were destroyed with dynamite in the middle of the night as key elements of a campaign of terror aimed at driving out the Muslim inhabitants. One of the best examples of this happened in the northern Bosnian city of Banja Luka. In Banja Luka, held by Serb nationalists from the beginning of the war, all sixteen historic mosques were destroyed. The main mosque Ferhadija, built in 1583, was completely destroyed by dynamite on the night of 7 May 1993 and its place, turned into a car park.

Mostar is still one of the best examples of this ideology of destruction, where the destruction of the Old Bridge and the Old Town became internationally recognised and analysed. While trying to explain the reason why he was trying to destroy the old Ottoman bridge in Mostar, one of the Bosnian Croat soldiers told a foreign journalist: "It is not enough to cleanse Mostar of the Muslims," he said, "the relics must also be destroyed" (Riedlmayer, 1995:4).

The Old Bridge, aged 427 years, and the whole surrounding area, with its different historical architectural elements, represents an outstanding example of a multicultural urban settlement. Before its destruction, on the 9th of November 1993, the Old Bridge's had historical and cultural significance to its city and its region, symbolizing the connection of the East and the West by linking two banks of Neretva River.

Exactly four years earlier the Berlin Wall fell. Both of these acts had a symbolic nature but very different meanings. The opening of the Berlin Wall symbolised the end of the division of Berlin and reunification of two Germanys, but the destruction of the Old Bridge symbolised the division of the city of Mostar into two sides, east and west, Muslim and Croat (Makas, 2007).

Since its brutal destruction, the Old Bridge has been argued to represent the destruction of cultural heritage in Bosnia and Herzegovina and beyond. Now with its reconstruction it has become a symbol of reconciliation, international cooperation and an attempt for a new coexistence of diverse cultural, ethnic and religious communities (Makas, 2007).

These examples illustrate but do not exhaust the events that took place in Bosnia and Herzegovina. They should, however, provide an understanding of the systematic destruction of a community's past in Bosnia and Herzegovina, its cultural monuments and its institutions and records.

Conclusion

It can be concluded that in the recent years one of the key element in achieving global stability and security in the world is cultural heritage and its role in postwar reconstruction. More preciously, the protection of cultural heritage becomes a key element in the economic, social and human development of a community and its recovery in postwar situations. For justification of this statement we need to underline that postwar heritage reconstruction does not represent a quick physical restoration; it rather requires a more complicated long development process that needs to be sustained through years of postwar recovery.

Furthermore, the motivation for reconstructing heritage and cities destroyed during conflicts are as complex as the motivations for their destruction. It can be said that destruction of built environment is often most visible, which could be one of the reasons why the reconstruction of built cultural heritage is one of the first priorities in the long recovery process. Here we can refer to Bosnia and Herzegovina, where the reconstruction of built cultural heritage was the first step in the postwar recovery process of the country.

Therefore, the role of cultural heritage represents a crucial factor in development in various manners such as: promoting peace and tolerance; preventing conflicts; preserving the cultural diversity and richness of people; contributing to economic growth at the local and national level; promoting and integrating the fragile categories of the population; promoting tolerance, intercultural and intercommunity dialogue; promoting good governance and strengthening citizenship; and contributing to tourism development. All these aspects are among the reasons why cultural heritage has become one of the key elements in the development process in postwar reconstruction.

References

Bevan, R. (2006) *The Destruction of Memory*. London: Reaktion Books

Bublin, M. (1999) *Gradovi Bosne i Hercegovine, milenijum razvoja i godine urbicida (The Cities of Bosnia and Herzegovina, a Millenium of Development and the Years of Urbicide)*. Sarajevo: Sarajevo Publishing.

De Condappa, P. (2006) 'Cultural Genocide in Bosnia-Herzegovina; Destroying Heritage, Destroying Identity', *Metamedia/Stanford University*, [online], Available: http://metamedia.stanford.edu/projects/culturesofcontact/121 [4 Nov 2011]

Harrison, R. (2009) 'What is Heritage?' [online], *BBC Open University*, available from: http://www.open2.net/savingbritainspast/what_is_heritage.html [04.11.2011].

Makas, Emily G. (2007) *Prepresenting Competing Identities: Building and Rebuilding in Postwar Mostar*, PhD Disertation-History of Architecture and Urbanis, Department of Architecture, Cornell University, New York.

Millar, S. (1989) *Heritage Management for Heritage Tourism*. Tourism Management.

Riedlmayer, A. (1995) *Killing Memory: The Targeting of Bosnia's Cultural Heritage*, Testimony Presented at a Hearing of the Commission on Security and Cooperation in Europe. U.S. Congress, April 4.

Riedlmayer, A. (2002) *Destruction of Cultural Heritage in Bosnia-Hercegovina, 1992-1996: A Post-war Survey of Selected Municipalities*. Cambridge, Massachusetts USA.

Stanley-Price, N. (2005) The thread of continuity: cultural heritage in post war recovery. *Conference Proceedings*, ICCROM FORUM, Rome, [Online], Available: http://www.iccrom.org/pdf/ICCROM_ICS06_CulturalHeritagePostwar_en.pdf [4 Nov 2011].

Turner, J. J. (1996) 'War for Cities and Noncombatant Immunity in the Bosnian Conflict', In *Religion and Justice in the War over Bosnia*, edited by Davis, G. Scott. New York: Routledge.

USING INFORMATION AND COMMUNICATION TECHNOLOGIES TO FOSTER SOCIAL ENCOUNTERS

Melgaço Silva Marques, Lorena[1]

Abstract

This paper proposes the discussion of temporary uses of spaces through the perspective of information and communication technology (ICT) employment, given its increasing importance in today's scenario of accelerated change. If on the one hand, the implementation of digital apparatuses in the urban sphere, especially in cities striving to be part of or to maintain themselves in the position of world capitals can be a high investment top-down strategy that aims to revitalise former industrial sites and, it can, on the other, present an alternative and more affordable means to using technology at-hand as to create social encounters in the urban sphere. In order to better explore the potential of those uses, the scope of this work draws on different concepts of the words "temporary," "culture" and "event" often present in urban studies literature, but seldom with the perspectives examined here. Baring those concepts in mind, this paper suggests that more versatile approaches to technology are more economically viable and effective in promoting social change and enhancing negotiations within the community.

Keywords: Information and Communication Technologies, Urban Development, Temporary Use of Spaces

---

1 M.Sc. International Cooperation and Urban Development; specialisation in Urbanism, Habitat and International Cooperation. Technische Universität Darmstadt, Darmstadt, Germany/ Université Pierre-Mendès-France, Grenoble, France. MArch. Escola de Arquitetura, Universidade Federal de Minas Gerais, Brazil. email: melgaco.lorena@gmail.com

Introduction

Many important academics believed in an important transition time, when the city as a spatial representation of society would give way to cybercities and every transaction and encounter would be done in the so-called cyberspace (Graham, 2004). Although such changes have not quite taken place, there has been an immense increase in the importance of these other spaces. Nevertheless the physical, palpable space is even more essential today once this "virtual" world only exists within an intricate and complex set of physical infrastructure (Sassen, 2004 and Graham, 2004). And this need demystifies the idea of a flat world, since even though the distances for those who have access to communication and transportation technologies have decreased, they have, for those who are not located in such privileged areas, in fact, stretched (Massey, 2006).

Regardless such ideas of a flat world, the development of information and communication technologies still influences the perception of cities, even if differently in different societies (Rapoport, 2008)[2]. From mobile phones to urban screens, we are experiencing what many scholars define as a mediated space.

> *As media become increasingly mobile and locative the opposing distinction of face-to-face and 'media' encounters is no longer useful; they are increasingly becoming overlaid and interwoven so that mediated behaviours increasingly impact on face-to-face encounters and vice-versa (Willis and Aurigi, 2011).*

For the last 25 years, major changes in the Western world, which led to economic, social and cultural changes, also affected urban politics and development. The shift from the Fordist city to the global city led cities to become "subject[s] to an increasing interurban competition and face the need to assert their position regarding a global 'space of flows' comprising the main elements of function, information and flow" (Groth and Corijn, 2005).

In such a scenario, former European industrial cities, such as Berlin, are striving to become informational poles. Highly dynamic, Berlin is hoping to sustain its "global media city" title by investing heavily in the transformation of its brown fields in different projects that rely mainly on high investments

---

2   Amos Rapoport points out how different societies absorb the same technologies, and such a phenomena is related to the cultural background, or what he calls "culture core and periphery."

from media enterprises (Krätke, 2004). Discussions around urban screens, out-of-home media that display cultural content, suggest that they can be powerful tools for promoting community cohesion. Nevertheless, they have not yet delivered on their promises.

Brazil, on the other hand, experiences a different situation but with similar outcomes. As a young "developing" country, it has not yet suffered from a strong deindustrialisation process; on the contrary, its construction industry is on the rise. But in this process, people are being displaced not only out of their homes, but also out of the public space where social encounters usually occur. These places are in a constant "meanwhile" state and, most of the time, they are not fully enjoyed by the community. Initiatives taken by the research group Lagear (Graphic Laboratory for the Experience of Architecture), such as "Long Distance Voodoo", aim at recovering this public sphere by temporary appropriations of public or common-use places through the creation of hybrid spaces, where technology becomes a means to promote broader dialogue between remote communities in a new, neutral shared space.

Who has the right to the city?

Harvey (2008: 23) argues that

> *the right to the city is [...] far more than a right of individual access to the resources that the city embodies: it is a right to change ourselves by changing the city more after our heart's desire. It is, moreover, a collective rather than an individual right since changing the city inevitably depends upon the exercise of a collective power over the processes of urbanisation.*

Soja (2009) and Marcuse (2008, 2009) point to the need to associate the right to the city with issues of spatial (in)justice. The most visible element of spatial injustice is the lack of access to land itself, which reinforces the cycle of urban injustice and segregation. Some individuals and communities have found *ad hoc* solutions by temporarily occupying idle areas in cities, and such an approach has been proven suitable for urban redevelopment in the recent context of economic crisis and therefore supported by many governments as a medium-term solution (BBSR, 2008; Department for Innovation, Universities and Skills, 2009 and SQW Consulting, 2010). Nevertheless as Soja (2008) points out, the right to a city is also related to the geographical distribution of its infrastructure, which encompasses, among other issues, the distribution of information and communication technologies. Not only the access to those technologies, but mostly how useful those technologies are on people's daily lives, is a key elements in determining whether someone can fully enjoy the city.

Brazil poses a clear example of this situation. According to studies, in 2008, 59% of Brazilians have never accessed the Internet or used a computer (BBC Digital Planet, 2008). The Brazilian government has decided to tackle "digital divide" issues by providing Internet Cafes (Baltazar, 2009), clearly defining the problem as the lack of access to the Internet. Although providing the tools is one solution, its access does not solve the wider problem, which is to make those tools useful[3]. More than a digital divide, the lack of access to useful ICT tools leads to a socio-cultural divide. Having access to computers and networks is unquestionably important; nevertheless it will not lead to automatic inclusion.

Lagear has been experimenting with low cost technology as to develop more appropriate strategies to target socio-cultural divide issues. The experiment *Ocupar Espaços*[4] (Occupying Spaces), held in 2006, for example

> aimed to enable socially excluded people from two remote favelas in Belo Horizonte to establish relationships by means of a hybrid of physical and digital spaces. The interfaces produced aimed to create a collaborative environment where people could interact among themselves and with the space that emerged from the juxtaposition of the physical space and the digital interfaces (Melgaço and Baltazar, to be published).

The mentioned interfaces were created using off-the-shelf software and hardware so that the two *favelas* could be connected and the community could create a new space for negotiation and fun. For that, they could gesture with coloured lights or even get involved with images projected in unexpected spaces (*Figure. 1*).

Although such a small experiment does not solve the problem of the digital divide (and it did not intend to), it goes beyond the current discussion of equipping communities and points to the possibilities of providing not tools, but means for people to be more conscious of their own socio-cultural space

---

3   There is a key difference between the terms "usability" and "usefulness," usually neglected by authors while dealing with issues of digital inclusion. "People might use whatever is available (usability), but the main question to be asked is: what are the actual benefits of this useable devices for people's socio-cultural inclusion (its usefulness)?" (Melgaço and Baltazar, to be published)

4   This project was developed in association with the NGO Oficina de Imagens.

regarding the problem as a socio-cultural issue. Through *Ocupar Espaços*, researchers concluded that new exploration of known places through the creation of new layers of interaction could contribute to reinforcing more cohesive communities.

> On the bottom line, technology itself is not the solution for inclusion issues, at least not the ones that really matter to people. Exclusion is a problem of lack of choice. By increasing the number of choices available, there could be a better opportunity for a community to decide what to trade off to promote their improvement. Traditional visions of digital inclusion might not be the most suitable approach for that. By providing people with the tools to set their own demands, we might also be surprised with how qualified they are to move towards their own autonomy (Melgaço and Baltazar, to be published).

Figure 1: Ocupar Espaços.
Source: Lagear Archive, 2006

"Culture", "temporary" and "event" analysed through another point of view

Although in urban planning literature, the words "culture", "temporary" and "event" usually relate to urban strategies for redevelopment, they do not often reflect other approaches that regard "culture" as the everyday, "temporary" as very ephemeral appropriations of the space and "event" as actualisations of virtualities associated to the place people are inhabiting. Those terms will be further developed in this section.

While a vast amount of literature dealing with issues of culture as a motor of development can be found (García, 2004) still only a few researchers regard culture as daily human production. Sharon Zukin (1995), for example, highlights the recent shift of analysis of cultures as aspects of everyday life to the focus on "Culture" as a collective of products fabricated according to the demands of patrons who compete to set symbols and, at the same time, the space to display them. As a consequence, "Culture," with a capital "C," reflected in museums, galleries and famous architecture, is seen as a motor of urban and economic development, not necessarily reflecting the "material civilisation that conceived and constructed them [great public spaces, statues, buildings]" (Zukin, 1995:113). Despite the promises of redevelopment and inclusion of cities in international tourism circuits, culture-based programmes have been criticised particularly concerning some outcomes that usually follow: gentrification, segregation and discrimination (Miles, 2005).

Figure 2 and 3: Long Distance Voodoo. Source: Lagear Archive, 2011

The word temporary usually qualifies interim uses of derelict or idle spaces, being those uses for cultural or economic purposes[5] and may generate activities such as indoor sports, cultural events, eating, markets for local people and attract visitors from other areas and involve the local community in redevelopment of residential areas (Hentila, 2002 and Blumner, 2006). These uses have been seen recently by governments and scholars as possibilities to grant given areas with redevelopment. Therefore, most literature produced in the planning field acknowledges temporary uses as non-permanent uses of emptied spaces, but usually such uses have a longer time-span and contribute to changing the character of the space over time. The temporary uses sought in this paper are either much shorter in time

---

5 There is a vast literature that explores the use of cultural assets for the development of a city. For an example, please refer to Andrés, L. (2010). Crises, disruptions and temporary uses: new challenges for planning practice and research?

and therefore do not reflect on the transformation of the built space or do not rely on high investments and planning. These uses aim to change the individual perception of the space (on a temporary or permanent basis), but do not always lead to the reconfiguration of the built environment.

It is also important to understand that the choice of the word "event" refers to the dichotomies of potential/real and virtual/actual, developed by Pierre Lévy (1996). For him, the term "event" means the "actualisation" of the virtualities of given situation. In architecture, that means possibilities allowed by the design of non-prescriptive spaces (Baltazar, 2009). This approach might also result in events in the traditional sense – such as a public or social occasion but is not based on it. On several occasions, vastly overlooked by researchers, they just reflect the way people appropriate the inhabited space and should, therefore, be seen as temporary and studied under other conditions rather than as more conventional cultural projects would be.

Technology in the urban sphere

The constant need of cities to compete in the international scenario has also been driven by technological investments. Besides the discussion of global financial cities, it is possible to find the pursuit of technologies as a landmark-setter, producing global media cities. According to Ursula Stalder (2011), the public sphere currently displays a variety of different media with different purposes, such as those to display information on screens, to exchange information (kiosk systems), to advertise (billboards) or to enhance architectural design (media façades). Some even propose to display public art (urban screens). As a result of such a heavy inclusion of technology in the urban spaces new social dynamics destabilise traditional hierarchies and question the symbolic role of the city. Besides, the development of media enabled by digital networks has allowed more decentralised forms of information distribution (McQuire, 2009).

Although technological apparatuses proliferate in urban spaces, the idea of a digital society independent of the urban centres has been proven wrong. Such as those of Marshall McLuhan, who suggested that "the city as a form of major dimensions must inevitably dissolve like the fading shot in a movie" and that the world would become a "global village" (Graham, 2004). The future of cities influenced by technological development and the fear of technological determinism[6] has been also depicted in many romances and movies, such as the seminal 1982 Blade Runner by Riddley Scott. The movie reflects on the consequences of technological determinism in our capitalist cities and alerts contemporary urban researchers of the importance of avoiding the logic of technological determinism by considering how technology should be used and not assuming it to be pre-established and untouchable.

Long Distance Voodoo: experimenting with technology in the city[7]

Long Distance Voodoo (FIG. 02 and 03) was an experiment that proposed the connection of two different places – the *Kauf dich Glücklich* Café in Berlin and the *Raul Soares* Square in Belo Horizonte, Brazil[8]. A third space for interaction was enabled for people located in remote physical spaces but engaged them in a common experience[9]. During this event, dancers from the Brazilian group "Contact and Improvisation" initiated their improvised dance from the inputs of participants in Berlin who, by punching a "voodoo doll," sent signals to cell phone vibrators located on the dancer's body. In general, this group initiates improvisations from the physical touch of other members. For this performance, though, touch was produced remotely to trigger the dancers. The use of off-the-shelf technology and open source programming tools create processes that can be easily re-created in other scenarios (This experiment has been already reproduced in two other

---

6   The term is defined by Rod Burgess (2005) as the view that social organisation and culture are predominantly and ultimately shaped by the technologies of production, exchange, communications and consumption. The author criticises this approach because it seems to neglect that technology is produced by men, and not by a superior force which we have to follow and should, therefore, be questioned.

7   Part of this argument was developed with Prof. Katharine Willis, submitted for publication in 2011.

8   This experiment was held in April 2011 and is part of a larger research called "Tripartite Networks" held at Lagear (Graphic Laboratory for the Experience of Architecture, Architecture school of the Federal University of Minas Gerais, Brazil), whose main goal is to investigate how remote actuation can amplify the senses of presence and belonging of participants in a hybrid space. It intends to question more traditional research approaches to presence which are, usually, based on the realistic representation the space. The Tripartite Networks project is supported by the Brazilian agency Fapemig, CAPES and CNPq.

9   This term was coined by Baltazar and Cabral Filho (2006) as to describe this space that is created from both digital and physical architectures and that will only exist as long as there is a connection between people located in different geographical spaces through the Internet, for example.

occasions: Interaction South America 2011 Conference, in Belo Horizonte and CulturaDigital.Br Festival in Rio de Janeiro, both in Brazil).

The name "Long Distance Voodoo" refers to the fostered remote communication and the possibility of triggering and acting on processes, playing on the phrase "Long Distance Call." It highlights the possibilities of technology-mediated encounters where no one has absolute control. The voodoo doll, as an inanimate object, embodies the possibility of influencing the improvisation of the dancer through its manipulation[10]. In this experiment, control was shared by participants. While Berliners could poke the dancer as desired, they could not predict the improvisations resulting from it, contradicting the principle of voodoo, where the person who owns the doll assumes immediate control over the body of the subject of his/her desire. Relations of control were reversed when the dancer challenged the participant to seek control of the next movement. It allowed, therefore, for a less traditional media to promote remote closeness, in a cybernetic relationship that could only happen during the experiment held in the mediated space formed by bringing together Berlin, Belo Horizonte and the Internet.

Experimenting with technology in the urban space in collective activities emphasises questions related to remoteness among urban inhabitants, according to Willis and Aurigi (2011). These are often related to the development of technologies and their role in metropolitan life as well as the common distinction of the "virtual" realm of technologies to "real" urban places (Crang, in Willis and Aurigi, 2011). Willis and Aurigi (2011) draw on Goffman's idea that performance in the public space refers to activities of an individual observed either by friends or strangers; which means that, in order for a performance to happen, often individuals unconsciously play a role that implicates their interaction in the event. Long Distance Voodoo fostered the *ad hoc* creation of what Schieck and Kostakos call a digital stage (in Willis, Aurigi, 2011:5):

> They point out the importance of creating settings for encounters and introduce the concept of a digital stage that can facilitate and encourage different types of social interactions, reinforcing the need for and relevance of 'place' as opposed to the simplistic view of displacement by media. Through proactive staging of encounters they create an urban performance that unfolds over time and the authors report that in order for this kind of

---

10 Lagear's Internal Report. For a video documentation, please refer to: Lautenschlaeger, G. (2011).

public display to be engaging the viewer needs to be able to construct a socially meaningful relationship of which the display and the human observer form a part.

Conclusions: from structural to approach decisions

Stalder (2011) points to the shift from the experience being part of the product to becoming the product. Most of the initiatives that relate to the use of ICTs in the urban spaces end up reinforcing products over processes and therefore, hindering the experience. Therefore, it is important to design tools that allow the experience itself to be a process that is only temporarily completed with the interaction of people. As much as Long Distance Voodoo explores alternative paths to using technology in the urban space, it still highlights issues relating to our technological fetish. Although it goes beyond automated responses of pre-defined mechanisms, it ultimately promotes a limited conversation stimulated more by the curiosity of the mechanism itself than by the possibility of getting in touch with the other.

Notwithstanding experiments such as Long Distance Voodoo explore the potential of temporary setups of information and communication technologies to foster social encounters and promote community building. They point to the benefits of substituting permanent solutions for more flexible ones in such a matter that a pattern of elements that promote social encounters can be created. More flexible approaches benefit from cheaper and easier means to adapting to unexpected changes in the conjuncture, allowing for ephemeral connections among different cities that experiment with bodily engagement and participation. Ideally, ICTs should become a means to an end, and not the end itself. Only in this way they will provide the tools for enhancing creativity and empowering individuals and communities.

Acknowledgements

This paper is a compilation of the master dissertation "Technospaces; Strategies of Urban Reconfiguration using Information and Communication Technologies in Berlin," supervised by Prof. PhD. Lauren Andrés. I would like to thank her careful supervision as well as the fruitful contribution of Prof. PhD. Katharine Willis, who has helped me shape and carry out my research.

The experiment Long Distance Voodoo was developed by Lagear's team: Marcela Alves de Almeida, Graziele Lautenschlaeger, Guilherme Ferreira de Arruda, Lorena Melgaço Silva Marques, Sergio de Lima Saraiva Junior, Marina Sanders Paolinelli, Tiago Cícero Alves, Estevam Gomes Quintino and Wallison Barbosa coordinated by Prof. PhD. Ana Paula Baltazar dos Santos and Prof. PhD. José dos Santos Cabral Filho.

References

Andrés, L. (2010) *Crises, disruptions and temporary uses: new challenges for planning practice and research?* [email] Message to Lauren Andres (l.andres@bham.ac.uk). Sent 23 February 2011.

Baltazar, A. P. (2009) *Cyberarchitecture: the virtualisation of architecture beyond representation towards interactivity.* unpublished PhD thesis, The Bartlett School of Architecture, University College London.

Baltazar, A. P. and Cabral Filho, J. (2006), 'Tenda Digital / Digital TENT (Technological Environment for Negotiated Topology) e suas possíveis implicações em contextos sociais'. *SIGraDi 2006 – congress proceedings*, 10th Iberoamerican Congress of Digital Graphics, Santiago: Faculdad de Arquitectura y Urbanismo, Univ. de Chile, pp. 346–49.

BBSR (2008) *The impact of temporary use of land and buildings on sustainable urban development*, [Online] Available: http://www.bbsr.bund.de/cln_032/nn_25904/BBSR/EN/RP/ExWoSt/Studies/TemporaryUse/01__Start.html [10 Jul 2011].

BBC Digital Planet (2008) 'Bridging the Digital Divide', *BBC News*, [Online], Available: http://news.bbc.co.uk/2/hi/technology/7647114.stm [10/08/2010].

Blumner, N. (2006) *Planning for the Unplanned: Tools and Techniques for interim use in Germany and the United States*, [Online], Available: www.difu.de/system/files/archiv/.../reihen/.../06-blumner_planning.pdf [3 Aug 2011].

Burgess, R. (2005) *Technological Determinism and Urban Fragmentation: a critical analysis. Explaining new concepts of the Urban Periphery* [Online], Available: http://ccs.ukzn.ac.za/files/Burgess%20against%20ltechnological%20determinism.pdf [10 Dec 2011].

Department for Innovation, Universities and skills (2009) *Looking after our town centres*, [Online], Available: http://www.communities.gov.uk/documents/planningandbuilding/pdf/1201258.pdf [10 Jul 2011].

García, B. (2004) 'Cultural Policy and Urban Regeneration in Western European Cities: Lessons from Experience, Prospects for the future'. *Local Economy*, vol. 19, no. 04, pp. 312-326.

Graham, S. (2004) 'Introduction' in Graham, S. (ed.) *The Cybercities Reader*, London: Routledge, 2004, pp. 03-29.

Groth, J., & Corijn, E. (2005) 'Reclaiming Urbanity: Indeterminate Spaces, Informal Actors and Urban Agenda Setting'. *Urban Studies*, vol. 42, no. 03, pp. 503-526.

Harvey, D. (2008) 'Right to the city'. *The new Left Review*, vol. 53, pp. 23-37.

Hentila, Helka-Liisa (2002) *Urban intensification strategies and promotion of temporary use* [online] Avaiable from: http://www.templace.com/think-pool/attach/download/5_H_Thinkurban_D_1002.docee13.pdf?object_id=3080&attachment_id=3087. [10/07/2011].

Krätke, S. (2004) 'City of Talents? Berlin's Regional Economy, Socio-Spatial Fabric and 'worst Practice' Urban Governance'. *International Journal of Urban and Regional Research* vol. 28, no. 03, pp. 511-29.

Lautenschlaeger, G. *Long Distance Voodoo* (2011) [Online video], Available: http://www.youtube.com/watch? v=H459OeyT7U8 [17 Jul 2011].

Lévy, P. (1996) *O que é Virtual?* São Paulo: Ed. 34.

Marcuse, P. (2008) 'Spatial Justice: Derivative but Causal of Social Injustice' *JSSJ*, [Online], Available: http://www.jssj.org/archives/01/media/dossier_focus_vo4.pdf [4 Jul 2011].

Marcuse, P. (2009) 'From Critical Urban Theory to the Right to the City'. *City*, vol. 13, pp.185-196.

Massey, D. (2006) 'Is the world really shrinking?' *Open Learn*, [Online], Available: www.open2.net/freethinking/oulecture_2006.html [10 May 2010].

McQuire, S. (2009) 'Mobility, cosmopolitanism and Public Space in the media city'. In: McQuire S. et al, *Urban Screens Reader*, Amsterdam: Institute of Network Cultures, pp. 45-64.

Melgaço, L. Baltazar, A. P. (to be published) 'The Museum of Today: towards bridging the socio-cultural gap in Brazil'. In: Abend, P. Haupts, T., Müller, C. (Hg.) *Medialität der Nähe. Situationen – Praktiken – Diskurse.* Bielefeld: Transcript Verlag.

Miles, M. (2005) 'Interruptions: Testing the Rhetoric of Culturally led Urban Development'. *Urban Studies*, vol. 42 no. 5/6, 889-911.

Sassen, S. (2004) 'Agglomeration in the digital era?' In S. Graham, *The cybercities reader*, London: Routledge, pp. 195-198.

Soja, E. (2008) 'The city and spatial justice', *JSSJ*, [Online], Available: http://www.jssj.org/archives/01/media/dossier_focus_vo5.pdf [4 Jul 2011].

SQW CONSULTING (2010) *Meanwhile uses: Business Case and Learning Points*, [Online], Available: http://www.meanwhile.org.uk/useful-info/misc/SQW%20-%20Meanwhile%20Use%20Report%20May%2010.pdf [10 Nov 2011].

Stalder, U. (2011) *Digital Out-of-Home Media: Towards a Better Understanding of Means and Effects of Digital Media in Public Space* [Online], Available: http://blog.hslu.ch/outofhomedisplays/files/2010/11/Stalder_2010_Pervasive-Advertising_Preversion.pdf [10 Nov 2011].

Willis, K., Aurigi. A. (2011) 'Hybrid Spaces: Presence, Rhythms and Performativity'. Conference Proceedings, Seventh International Conference on Intelligent Environments, Nottingham, pp. 100-106.

Willis, K.; Melgaço, L (under review) *Long Distance Voodoo – Experiences of embodied presence and urban media in urban public* space.

Zukin, S. (1995) *The cultures of the cities*, Oxford: Willey-Blackwell Publishing.

APPRAISAL OF THE EFFECTS OF NON-PERFORMING POLICIES. HOUSING DEVELOPMENT IN A NEW PLANNED CITY, NAYA RAIPUR, INDIA

Rajasekharan, Rajesh[1]

Abstract

The need to adopt sustainable urban development practices is inevitable for South Asian cities that are being plagued by rapid, massive and unplanned urban expansion. Economic growth has resulted in the development of urban centres characterised by inefficient urban infrastructure, transportation and traffic issues, environmental degradation and, most importantly, a deficit of affordable housing. Cities and towns of India amply illustrate all these aspects and developments in India's housing sector, in particular, present a very dismal performance. The situation is attributable to faulty policy decisions, a dearth of clear-cut policy guidelines and policy instruments, and an absence of adequate regulations.

Planning and development of a new city provides an opportunity to sustainably plan housing sector development and Naya Raipur, the new capital of Chhattisgarh state, presents just this occasion. However, a critical appraisal of the Government of India's national housing policy, the housing policy of Chhattisgarh state and the development regulations for Naya Raipur City reveals: (1) Lack of clear cut policy initiatives, regulations and controls on part of national and state governments, (2) promotion of manipulative open market system favouring private players.

Keywords: Sustainable Urban Development, Housing Sector Development, Housing Policies, Policy Instruments

---

1 M.Sc. International Cooperation and Urban Development; specialisation in Sustainable Emergency Architecture. Technische Universität Darmstadt/ Universitat Internacional de Catalunya . email: rajesh3797@hotmail.com

Challenges of urbanisation and housing sector development in India

History has shown urbanisation to be an inevitable phenomenon part of the modernisation and economic growth of a country/region. In the last six decades, throughout the world, a large rural-to-urban population shift has occurred and studies project that by 2030 the world's urban population will reach almost 5 billion. The developing world, in particular, will experience an unprecedented scale of urban growth in the developing world. A further urban increment of 1.8 billion people is expected globally during 2025-2050, with India being the major contributor (377 million) and China following (205 million) (United Nations, 2007). Therefore urbanisation presents unique challenges as well as opportunities for these countries, especially India.

India has a population of 1.21 billion and the Indian economy is one of the fastest growing in the world; characterised by a large skilled workforce employed in a variety of sectors. As mentioned above, the country is undergoing rapid urbanisation, with the urban population increasing at a faster rate than its total population. By 2030, with 575 million urban dwellers, India will have 41% of its population living in cities and towns (India: Urban Poverty Report, 2009).

To accommodate these additional millions into the urban system, in a sustainable way, the urban development processes in India will have to undergo significant remodelling and restructuring and entirely new cities and towns will have to be planned and developed. But there is currently limited awareness of the scale of the challenges ahead and grossly inadequate systems remain in place to handle the task. One of the main impediment in sustainable growth of cities and towns in India is the scarcity of land available for building physical infrastructure. Roots of these problems can be found in inadequate and inefficient land policies of the country.

At present, Indian cities are characterised by high densities of population, extreme poverty, unequal social infrastructure, inefficient urban infrastructure, inadequate urban services, environmental issues etc. Planning of cities and towns in India has, until now, failed to create an inclusive model of sustainable urbanism. The widening gap between the demand for urban infrastructure and capacity to supply what is needed remains a major constraint for sustainable development.

According to the Indian Constitution, responsibility for urban development and housing rests with State governments. Thus, while the policy framework comes from Central Government, State governments provide a legislative background within which the local bodies and development authorities regulate urban development activities (Adusumilli et Al., 2004). But policymakers have usually been unwilling to accept the phenomenon of urban growth and have attempted to counteract it by simply attempting to reduce rural-urban migration.

Housing is a principle theme in sustainable urban development. Aiming to fulfil a key aspect of living in an urban area - the provision of decent shelter for thousands of residents - housing sector development is guided by national and regional housing policies, specific sectoral development programmes, action plans, specific measures and projects in tandem with need. In urban centres of India, less than 10 per cent of the total housing stock is provided by public agencies. Over the past 20 years, since the implementation of economic reforms, public sector agencies have become reluctant to fulfil growing housing demands. In effect, housing sector development is now managed and controlled by private players.

Provision of affordable housing is one of the most formidable challenges that urban development in India has to deliver. Technical group set up by the Government of India in 2007 estimated the urban housing shortage to

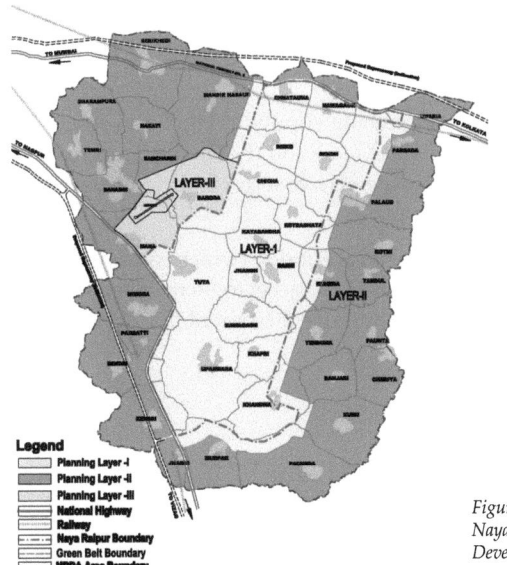

Figure 1: NRDA PLanning Area for Naya Raipur. Source: Naya Raipur Development Authority.

be 24.7 million units. Of this shortage, 99% is related to the "Economically Weaker Section" and "Low Income Group" segments (Ministry of Housing & Urban Poverty Alleviation, 2009). Need for affordable housing will be a crucial urban development challenge for India considering growing demand and escalating land prices in urban centres. The rate of housing development and provision has not been commensurate with the rate of population growth in the urban areas. An overview of the sector reveals that the demand pattern and affordability criteria of different sections' of urban dwellers are not taken into consideration, particularly those in the middle and lower income strata for which there is a scarcity of affordable housing. Governments are unable to provide housing and desirable urban services to most of the urban poor, leaving the sector entirely unregulated and in the hands of private sector with no policy direction or regulation mechanism.

Policy Directions in the Housing Sector –The Government of India's position on the housing sector is conveyed through the National Urban Housing and Habitat Policy (NUHHP) of 2007.

Some features of the policy are:

- Integrating housing provision to urban poor into the objectives of the Jawaharlal Nehru National Urban Renewal Mission (JNNURM[2]), Development of urban areas must be in line with the objectives of the 74th Constitution Amendment Act[3].

- Focus on urban planning, increasing supply of land, use of spatial incentives like additional Floor Area Ratio (FAR) and Transferable Development Rights etc. Allowing private sector to do land assembly within the purview of master plans.

- 10-15% of land or 20-25% floor space index (whichever is greater) in every new public/private housing projects to be reserved for low income group housing through appropriate spatial incentives.

---

2   Jawaharlal Nehru National Urban Renewal Mission (JNNURM) is the urban development programme launched by Government of India in 2005 for regeneration of Cities with financial assistance from the central government.

3   Constitutional Amendment to strengthen municipal governance The important provisions specified in the Act include constitution of three types of municipalities, devolution of greater functional responsibilities and financial powers to municipalities

In a way, the policy unambiguously delegates open market solution for housing sector development and expects private players to define the whole sector according to market conditions. One aspect that is very clear - the central government seeks to play the role of an 'enabler' and 'facilitator' under a policy that does not specify any precise instruments to achieve its stated objectives. The National Urban Housing and Habitat Policy of 2007 provides an impression that housing policies and programmes are formulated on the basis of political expediency and bureaucratic notions rather than a structural analysis of issues and challenges in urban development, including housing.

Chhattisgarh state housing policy

The Government of Chhattisgarh's policy position states that it 'will assist' all citizens, in particular the rural poor, to secure for themselves affordable dwellings with the government active as a facilitator (Housing Policy of Chhattisgarh).

Main features of the policy are: Legal and regulatory reforms, Active participation of cooperative sector in housing development, strengthening the role of government as facilitator

The State Government of Chhattisgarh's housing policy is very much in line with the national housing policy of India with many crucial areas of housing development having been delegated to the private sector. The State has proposed a series of actions - procedural simplification, legal and regulatory reforms, mandatory allocation of 25% of housing for economically weaker sections - but all of these are too modest to recuperate the housing sector from existing practices and to ensure equity for all economic and social groups. Also planning agencies at state and local levels do not have the capacity to systematically carry forward many of the aforementioned reforms. Effectively, following the footsteps of the national housing policy, the state government has also in the pretext of public-private participation created more space for a de-regulated open market system.

Housing Development in the New Planned City of Naya Raipur

The State of Chhattisgarh was formed in the year 2000, with Raipur as the capital city. Yet due to existing urban expansion and development problems faced in Raipur, it was decided to establish a new capital city: Naya Raipur. This new planned city is envisaged with multiple roles in economic growth and development of the state. The move to create a new city is highly commendable; firstly it will definitely ease the pressure on Raipur, which is heavily wanting for performance; also it will help remodel the economic strategy of this predominantly tribal state endowed with a large reserve of natural resources. Naya Raipur Development Authority (NRDA) has been appointed as the nodal agency for development and administration of Naya Raipur. The development plan for Naya Raipur covers a total area of 237.42 km², out of which the core area is 80.13 km², and the new city will be developed in three phases to a target population of 560 000 by 2031.

Land use in Naya Raipur

The total planning area for the city consists of 23 742.63 Hectares. The proposed land use plan, slated to be completely functional by 2031, has focused heavily on recreational, public and semi-public spaces, which together will cover nearly 50% of total land. This planning decision will lead directly to horizontal spread; expansion of the physical scale is very much questionable in such climatic region, where temperature in peak summer reaches 44 degree Celsius. *Table 1* gives the detail of proposed land use in Naya Raipur

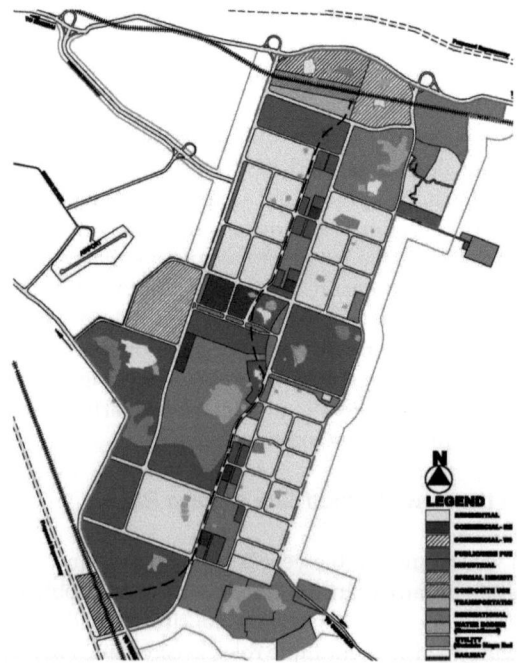

Figure 2: Land Use Zoning Plan for Naya Raipur. Source: Naya Raipur Development Authority.

Table 1 - Proposed Land Use in Naya Raipur by 2031

Land Use	Area in Hectare	Percentage
Residential	2113.39	26.37
Commercial - Retail	146.67	1.81
Commercial - Wholesale	130.67	1.63
Industrial	196.13	2.42
Special Industry	263.05	3.28
Public & Semi Public	1846.38	23.04
Recreational	2137.44	26.67
Transport	1005.77	12.55
Composite Use	177.6	2.22
Total	8013.1	100

Source: Naya Raipur Development Authority, 2010:xix

Housing development in Naya Raipur

Development guidelines, regulations, land tenure acts and the role played by Naya Raipur Development Authority will determine housing sector development in Naya Raipur. The population projection for Naya Raipur by 2030 is 560,000 persons and the housing sub-system defined by the development plan forecasts the requirement of 123 860 dwelling units, of which 46% would be constituted by 1 to 2 room units. According to projected housing sub-system, the maximum share of housing will be fulfilled by private housing i.e. individual houses, apartments, housing colonies, housing societies etc. This implies that private players will have an increasing stake in housing sector development.

The city has been divided into 21 residential sectors and the conceived population structure is: 600 000 at the city level, 150 000 at the community level, and 15 000 – 20 000 persons at the neighbourhood level. Housing areas will have a shared facility core at the neighbourhood level, in addition to the area level facilities. Projected net residential density is 93 households per hectare with a gross density of 250 persons per hectare. As per the Public Private Partnership model, government acquired land will be sold or leased to developers or would be allotted to housing societies for further development. The development plan states that the "private sector would be the main implementer, that is to say responsible for capital resource generation and the management of the implementation. The public authority would be the facilitator and protector of overall social objective of equity". What remains uncertain is the role of protector of the social objective in a premise controlled by open market without any decisive regulatory framework.

Regarding urban poor, the development plan says that "the development of the new Capital City characterised by a high level of construction activity will attract a significant number of construction workers. Providing suitable housing to the population is thus an important issue". Beyond this, housing development for urban poor is not defined by the planning agencies. The existing village within the planning area of Naya Raipur will be declared an urban village; (which is a good planning decision to incorporate the villages into the urban fabric instead of forcibly shifting them out of the newly developed area.

Any new construction within the village settlement shall be subject to approval from the concerned local body. This move is severely questionable, provided that these villages already have certain housing patterns suited to their context. Imposing new stringent regulations might have an adverse impact on processes of a sustainable amalgamation of these settlement areas into the new urban fabric.

Socio-economic aspects of housing development

an important feature of sustainable housing sector development is the presence of affordable and need based housing for the large section of urban working groups. It is necessary to retain all the sections of society for promoting community development and social inclusion. In the case of Naya Raipur there is almost no provision for economically regulated affordable housing for working families, considering that the number of entry level jobs will be sizeable. Eventually the communities will be forced to leave for peri-urban, suburban areas or even Raipur, thereby creating a travel cycle over long distance; directly affecting productivity in all sectors.

Naya Raipur faces many challenges; specifically with the scale of planning for independent sectors. As in other cities, gentrification is poised to become a serious social issue if housing sector development disregards the economic profile and social reality of the place. Climatic suitability of wider roads, large avenues and boulevards, and a large quantity of open spaces raises serious questions over the sustainability attributes being claimed by planners and development agencies.

Reflections on urban development and housing policies in India

Housing sector development in India portrays enormous disparity in need, affordability and availability. For sustaining balanced economic growth in cities it is necessary to develop a socially and economically accessible housing that is part of an urban development strategy. A wider range of housing options, types, prices levels and tenures needs to be developed in residential sectors. Housing policy has to exert a controlling influence on housing markets by means of policy and economic instruments and be carried out, on the one hand, by the establishment of a basic legal framework. In India policies do not translate completely as programmes and projects bring in desired results. Policy drafts based on a quantitative analysis of scarcity, and treatment of housing as a mere commodity, will lead to 'nowhere'. Policies should mandate specific time bound action plans so as to correct the arbitrariness in housing development practises. For this, it is necessary to have policy instruments that will guide programmes and projects through a regulatory framework.

Regulations need to reflect larger aspirations pronounced through policies at national and regional levels. These housing policy measures have to be backed up by urban development strategies which are directed, above all, at improvement of the living environment. India has to strengthen the institutional norms in the housing sector through an appropriate regulatory framework instead of searching answers in the housing sector only through an open market strategy. Regulatory frameworks have a significant bearing on urban development in general and, in particular, on planning, zoning, land use and plot development, space standards and infrastructure services. A regulatory framework is also one of the few instruments available to governments to influence urban land and housing markets and the investment decisions of private sector developers (Payne, G. Majale, M., 2004:25).

Lessons from Naya Raipur Model

The urban development model for Naya Raipur could lead to urban sprawl, having greater negative effects on the overall development of this city in the future. Public-private partnerships are desirable and required in housing sector in developing countries with limited economic resources. But interpreting public-private partnership as a policy instrument/initiative that paves way for a completely non-regulated open market system, disowning the State's responsibility, will prove detrimental not only for policy makers and the bureaucracy but for the urban dwellers, as well. This is especially true for the middle income group and increasingly so for those economically weaker.

Projection by development plan is that demand for dwelling units of smaller size would be high. This can be attributed to the sizeable presence of entry level workers, middle and lower middle income groups, single occupancy tenants etc. It needs to be assessed on the ground, to what extent private players will be interested in this section of society. Reason being that, for this section, there would be a need to create a variety of new housing options and tenures. Government has made its stand very clear, but what remains uncertain is how far the role of protector of social objective of equity will be effective in an open market system devoid of any regulatory framework. It is highly unlikely that the economic model for housing sectors or neighbourhoods would be accessible to all sections of society.

The process of housing development in any urban area has to be people-centred. To achieve the goals and objectives of the housing policy, subsequent programmes and projects should be generated to meet the actual needs of urban dwellers and strategies formulated to address their problems. The housing policy of the Government of Chhattisgarh follows the National Urban Housing and Habitat Policy, 2007, formulated by Government of India. Obviously, private players will have larger stake in housing development of Naya Raipur therefore, not mere guidelines, but a regulatory framework is crucial to ensure the realisation of policy objectives.

As a policy intervention, the state agency - Chhattisgarh State Housing Board (CSHB) - should be entrusted with more power and responsibilities in developing the housing sector of Naya Raipur. Essentially as policy instrument, the institutional bodies of planning and development under the State should be strengthened and professionally equipped to:

- Implement legal and regulatory reforms.
- Provide adequate need based affordable housing through wider housing types and tenures within present sectors.
- Ensure active participation of cooperative sector in housing development.

Formulate real estate codes and frame a state Real Estate Act with the objective of regulating operations of developers and builders.

References

Adusumilli, U. Shekdar, D. (2004) 'Regulatory Guidelines for Affordable Shelter - Case studies of Navi Mumbai and Hyderabad, India', in Payne G., Majale M. *The Urban Housing Manual, Making Regulatory Frameworks Work for the Poor.*

Chattopadhyay, B. (n.d.) *Sustainable urban development in India* - Some issues, NIUA.

Government of Chhattisgarh, India (2010) [Online], Available: http://cghb.gov.in/ [10 Nov 2011].

Government of India & UNDP (2009) *Urban poverty report,* India.

Grant Thornton India (2010) 'Growth & Governance', *Indian Real Estate - Vision 2020.*

Ministry of Housing & Urban Poverty Alleviation (2007) *National Urban Housing and Habitat Policy*, Government of India.

Ministry of Housing & Urban Poverty Alleviation (2009) *Annual Report 2008-09.* Government of India.

Naya Raipur Development Authority (NRDA), (2010) *Naya Raipur Development Plan-2031,* [Online], Available: http://www.nayaraipur.com/, http://raipur.gov.in/ [10 Nov 2011].

Payne, G., Majale, M. (2004) *The Urban Housing Manual, Making Regulatory Frameworks Work for the Poor.*

UN HABITAT, *National Trends in Housing Production Practises, Volume 1.* India.

United Nations (2008) *World Urbanization Prospects The 2007 Revision*, Department of Economic and Social Affairs Population Division, United Nations, New York

UNDP (n.d.) *Country Programme for India,* 2008-2012.

UNFPA (2007) *State of World Population 2007, Unleashing the Potential of Urban Growth.*

. (re) pensando o desenvolvimento urbano . penilaian semula pembangunan b
pment urbain . (ri) pensare lo sviluppo urbano . (re) thinking urban development . (re) pensando el desarrollo
um) denken . (re) pensando o desenvolvimento urbano . penilaian semula pembangunan bandar . (re) penser le
ensare lo sviluppo urbano . (re) thinking urban development . (re) pensando el desarrollo urbano . Stadtentwicklung
ndo o desenvolvimento urbano . penilaian semula pembangunan bandar . (re) penser le développment u
po urbano . (re) thinking urban development . (re) pensando el desarrollo urbano . Stadtentwicklung (um) de
volvimento urbano . penilaian semula pembangunan bandar . (re) penser le développment urbain . (ri) pensa
inking urban development . (re) pensando el desarrollo urbano . Stadtentwicklung (um) denken . (re) pensar
o . penilaian semula pembangunan bandar . (re) penser le développment urbain . (ri) pensare lo sviluppo urba
opment . (re) pensando el desarrollo urbano . Stadtentwicklung (um) denken . (re) pensando o desenvolvime
la pembangunan bandar . (re) penser le développment urbain . (ri) pensare lo sviluppo urbano . (re) thinking ur
ndo el desarrollo urbano . Stadtentwicklung (um) denken . (re) pensando o desenvolvimento urbano . penilai
andar . (re) penser le développment urbain . (ri) pensare lo sviluppo urbano . (re) thinking urban development .
rbano . Stadtentwicklung (um) denken . (re) pensando o desenvolvimento urbano . penilaian semula pemb
er le développment urbain . (ri) pensare lo sviluppo urbano . (re) thinking urban development . (re) pensando
entwicklung (um) denken . (re) pensando o desenvolvimento urbano . penilaian semula pembangunan b
oppment urbain . (ri) pensare lo sviluppo urbano . (re) thinking urban development . (re) pensando el desarrollo
um) denken . (re) pensando o desenvolvimento urbano . penilaian semula pembangunan bandar . (re) penser le
ensare lo sviluppo urbano . (re) thinking urban development . (re) pensando el desarrollo urbano . Stadtentwick
ndo o desenvolvimento urbano . penilaian semula pembangunan bandar . (re) penser le développment u
po urbano . (re) thinking urban development . (re) pensando el desarrollo urbano . Stadtentwicklung (um) de
volvimento urbano . penilaian semula pembangunan bandar . (re) penser le développment urbain . (ri) pensa
inking urban development . (re) pensando el desarrollo urbano . Stadtentwicklung (um) denken . (re) pensan
o . penilaian semula pembangunan bandar . (re) penser le développment urbain . (ri) pensare lo sviluppo urba
opment . (re) pensando el desarrollo urbano . Stadtentwicklung (um) denken . (re) pensando o desenvolvime
a pembangunan bandar . (re) penser le développment urbain . (ri) pensare lo sviluppo urbano . (re) thinking ur
ndo el desarrollo urbano . Stadtentwicklung (um) denken . (re) pensando o desenvolvimento urbano . penilai
andar . (re) penser le développment urbain . (ri) pensare lo sviluppo urbano . (re) thinking urban development .
rbano . Stadtentwicklung (um) denken . (re) pensando o desenvolvimento urbano . penilaian semula pemb
r le développment urbain . (ri) pensare lo sviluppo urbano . (re) thinking urban development . (re) pensando
entwicklung (um) denken . (re) pensando o desenvolvimento urbano . penilaian semula pembangunan b
oppment urbain . (ri) pensare lo sviluppo urbano . (re) thinking urban development . (re) pensando el desarrollo
um) denken . (re) pensando o desenvolvimento urbano . penilaian semula pembangunan bandar . (re) penser le
ensare lo sviluppo urbano . (re) thinking urban development . (re) pensando el desarrollo urbano . Stadtentwick
ndo o desenvolvimento urbano . penilaian semula pembangunan bandar . (re) penser le développment u
po urbano . (re) thinking urban development . (re) pensando el desarrollo urbano . Stadtentwicklung (um) der
volvimento urbano . penilaian semula pembangunan bandar . (re) penser le développment urbain . (ri) pensa
inking urban development . (re) pensando el desarrollo urbano . Stadtentwicklung (um) denken . (re) pensan
o . penilaian semula pembangunan bandar . (re) penser le développment urbain . (ri) pensare lo sviluppo urba
opment . (re) pensando el desarrollo urbano . Stadtentwicklung (um) denken . (re) pensando o desenvolvime
a pembangunan bandar . (re) penser le développment urbain . (ri) pensare lo sviluppo urbano . (re) thinking ur
ndo el desarrollo urbano . Stadtentwicklung (um) denken . (re) pensando o desenvolvimento urbano . penilai
andar . (re) penser le développment urbain . (ri) pensare lo sviluppo urbano . (re) thinking urban development .
rbano . Stadtentwicklung (um) denken . (re) pensando o desenvolvimento urbano . penilaian semula pemb
r le développment urbain . (ri) pensare lo sviluppo urbano . (re) thinking urban development . (re) pensando
entwicklung (um) denken . (re) pensando o desenvolvimento urbano . penilaian semula pembangunan b
oppment urbain . (ri) pensare lo sviluppo urbano . (re) thinking urban development . (re) pensando el desarrollo
um) denken . (re) pensando o desenvolvimento urbano . penilaian semula pembangunan bandar . (re) penser le
ensare lo sviluppo urbano . (re) thinking urban development . (re) pensando el desarrollo urbano . Stadtentwick
ndo o desenvolvimento urbano . penilaian semula pembangunan bandar . (re) penser le développment u
po urbano . (re) thinking urban development . (re) pensando el desarrollo urbano . Stadtentwicklung (um) der
volvimento urbano . penilaian semula pembangunan bandar . (re) penser le développment urbain . (ri) pensa

CHAPTER II

URBAN GOVERNANCE, MANAGEMENT AND SOCIAL CHALLENGES IN PLANNING

Prof. Jaqueline Polvora
Carolina Guimaraes
Luana Xavier Pinto Coelho
Lim Hui Ling
Kari Smith

URBAN GOVERNANCE AND SOCIAL CHALLENGES IN PLANNING. OLD THEMES FOR NEW REALITIES: INTRODUCTION

Prof. Britto Pólvora, Jacqueline[1]

Abstract

This paper discusses social challenges in urban governance, departing from classic studies in urban sociology. It departs from elements such as diversity, heterogeneity and exclusion as engines for claims and changes in urban contexts. It continues discussing them as challenges in contemporary urban politics.

Keywords: Urban Studies; Urban Politics; Democracy; Social Exclusion.

Urban realities have been the focus of study in the social sciences since the Chicago School in the beginning of the 20th Century, along with the urbanisation processes occurring in the United States. This sociological school introduced the debate about urban processes and has contributed to our better understanding of the complexity of urban social realities. Many decades later, social scientists still incorporate theories and knowledge generated by this school. Amongst many important contributions, the Chicago school raised a crucial point – they acknowledged cities as heterogeneous spaces where different groups of individuals intermingle, even if sometimes segregated from each other and not necessarily forming communities. Heterogeneity and diversity of urban realities are key points

---

[1] Brazilian urban anthropologist working on poverty and urban exclusion. She obtained her university education in Porto Alegre (PUCRS, UFRGS), Brazil, and her Ph.D. in the U.S. from the University of Texas at Austin, where she specialised in African Diaspora Studies. Ms. Pólvora's research focuses on the disputes between "formal" and "informal" city in countries of the South hemisphere. Currently, she collaborates with the Graduate Programme in Social Sciences of the University of Cape Verde, teaching and researching

that have been studied by urban social scientists since then. In order to debate the challenges in urban planning for cities' governance, this article departs from these elements – diversity, heterogeneity and exclusion – as engines for claims and changes. It will continue discussing concerns and challenges in contemporary urban politics.

Since Henri Lefébvre wrote *La Production de l'Espace* (1974), we learned to think about space as "a social product" and thus another element of social life composed by collective values and meanings. In the case of urban space, Lefébvre visions it as a capitalist product and producer of (capitalistic) meanings and values. This means that according to its economic mode of production, every society produces an urban model that corresponds to the reproduction of its cultural and economic values. For contemporary capitalist societies, marketing and entrepreneurialism are main values that are in tune with actions and policies; consequently, politics played in urban spaces are oriented to capitalist purposes. Following these lines, contemporary urban politics conceive and generate urban land as valuable and main merchandise for contemporary cities.

Given these structural forces, "urbanisation has always been a class phenomenon" (Harvey 2008: 24), for the privatisation of public spaces has been the rule in contemporary liberal cities in both developed as well as in developing countries. The internationalisation of the privatisation-rule follows the bigger global economic restructuring of urban geographies, and poor countries reproduce the same disparities in their cities between poor and rich areas (Sassen 2000). In this sense, phenomenon such as gated communities, an extreme example of the privatisation of public spaces, is also present in the routine of peripheral cities in poor countries. In these places, not only the privatisation of public areas endures in urban politics, but also a sophisticated division of the space between different classes and social identities takes place while urban reforms are implemented (Caldeira 2000).

The over-valuation of urban land and the consequent demand for it for business takes place because cities are important economic engines in both the developed and developing world. Cities receive financial capital with different purposes; these financial investments are dynamic and valorised goals from which local governments are benefiting to promote urban reforms, often increasing the gap between rich and poor people. These investments are repeatedly concentrated in real estate business in which only a certain class of people can participate. As the literature has been exhaustively pointing out, these investments often appear dressed with technical language under the label of upgrading and/or the expansion of certain areas, but in fact they exclude and segregate even more dispossessed people (conf. Florin 2005; Harvey 2008; Holston 2008; Sassen 2007; Caldeira 2000, amongst others). Additionally, new "castes" of employees – mainly international businessmen – emerge in urban areas of both developed and developing countries, increasing the differences between "important" and "non-important" professional activities. And yet, in urban areas all over the world the amount of well-paid (often over-paid) people shrinks as it increases the number of low-paid workers (Sassen 2000: 210).

All these aspects provide enough material to contradict the argument of the improvement and upgrading of urban areas and of people so that, inevitably, this contradictory phenomenon creates occasions for pressure and claims. As economic power concentrates in the hands of a few, cities' governments have to support the augmentation of gentrified spaces for a certain elite, either national or international. At the same time, governments have to deal with the (dis)proportionate augmentation of people who make their living from informal activities, such as street children and rag pickers, as well as with the increasing number of people living in informal and poor areas, frequently in slums. Thus, urban politics that apparently exist for the sake of the whole city, in fact promote an *embourgeoisement* of urban life, clearly spreading this lifestyle for citizens who are thought to belong to it. This social exclusion process is a global phenomenon that accompanies cities throughout the world, because they themselves are the centres where international financial capital operates (Sassen 2007; Holston 2008).

Given this reality, I propose to recapitulate the analysis, returning to what was already underlined by the sociological school of Chicago: the structural heterogeneity of urban spaces and the exclusion of part of their inhabitants, instead of assuming an "ideal" homogeneity (in economic, cultural, ethnic or gender terms). This has been the Achilles' heel of urban governments: how to govern so that urban politics respond to the heterogeneity of cities' populations? How to promote policies that respond to the financial pressures – since these transactions are the ones that pay the tax revenues of cities – and, at the same time, respond to the dispossessed whose necessities of land, housing, jobs, and consumption are clearly different and put pressure on governmental actions and decisions? In the end, the underprivileged also want to be included in the presumed goodness of urban scenarios promoted by governments.

One fashionable way of responding to the above challenge is to make people feel included through democratic-type governance. Very often more a rhetorical artifice than a practice, democratic governance has been included in the U.N. discourses and documents, as well as for development agencies and financial institutions like the IMF. These organisations are engaged in supporting projects that promote civic participation, the development of transparent and democratic institutions, the prevention and elimination of corruption, amongst others. All these determinations and goals demand people's participation, as democracy is the political principle for modern societies in which equality, justice, and human rights should guarantee the organisation of differences (Holston 2008: 03). In this sense, modern cities became the scenario in which these forms of governance must be played, as they are the *loci* where inequalities, exclusion, and marginalisation are more evidently manifested. Thus, one role of those who govern is to balance between the business mentalities that predominate in urban centres, and the claims and demands of those excluded from it.

Following the democratic principle of equality is not an easy task as it presupposes the redistribution of power, so that dispossessed people can participate in political and economic decisions. Several alternatives have been emerging to respond to this challenge, as some articles in this section demonstrate. Participatory budget is probably the most known in literature, as well as in political circles and in the organisations mentioned before. Many other different attempts of democratic governance are happening in different cities on different continents. Without entering in the merit of whether they are working or not – and accepting that some are – positive experiences offer examples of urban politics being open to the different demands in the city. Ideally, they carry the implicit acceptation that people have not only problems to resolve, but also solutions for them. This determination to redistribute power within cities' heterogeneity implies an acceptance that people can deal with the power to make political and economic decisions. Ideally, political decisions entail to redistribute power beyond political comrades.

Again, the school of Chicago serves us as a guide for thinking about the exclusion and redistribution of power in the city, since their studies recognised the abundant presence of "marginalised people" in North-American cities (especially R. Park and L. Wirth). Also, other sociological studies acknowledged the reality of cities which were divided by racialised ghettoes (Du Bois 1899; St. Clair Drake 1945). Two decades ago, discussions lead by feminist studies theorised cities as places where male activities and benefits prevail and women became more excluded (Wilson 1991; Spain 1992; Massey 1994; Hayden 1995). The process of the exclusion of women and other political minorities has to do, amongst other factors, with a certain type of urban politics that excludes those who are not wealthy and powerful. A more recent factor has been the economic global liberalization that promotes brutal divisions in both rural and urban spheres, and whose consequences can be seen more explicitly in urban scenarios. In this sense, urban exclusion is not a new phenomenon because the number of excluded people has increased along with the urbanisation of the world. What is new in this phenomenon, however, is the diversity of excluded people. The world as a big slum is the image given to us by Mike Davis (2006), referring to the disparate growth of deteriorated urban populations in developing countries.

In this sense, the only response for cities is to become spaces where democracy – and the struggle for it – is claimed. This does not mean that all over the world people are organizing and urban social movements are becoming an important force of pressure. Today's urban conditions – increasing exclusion of people, impoverishment and informalisation of urban life – on the contrary, should be seen as urgent pressures for inclusion of socially excluded people. Recent manifestations on the streets of Cairo and Tunis, in London last year, and in Paris in 2005, are the manifestation of political pressure on local governments, and, as the ongoing results show, they should not be minimised. There is, however, the reality of excluded families evident in informal ways of life which, notwithstanding their silent struggle for daily life, challenges urban governments to recognise and redistribute available resources and benefits. Informal electricity and water connections, land squatting and the creation of new informal houses and settlements are challenges that cities' governments treat as disturbances, when in fact these are ways of life that the excluded have found in order to live in contemporary cities (AlSayyad 2004).

Recognizing people's excluded reality means that urban planning is the first idea to be challenged. Including excluded people in this agenda means to be open to include in the very notion of "planning" different and often conflictive aspects of urban realities. Besides the political agenda, technical measures, and economic interests of progressive parties or alliances, planning should take into account the redistribution of goodness, which is nothing other than incorporating into planned space excluded parts of urban everyday life. Good governance should mean the guarantee of the exercise of different identities and, at the same time, the promotion of ties between people. More than that, it should also promote economic prosperity, political inclusion, environmental care, and basic urban benefits, amongst other rights. These are essential aspects that should be included in contemporary debates on urban governance.

References

AlSayyad, N. (2004) 'Urban informality as a "new" way of life.' AlSayyad, Nezar, Roy, Anania. *Urban Informality. Transnational Perspectives from the Middle East, Latin America, and South Asia.* Oxford: Lexington Books, pp. 7 - 32.

Caldeira, T. P. (2000) *City of Walls. Crime, Segregation, and Citizenship in São Paulo.* Berkeley and Los Angeles: University of California Press.

Davis, M. (2006) *Planet of Slums.* London, New York: Verso.

Drake, S. C. (1945) *Black Metropolis. A Study of Negro Life in a Northern City.* New York: Brace and Company.

Du Bois, W.E.B. ([1899]1967) *The Philadelphia Negro. A Social Study.* New York: Schocken Books.

Florin, B. (2005) 'Urban Policies in Cairo: from speeches on new cities to the adjustment practices of ordinary city dwellers' Simone, Abdoumaliq and Abdelghani Abouhain. *Urban Africa. Changing Contours of Survival in the City.* Dakar: CODESRIA.

Harvey, D. (2008) 'The Right to The City.' *New Left Review* 23, pp. 23 - 40.

Hayden, D. (1996) *The Power of Place. Urban Landscape as Public History.* Cambridge, Mass., London: The MIT Press.

Holston, J. (2008) *Insurgent Citizenship. Disjunctions of Democracy and Modernity in Brazil.* Princeton: Princeton University Press.

Lefèbvre, H. (1974) *La Production de l'Espace.* Paris: Anthropos.

Massey, D. (1994) *Space, Place, and Gender.* Minneapolis: University of Minnesota Press.

Sassen, S. (2000) 'A New Geography of Centres and Margins: Summary and Implications.' LeGates, Richard. *The City Reader.* London and New York: Routledge, pp. 208 - 212.

Sassen, S. (2007) 'The Global City: Recovering Place and Social Practices.' Sassen, Saskia. *Sociology of Globalization.* New York: Norton, pp. 97 - 128.

Spain, D. (1992) Gendered Spaces. Chapel Hill: University of North Carolina Press.

Wilson, E. (1991) *The Sphinx in the City. Urban Life, the Control of Disorder, and Women.* London: Virago Press.

SOCIAL MEDIA: A NEW TOOL FOR PUBLIC ORGANISATIONS

Guimaraes, Carolina[1]

Abstract

Social media has grown not only in terms of numbers of users worldwide but also in influence. Its interactive and social nature provides opportunities for public organisations and reinforces commitments to transparency, accountability and participation. This paper identifies six benefits for using social media by public organisations: information and participation improvement, image change, marketing, transparency, advice giving, and connecting with other organisations. This research was supported by two questionnaires answered by fifteen public organisations from Germany (13), United Sates (1) and Canada (1). The main finding of the first questionnaire validated 'Information and participation improvement' as the main objective pursued by most organisations in social media. Provided the wide definition of 'participation', the author designed a social media participation model, categorised in three levels: information sharing, opinion making and collaboration to decision-making. Through the aid of a second questionnaire, social media participation levels were analysed. Results show that most organisations are carrying out opinion making activities (11 out of 15), and hold mixed views regarding pursuing higher levels of social media participation (namely decision-making). The research concludes by identifying the present challenges and providing further recommendations for achieving further participation via social media.

Keywords: Web 2.0, Social Media, Public Organisations, Social Participation

---

1 M.Sc. International Cooperation and Urban Development, Technische Universität Darmstadt. Darmstadt, Germany. B.A. in Economics and Political Sciences, University of British Columbia, Vancouver, Canada. email: carguima@yahoo.com.br

Introduction

The explosions of social media platforms have moved from the personal to private sector to public domains. Social media refers to platforms that facilitate sharing, dialogue and collaboration between people, here referred as the various platforms that take advantage of Web 2.0 philosophy[2]. Social media has become a significant topic in the landscape of technology, communication, media and participation. While social media platforms have proven to hold significant value during political campaigns and civil society demonstrations, this article will focus on how it can be used by public organisations on a daily basis as a vehicle for sharing information, delivering transparent services, enabling dialogue and participation between various audiences and harnessing collective intelligence for ultimate decision-making. It is important to highlight that the research below is a short version of a much more comprehensive research carried out by the author; for further information please contact the author.

This research weaves together academic and reports on the subject with practical surveys, in order to balance theory with practice to shed light on the current practices of the pertinent target group. The first part provides an introduction regarding public organisations and social media, followed by a review of the initial survey carried out with public organisations. The second part elaborates on the findings of questionnaire one, developing a participation model that is further proofed with a second questionnaire, which entails a more in-depth analysis of social media participation by public organisations. Based on the analysis between findings from questionnaires one and two, challenges are outlined and recommendations are provided.

Public organisations and social media

Is the use of social media in the public sector an oxymoron? It is more likely to conceive that the private sector might find it easier to integrate innovation than its counterparts. Public organisations by nature count with regulations, bureaucracy and tradition, which can often serve as deterrents for leveraging greater transparency, communication, collaboration, accountability and stimulating greater levels of civic

---

[2] *Web 2.0 is a boundary-less concept characterised by many principles and practices that possess varying levels of importance some important characteristics are: cost-effective scalability, remix able data source and data transformation, a framework of participation, decentralisation of information and creativity of services, among others. (O'Reilly, 2005)*

engagement (Mergel, Shweik, and Fountain, 2009). In addition, social media platforms are continuously growing and changing; this dynamic movement might present a challenge to organisations not used to fast-paced changes.

Within Web 2.0 lies a series of potentials for what public organisations 'could be.' While Web 1.0 might be fully or almost fully embedded in public organisations activities, Web 2.0 requires a paradigm shift in terms of how public organisations perceive themselves and the way they interact with their audiences (Bruns, 2007).

Participation and information sharing

With the public organisation perspective in mind, in other words aware of its services delivery and organisational constraints, six perceived benefits for the use social media were put forth: information and participation improvement; image change of your organisation; marketing; advice giving; transparency and credibility; and better exchange of information with other local and international organisations. These six benefits were inquired about through a questionnaire sent to 22 public organisations in Germany, Canada and the United States, with a successful response rate of 68% (15 respondents). Each benefit highlights a different incentive for undertaking social media; they are not mutually exclusive, but instead support one another. Out of the fifteen respondents, thirteen were German organisations and two were international organisations (Metrodenver and Metro Vancouver).

The organisations chosen all have in common a conservative nature, are mostly followers of innovation, are required to consider various perspectives and angles of various subjects and issues, are accountable either to the public directly or to another public organisation and have bureaucratic processes. They can be divided into four sub-categories: governmental organisations [Goethe Institute, Institut Stadt Geschichte (ISG)], semi-public/semi-private (Hamburg Tourism), city administration (Kassel, Ingolstadt, Bremen, Gross Gerau, Nürnberg, Frankfurt) and metropolitan region [Ruhr, Rhein Neckar, Hamburg, Metrodenver, Metro Vancouver, Nürnberg)].

The objective of questionnaire was to gain a more refined understanding of the reasons, perceptions and objectives of social media usage by public institutions. For the focus of this article, only a few questions will be expanded upon.

Through the questionnaire, it became evident that social media is still a very young tool for public organisations; 10 out of the 15 participants had their first contact with it in 2010. Among the six main benefit outlined above, the most popular reasoning behind organisations' social media presence was information and participation improvement with 12 ticks.

Also, provide the hype of social media, it could be said that many organisations 'dove' into it, or followed a bandwagon without really understanding the meaning and expectations behind it. Interestingly, however, 43% affirmed that social media was indeed framed within a communication strategy, refuting the principle that all organisations had treated social media in isolation to participation and communication strategies.

While, the first questionnaire offered a positive overview of social media for public organisations' use, it did not give much insight in terms of the level, meaning and commitment of social media participation by the organisations. It left the reader unclear to what extent organisations were taking into account user perspective and how this perspective was actually percolating down the organisation communication chain. Therefore, the need for more in-depth investigation was warranted, leading to continuous research and a second questionnaire.

What kind of social media participation?

For a better understanding of the stated objective pursued by public organisations via social media: information and participation improvement, further study was pursued on it. This paper defines participation in general terms by an engagement process between public organisations and its direct users/constituents/citizens within the urban context in a flexible, informal, constant manner and up to speed with local and global complexities.

I WRITE
YOU SHARE
HE/SHE COMMENTS
WE THINK
YOU COLLABORATE

Figure 1.
Source: Bianca Guimaraes, 2012.

At the present time and for the sake of this paper, social media should be regarded as a supplement to informal participatory processes as opposed to referendums and political elections, for example. It has already been utilised as it could be successfully noted in: Talk Green (Vancouver, Canada)[3] and participatory budgeting[4] (Cologne, Germany), both very recent and on-going processes.

Two-way interaction, be it on- or off-line, is important to produce insightful reflections and outcomes especially. It is through these exchanges that people educate themselves about the various implications and consequences of different issues: "Actively engaging the sometimes crowd can actually enhance government's problem-solving ability and is an enriching aspect of democracy." (Goldsmith, 2011)

Communication is vital when contemplating democracy; therefore it is important to create various channels for interaction is important. Social media as a growing tool of communication can definitely assist public organisations in opening up and diversifying their communication channels. However, for significant exchange to materialise into something substantial (be it a theme to be discussed by higher-ups in public organisation or law, policy, etc.), instead of getting lost in informal conversation, social media exchange must be accompanied by action and commitment from the public side.

As it can be arbitrarily used to serve specific purposes, it is important to highlight the varying levels of participation. Hidden under a broad umbrella term, participation can range from very superficial interaction, disguise under 'education or curing' participants to real participatory action with higher levels of 'decision-making clouts' (Arnstein 1969). Based primarily on Arnstein and Shirky ideas, but as well as other participation and social media concepts, the below model was created by the author to facilitate the categorisation of social media participation, while also serving as an implementation model for organisations to progress to higher levels of participation.

As the model becomes more complex and organisations move further, the higher risks, assumed owing to power sharing as well as the increased work of trying to capture and consider different views, are matched by increased trust, empowered citizens and more accepted and widely adopted solutions.

---

3   For more information: http://talkgreenvancouver.ca/
4   For more information: https://buergerhaushalt.stadt-koeln.de/2012/

The model is divided into three levels: *information sharing, dialogue and opinion making and ultimately collaboration to decision making.*

Information sharing is nested in transparency, where all users are respected as important producers of information. Towards this aim, the continuous exercise of sharing hopes to break a cycle of information asymmetry by increasing the number of people that have access to information and are therefore able to make more informed decisions.

Once information sharing is more widely incorporated, conversation is added to the set of benefits provided by social media. At the 'Dialogue and Opinion Making' stage, both sides of the equation are exchanging at the same level, horizontally, and trying to understand each other's perspectives and opinions. A greater sense of community is fostered and the 'my side' and 'their side' is slowly replaced by 'our' idea and/or views. Public employee moderation is gradually replaced by user engagement. Ultimately, at the 'Collaboration to Decision Making' stage, public organisations are taking bigger steps in the name of participation and are more open for interaction and internal discussion regarding social media exchange. In addition, they are increasingly willing to incorporate more tailored social media platforms, for example, using crowdsourcing tools for specific exercise of collaboration.

After the elaboration of this model, the author approached the same organisations from questionnaire one, to better understand their participation status. In this way, the survey sought to investigate how these organisations were responding to, integrating and internally discussing comments, opinions, and suggestions exchanged through the use of social media. Organisations were also asked to categorise their own participation level in social media by inquiring as to whether or not they were carrying out opinion- or decision-making activities.

While much could be said regarding the results of the survey, this article would like to focus on whether they were pursuing opinion-making or decision-making activities. The assumption that all organisations were carrying out activities in social media beyond information sharing proved to be wrong. Organisations were only given the chance to self-assess between opinion-making and decision-making and most organisations, 11 out of 15, selected the former. Three organisations clearly expressed that they were pursuing informational activities only through social media (Metropol Ruhr, Hamburg Tourism and Metropolitan Hamburg).

This research gauged whether opinions coming through social media platforms were percolating down the organisational structure and being used for decision-making purposes or as content for internal discussion. The various replies demonstrated that only on rare occasions did information and public opinion reach decision makers, a reality that was reinforced by the organisations themselves when they selected opinion-making as the main pursuit in social media in their response to the self-assessment question.

No organisations affirmed that they were carrying out decision-making activities through social media. Some organisations mentioned that social media was relevant in 'soft' decisions (words used by the city of Bremen), for example in page design details (City of Bremen) or event locations (city of Nürnberg). However, no exercise that could lead to decision-making, such as discussing social media content with internal employees (especially decision-makers), asking a question to users regarding a specific topic or creating a platform to harness collective ideas, were conducted via social media.

In some cases, there were some discrepancies between an organisation's own opinion of their activity and the perception by the author based on their replies and observation of their social media platforms interactions; for example, ISG, City of Gross Gerau and City of Hamburg, that stated their were acting on a level higher that it could be noticed on their social media platforms.

This questionnaire shed light that the mentioned social media strategy cited on the initial questionnaire proved to be rather limited, provided the replies to the second questionnaire, insinuating a contradiction or even a differentiation of thinking. While a strategy can be thought of as an encompassing framework, it can also be a simple document that states a few rules for liability purposes. Overall, it seemed that the above mentioned strategy was far from addressing how social media could be used to leverage participation, or how such comments and feedback could be integrate on the organisational structure to reach decision-makers. Most organisations were perceived as 'free floaters' in the realm of social media, which lacked a structural afterthought.

The findings uncovered various intrinsic organisational challenges to the extended use of social media. The combination of fear of soliciting too many opinions, power-sharing, lack of human resources and know-how and a disbelief in the power of social media were shown as the main obstacles hindering further social media usage and organisational adherence to achieve higher levels of participation. These mentioned challenges should be tackled by following recommendations in order to bridge the gap between status quo and increased social media participation. One of the biggest challenges and greatest opportunities in social media for public organisations is to be authentic, which provides the user with a real perception of organisations' intentions and credibility in their mission statement.

Steps forward

Participation should be thought of as an organisational philosophy as opposed to sporadic events of dialogue that are neither cohesive nor frequent. Employees who are already working on the 'front line' with social media should be praised and asked to provide organisational insight on how to further social media participation for other activities and departments. Also, crowd wisdom should be recognised as an important tool for reaching a common goal, where there is a mix between content and context expertise.

While a framework for dealing with social media in public organisations should be created, it should be such that it does not stifle creativity and interdisciplinary work, and also follows the pace and objectives of each organisation's culture. Employees should be given the opportunity to think about how such tools could be an advantage to their work and ultimately the work of the organisation in general.

Figure 2: Social media: the oil that lubricates the system. Source: Bianca Guimaraes, 2012.

Conclusion: where are we at?

This research aimed at analysing the reasons behind public organisations pursuing social media platforms primarily in Germany, but also in Canada and the United States. While various reasons were found, information and participation improvement was realised as the primary objective. While only a small number of case studies were investigated, the results of this research provide the reader with a general perception of the status of social media in public organisations.

Social media provides an opportunity for improving participation through providing clarity, speed, accessibility and quantity of information exchanged and debated, generating dialogue and facilitating decision-making activities.

As a general rule, public organisations are engaging in social media as they realise the apparent need to create, distribute and exchange information, opinions and dialogue. However, when participation was further investigated and broken down into stages, it was revealed that social media remains an opinion-making platform and is sometimes even used for basic information dissemination purposes. Moving from Questionnaire 1 to Questionnaire 2, it was possible to perceive nuances in the definition of participation previously packaged under 'information and participation improvement.' The role of social media as a decision making tool still proves to be underutilised. Social media is mostly being used by the respondents as an additional communication platform and the content exchange is neither reaching far nor wide within the organisations' hierarchies. Social media comments are normally feared and hold negative connotations; when not, they are found in creative organisational sectors cultivated by inspired staff willing to harness a virtual sense of community, though often in an isolated manner.

New complexities and issues brought by the 21st century (budget cuts, loss of welfare state, climate change, immigration, etc.) will require new ways of conducting business, delivering services and interacting with users/citizens. In combination with technological change, which has brought new duties and priorities for public organisations, the response to this requirement is likely to demand more engagement, participation and interaction that is flexible, horizontal, constant and responsive in order to answer to rapidly changing context and population needs. Social media provides great potential in fulfilling the need to build with the public instead of fixating about the need to release only a finished product. The dialogue along the way is rich in user experience with the potential to continue to polish the end product in addition to being in agreement with technological realities. These digital networks and platforms have provided new rules in the urban context in terms of speed, quality and quantity of information, feedback and dialogue. This research put forth a technology-driven alternative to the traditional public participation processes that favours a new and user-centred tool.

References

Arnstein, S. R. (1969) 'A Ladder of Citizen Participation'. *Journal of American Institute Planners,* vol. 35, no. 4, pp. 216-224.

Bruns, A. (2007) 'Produsage: Towards a Broader Framework for User-Led Content Creation' *Creativity and Cognition – Conference proceedings,* 6th ACM SIGCHI conference on Creativity & cognition, ACM, Washington, DC, pp. 1-7.

Goldsmith, S. (2011) 'The Wisdom of the Crowd in New York City', *Connecting American Leaders,* Governing, February, 16. [Online], Available: http://www.governing.com/blogs/bfc/wisdom-crow=d-new-york-city.html [16 Feb 2011].

Hartley, H., Nordstrom, A. F. (2010) 'From Gov 2.0 - eGovernment Social Media Platform Deployments and Future Opportunities', *Slideshare,* [Online], Available: http://www.slideshare.net/egov/gov-20-egovernment-social-media-platform-deployments-and-future-opportunities [8 Feb 2011].

Mergel, I., Shweik, C., Fountain, J. (2009) *The Tansformational Effect of Web 2.0 Techonlogies on Government.* Social Science Research Network.

Shirky, C. (2008) *Here Comes Everybody: The Power of Organizing Without Organizations.* New York: The Penguin Press.

Shirky C., (2009) 'How social media can make history', TED Talks [Online video], Available: http://www.ted.com/talks/clay_shirky_how_cellphones_twitter_facebook_can_make_history.html [8 Feb 2011]

PARTICIPATORY BUDGETING IN SOUTH AMERICA AND EUROPE: A SOCIAL INCLUSION PERSPECTIVE

Xavier Pinto Coelho, Luana[1]

Abstract

This paper discusses how differently participatory budgeting has been interpreted by local governments as it is replicated in South America and Europe, taking into account its strong link to urban social inclusion that marks its origins especially in the Brazilian initiatives which started in the '90s. In order to assess this statement, a research was conducted in 24 cities on participatory budget's regulations, searching for their justification for implementing the project and the format given to it. Three big groups of objectives associated with the implementation of participatory budgeting were identified: *government efficiency, citizenship and democracy* and *social inclusion and urban solidarity*. The comparison of the participatory programmes in cities of Europe and South America has revealed that European cities barely relate participatory budgeting with urban social inclusion, but rather they put their focus on gains in administrative efficiency and the restoration of local politics' legitimacy. South American cities often relate participatory budgeting with social inclusion and have made advancements in the recognition and redistribution of resources for excluded groups within participatory budgeting, creating specific mechanisms of affirmative action in order to realise those objectives.

Keywords: Participatory Budgeting, Social Inclusion, Project Replication, Citizenship, Local Democracy, Europe and South America

---

1   M.Sc. International Cooperation and Urban Development; specialisation in Urbanism, Habitat and International Cooperation. Technische Universität Darmstadt, Darmstadt, Germany/Université Pierre-Mendès-France, Grenoble, France. Graduated in Law, Ouro Preto, Brazil. email: luanaop@yahoo.com.br

Introduction

The potential of participatory budgeting for social inclusion has been pointed out by several studies and researchers dealing with urban development[2]. In its origin in Porto Alegre,[3] participatory budgeting has aimed to transform social reality, mainly by inverting the priorities of city investment according to the population's needs. This ideal is not easily found in later replications of the process by other local governments.

Participatory budgeting is a process that aims to involve citizens in the deliberations upon what the next year's investment plan for the city will be. Instead of being a unilateral decision from local government, the construction of the budget becomes a collective decision. However, citizens and the public administration do not debate about the "budget" or finance; rather, citizens deliberate about their neighbourhood, their city, their street and their needs and wishes from infrastructure to services and the public administration intervenes to transform those discussions into budgetary plans.

This paper critically discusses how differently the project or idea of participatory budgeting has been interpreted by local governments, particularly in South America and in Europe, where it has been highly utilised. This analysis is done from the perspective of *social inclusion*.

Being socially excluded means to be denied the access to what the collectivity can provide so as to guarantee freedom and decent conditions of life. Or rather, according to Castells (1999: 8), social exclusion is defined as 'the process by which certain individuals or groups are barred from access to social positions that would entitle them to provide for themselves adequately, in an autonomous way, within the context of prevailing institutions and values'.

The relevance of social inclusion to the analysis of participatory budgeting is identified on two different fronts: first, as a participatory experience itself

---

2   Abers 2003; Avritzer 2003; Baiocchi 2003; Cabannes 2004; Cavalcante 2007; Ciciliani 2008; Hernándes-Medina 2010; Santos 2003; Sintomer e Allegretti 2009; Wampler 2007; Souza 2001; Sintomer, Herzberg and Röcke, 2011.

3   The reference of participatory budgeting worldwide is the experience of Porto Alegre in Brazil. Even if a few cities in Brazil attempted to implement participatory budgeting before Porto Alegre, some of them during the dictatorial regime, such as the case of Piracicaba (1977-1982) and Lages (Souza, 2001), it is with Porto Alegre that the initiative came to transform the way of governing.

which allows learning by doing, associated with the exercise of citizenship and the political inclusion of marginalised groups often subjected to relations of patronage. Second, as a practice that has directly aimed to invert the priorities of local budget allocations and to include excluded social groups by creating mechanisms for doing so. Then, it attempts to tackle social inequalities by incorporating into its process two necessary dimensions of inclusion: recognition and redistribution (Fraser, 2003).

The comparative analysis of the regulations of participatory budgets conducted in South America and in Europe revealed differences in the conception of the programmes. It was found that there was a great variety of objectives listed by local governments to justify the implementation of the initiatives. This research was conducted on 24 cities' regulations (using secondary sources[4]) that, during the period of the investigation (2011), had active projects of participatory budgeting, both in South America and in Europe.

The scope of the research was to verify the projects' regulations available online and the information accessible through official websites such as publications, manuals, presentations and reports. The main goal was to assess local governments' objectives in implementing participatory budgets, as listed in their regulatory documents, and to remark on the presence (or absence) of *social inclusion* as one of those objectives.

The cities researched were: 1) in South America: Belo Horizonte (BR), Cordoba (AR), El Salvador (PE), Fortaleza (BR), Montevideo (UR), Porto Alegre (BR), Recife (BR), Rosario (AR), Puerto Montt (CL), Rancagua (CL),

---

4 Reglamento del presupuesto participativo de la comuna de Rancagua 20.17.0.0.1; Resolução de 5/10/2010 sobre as normas para execução do Programa do Orçamento Participativo de São Carlos; Regimento Interno 2010/2011 do Orçamento Participativo de Porto Alegre; Ordenanza Municipal n. 191 MVES Villa El Salvador; D'org di data 19/09/2008 Linea Guida per Le sperimentazione de Bilancio Partecipativo Del Comune di Udine; Ordenanza 11.499 de 22/07/2008 cuidade de Córdoba, Argentina; Caderno de diretrizes e metodologia do Orçamento Participativo 2009/2010 Belo Horizonte; Regimento do Orçamento Participativo da Cidade de Fortaleza; Regimento Interno do Orçamento Participativo de Guarulhos; Carta de Princípios do Orçamento Participativo de Lisboa, Regimento Interno do Orçamento Participativo de Recife, Ordenanza n. 7326/2002 da Cuidad de Rosário; Regolamento Dell Bilancio Partecipativo Parma, Itália, 2010; Reglamento Presupuesto Participativo 2011 Puerto Montt; Regulamento OPJovem da Trofa 02/2011; Normas de funcionamiento de los PP 2010.02.03 Málaga; Regeln Bungerhaushalt 2010 Cöln; Règles du Budget Participatif Saint-Denis 2010; Reglamento Presupuesto Participativo Sevilla; Charte de Partenariat pour la maîtrise par le Conseil Local de la Vie Associative du Budget Participatif de Aubagne; Hildener Bürgerhaushalt 2010.

Guarulhos (BR) and Sao Carlos (BR) and 2) in Europe: Aubagne (FR), Corboda (ES), Lisboa (PO), Málaga (ES), Parma (IT), Grottammare (IT), Saint Denis (FR), Sevilla (ES), Trofa (PO), Udine (IT), Cologne (GE) and Hilden (GE).

Participatory budgeting in South America and in Europe: convergence or divergence?

The research produced a list of 30 different objectives behind the implementation of participatory budgeting, as identified in local regulations. They were classified under three themes, as shown in *Table 1*.

Table 1 - Objectives of participatory budgeting

Government Efficiency	Citizenship and democracy	Social inclusion and urban solidarity
improve public administration's efficiency	promote citizen participation	invert social priorities
accountability	deepen democracy	promote social solidarity within the city
transparency	strengthen social links	equity in allocation of public resources
Inform population about public finance	school of citizenship/ democracy	rescue of people's citizenship
build trust between citizens and government	self-ruling procedures	tackle social inequalities
facilitate control over government	enhance a global vision of the city	promote social inclusion
better use of local resources	direct participation	allow different social segments to present demands
overcome corruption and clientelism	promote active citizenship / empower citizens	promote social justice
co-decision/ co-management on public expenditures	promote sense of belonging	improve quality of life
improve communication, promote dialogue between government, technicians and people		promote tolerance, peace and respect of diversity
create public policies which meet people's expectations		

Source: Xavier Pinto Coelho, 2011

In the 24 cities studied, references to gains in three macro-categories (named *government efficiency, citizenship and democracy* and *social inclusion and urban solidarity*) were identified. The analysis of the relationship between participatory budgeting and those ideals will be further developed.

Objectives put into *government efficiency* relate to the implementation of participatory budgeting to gains in the public administration's own machinery and the relation between politicians and public administrators with citizens. It relates to an open debate on the public budget as a pre-condition for the creation of policies which meet peoples' expectations and as a process of co-decision on the best use of local resources. This open debate is considered to be a facilitator of popular control upon elected representatives, acting as a tool against corruption at the same time.

The objectives compiled under the name of *citizenship and democracy* are mainly related to participatory budgeting's potential to deepen democracy or enhance the quality of democracy, while direct citizens' participation is promoted. Some localities recognise participatory experiences as 'schools of citizenship' and 'schools of democracy,' as the deliberation empowers citizens and strengthens social links. Those social links often refer to the associative tissue, which becomes stronger as well.

As far as *social inclusion and urban solidarity* is concerned, the main objective identified was the possibility to tackle social inequality through an equitable allocation of public resources while inverting priorities voted on by citizens themselves according to social criteria. Objectives such as promoting social solidarity within the city or fostering social justice show how those municipalities see participation as a way to break the urban divide in extremely unequal contexts. Additionally, there is also a concern with the inclusion of vulnerable social groups, in a way to allow them to present their demands.

As far as the part of the study that includes the research findings in the 24 cities is concerned, the objectives related to *government efficiency* corresponded to 46% (forty-six percent) of the overall justification (formal) for implementing participatory budgeting, while *deepening democracy* appears in 37% (thirty-seven percent) and *social inclusion* in 17% (seventeen percent) of presented objectives.

From the 24 cities, 11 had *social inclusion* as a clear objective for implementing the project and as a goal of the policy in itself, from which nine were located in South America. In Europe, just two cities see participatory budgeting as a tool to foster inclusion and fight against inequalities, both being in Spain[5].

In *Table 2*, it is possible to make a overview comparison between the European cities and the South America cities, according to the predominance of groups of objectives.

As the table shows, objectives related to *social inclusion* are predominant in South America and they appear in Europe only in the Spanish cities. On the other hand, objectives related to *government efficiency* are more predominant in European cities. Objectives related to *deepening democracy* are more balanced between the cities on both continents.

Table 2 - Groups of objectives by continent.

Source: Xavier Pinto Coelho, 2011

There are also substantial differences in the approach to how to reach the main 'theme objective' within the same groups of objectives. For instance, the objective of *facilitate control over government* appears eight times in the South American cities' discourse and only once in Europe. Here, participatory mechanisms are still strongly related to the possibility of overcoming the dominant structure of power by allowing the 'people' – a concept with a

---

5   The regulations researched provided clauses disposing the main goal being implementing the policy and for this reason it was possible to conclude which governments used "social inclusion" as one of the main reasons.

strong ideological perception – to be part of the political life. On the other hand, *improve communication and promote dialogue between government, technicians and people* appears mainly in the European context.

Another difference, even within the same theme group, is that *deepen democracy* is overall more predominant in Europe, whereas *empower citizens and promote active citizenship* appears in prevalence in South American cities. It is clear that the presence of an element of 'pedagogy' or 'empowerment' in the discourse in South American cities towards the participants, which also relates to the belief in the pedagogical aspect of participatory budgeting on building up citizenship awareness.

Differences in projects' conceptualisation: objectives vs. mechanisms

The study of participatory budgeting's objectives listed in the policy's regulation was relevant to show how the format or the conceptualisation of the project would vary according to the justification given by local governments for its implementation. The studied cities where social inclusion is a clear objective have worked to create mechanisms to guarantee that this aspiration would be reached.

As stated before, among the 24 cities studied, eleven had social inclusion as a clear objective of the programme[6]. Thus, many different methods were identified to guarantee that vulnerable social groups could benefit and that some territorial redistribution could happen to benefit poor regions. Those mechanisms will be briefly described.

In order to guarantee an equitable resource distribution within participatory budgeting, the municipality of Belo Horizonte came up with an index, the so-called IQVU (*Índice de Qualidade de Vida Urbano*), which means "quality of urban life index," based on a set of 38 indicators (including access to health, education, urban infrastructure and housing, for instance). This index was given to each zone of the city as a criterion for resource distribution associated to size of population. The lower the IQVU and the bigger the population, greater are the resources allocated to the region for deliberation in the participatory budget assemblies. The city of Rosario in Argentina has also developed a "privation index" (*Índice de Carencia*), with similar criteria.

---

6 *Belo Horizonte, Cordoba (Argentina), Corboda (Spain), El Salvador, Fortaleza, Málaga, Montevideo, Porto Alegre, Recife, Rosario, Sao Carlos.*

The city of El Salvador in Peru gives priorities to regions according to population size and the privation of basic needs, which is a similar mechanism also used in Porto Alegre, with the difference being that, in the later, the participants during the assemblies make decisions about priorities. The cities of Recife, Cordoba-AR and Fortaleza have also adopted the mechanism of "election of priorities" to drive resource allocation.

The European cities of Cordoba and Málaga in Spain have adopted criteria for resource allocation as well. In Málaga, resources are distributed according to infrastructure availability in the region, urgency or general interest, whereas in Cordoba the priority is given to proposals in territorial areas with a lack of investment or areas that suffer from social exclusion and proposals that affect greater proportion of population.

Besides the criteria of resource allocation, the city of Belo Horizonte has also included into the process a mechanism to foster urban solidarity, which is called the caravan of priorities (*caravana de prioridades*). The regional delegates selected by the community go around the city to visit the places of projects proposed during the meetings, in order to give them ground to decide on priorities. This mechanism allows the participants to understand other realities and to better judge which district is more in need of investment. The city of Guarulhos has also adopted the caravans of priorities in its process.

Mechanisms to enhance gender equality are present within the studied cities as well. In El Salvador and Córdoba-AR, the number of female and male delegates must be equivalent. Other cities, such as Rosario, Recife and Fortaleza, have chosen to approach gender inequality by conceiving separate participatory arenas for the debate on the issues concerned.

Cities such as Sao Carlos, Rosario, Fortaleza, Málaga, Trofa, Lisboa and Puerto Montt have participatory budget projects running simultaneously just for youth and kids. Trofa is the only case in which participatory budgeting targets just the youth. In Sevilla, Spain, kids from the age of ten years can present proposals and vote. Their assemblies happen separately, but they present and defend their proposals to the regular assemblies with the adults.

Other vulnerable social groups also have special spaces for participating in the debate, such as the elderly people, who have a thematic assembly in São Carlos and Fortaleza; the black population and GLBT[7] in Recife and Fortaleza; and people with disabilities in Fortaleza. The city of Montevideo, despite presenting social inclusion as a clear justification of implementing the project, has no specific mechanisms to foster this objective.

Some sort of registration is required for citizens to participate in all cities of the research sample, so that repetitions of voting can be avoided. But no city relates participation in participatory budgeting with electoral procedures. Such measure can be identified as an inclusive factor, especially in Europe, since it allows immigrants to participate. The city of Udine, in Italy, expressly states the possibility of foreigners to participate by just presenting any identification document.

In many of the studied cities in Europe, the participatory budget was only one of many participatory tools available in the local administration. In France, for instance, the *"ateliers participative"* or *"les outils de la démocratie participative"* are part of a greater project of participatory democracy implemented by local governments. Citizens' participation there intends to foster a proximity management or *gestion de proximité*. From the social perspective, participation serves to reinforce the social links, envisioning a *ville solidaire*. (Sintomer et Hammo 2005).

Conversely, the case of Cologne in Germany shows how participatory budgeting or *Bürgerhaushalt*, exists mainly in the governmental dimension; that is to say, the public consultation on municipal finance is seen as a tool to reach public administration's efficiency and modernisation. In the analysed German cities, the participants can present proposals online according to the themes the municipality has already chosen. Their participation is consultative and not enforceable.

Conclusion

The data shows that, according to the objectives given to participatory budgeting by the local governments, the format of the processes changes accord. As the objective of *social inclusion* is mainly present in South American cities; the study assessed how the project has changed in format considering its beginning in South America and its later replications in Europe[8]. Even though the research focused only on the regulatory level, that

---

7 *Gays, lesbians, bisexuals and transsexuals.*

8 *Even though some authors argue that most of the participatory budgets in Europe have no direct relation with the Brazilian experience. (Sintomer e Allegretti 2009)*

is to say, on the theoretical rather than empirical elements of the projects' conceptualisation, it was possible to infer that, ideally, if the project aims to tackle social inequality, it will most likely also contain mechanisms to foster such a goal.

Through the research, the assumption that in European cities such an emphasis on social inclusion would not be overall present in implementing participatory budgeting was proven to be accurate. In Europe, local governments' regulations justify citizens' participation more in terms of public administration's efficiency and open dialogue with citizens to foster transparency and accountability. Participatory budgeting in this case is more within trends to modernise public administration and face current political legitimacy crises.

As far as the experiences studied in South America are concerned, the association between participatory budgeting and social inclusion is clear. Local governments have implemented projects with a clear aim of making a democratic revolution, empowering citizens and transforming the urban social reality, which was clear in the regulatory documents reviewed. However, how far those goals can really be achieved depends on how the administration seeks to realise the social objectives, how much of the budget is going to be allocated to public deliberation and which mechanisms are going to guarantee an equitable distribution of resources.

The research observed that the intentions behind the implementation of participatory budgeting varies enormously from cities in South America and cities in Europe. The differences in social realities may justify the differences in the discourse on the two continents. The urge for social inclusion in South America is higher, where the inequalities are outstanding. However, even if the degree of inequalities are not comparable in both continents, participatory budgeting has proven to be an important tool to redirect priorities of investment to areas and people more in need.

Acknowledgements

This paper is an excerpt of the master dissertation presented to the Institute d'Urbanisme de Grenoble to be granted the title of Master in "Habitat, Urbanisme et Coopération International". I would like to thank Giovanni Allegretti and Yves Cabannes for the support, comments and valuable time.

References

Abers, R. (2003) 'Reflections on what makes empowered participatory Governance Happen', in Fung, A., Wright, E., *Deepening democracy: institutional innovation in empowered participatory governance*, London: Verso, pp. 200-207.

Avritzer, L. (2003) 'Modelos de deliberação democrática: uma análise do orçamento participativo no Brasil', in Santos, B. *Democratizar a democracia: os caminhos da democracia participativa*, Porto: Edições Afrontamento.

Baiocchi, G. (2003) 'Participation, activism, and politics: The Porto Alegre experiment', in Fung, A. and Wright, E., *Deepening democracy: institutional innovation in empowered participatory governance,* London: Verso.

Cabannes, Y., (2007) *Instruments and mechanisms linking physical planning and participatory budgeting.* Working paper, Belo Horizonte: SEGRAC.

Cabannes, Y. (2004) 'Participatory Budgeting: A significant contribution to participatory democracy'. *Environment and Urbanization*, vol.16, no. 1, April, pp. 27-46.

Cavalcante, P. (2007) 'O Orçamento Participativo: estratégia rumo à gestão pública mais legítima e democrática', *Revista de Polícas Públicas e Gestão Governamental*, edição: Anesp, vol. 6, no. 2 jul/dez, pp.11-28.

Castells, M. (1999) 'Information Technology, Globalization and Social Development' *UNRISD Discussion,* Geneva: United Nations Research Institute for Social Development, paper No. 114.

Ciciliani, G. (2011) *Presupuesto Participativo desde una perspectiva de género.* Experiencia de la Municipalidad de Rosario, Argentina, [Online], Available: http://www.rosario.gov.ar/sitio/verArchivo?id=4514&tipo=objetoMultimedia, [15 May 2011].

Fanesi, P. (2005) 'Case Studies: Grottammare' in Sintomer, Y, Herzberg, C. and Röcke, A., *Participatory budgets in a European comparative approach*,Berlin: Hans Böckler Stiftung, pp. 367-391.

Hernándes-Medina, E. (2010) 'Social inclusion through participation: the case of the participatory budget in Sao Paulo', *International Journal of Urban and Reginal Research*, vol. 34.3, September, pp. 512-32.

Nez, H. (2009) 'La démocratie participative face à l'idéal d'inclusion politique et sociale: une comparaison des assises de ville à Bobigny et du budget participatif à Belo Horizonte', *Cahier du Brèsil Contemporain*, pp. 257-282.

Observatorio Internacional de la Democracia Participativa (OIDP), (2006) *Processes and mechnisms for the inclusion of indigenous women in local management. Cotacachi participatory budget*, Cotacachi.

Santos, B. (org.). (2003) *Democratizar a democracia: os caminhos da democracia participativa.* Porto: Edições Afrontamento.

Silva, T. (2003) 'Da participação que temos à que queremos: O processo do Orçamento Participativo na cidade de Recife', in Avritzer, L. and Navarro, Z. , *A inovação democrática no Brasil*, PP. 297-334. São Paulo: Cortez.

Sintomer, Y., Herzberg, C., and Röcke, A. (2001) *From Porto Alegre to Europe: Potentials and Limitations of Participatory* [Online], Available: www.dpwg-lgd.org/cms/upload/pdf/participatory_budgeting.pdf [27 Apr 2011].

Sintomer, Y. and Allegretti, G. (2009) *I bilanci partecipativi in Europa: nuove esperienze democratiche del vecchio continente.* Roma: Ediesse.

Sintomer, Y., and Ben Hammo, M. (2005), 'Saint Danis, chapter of the report', in Sintomer, Y, Herzberg, C. and Röcke, A., *Participatory budgets in a European comparative approach,* pp. 218-243. Berlin: Hans Böckler Stiftung.

Souza, C. (2001) 'Participatory Budgeting in Brazilian Cities: Limits and Possibilities in Building Democratic Institutions', *Enviroment and Urbanization,* vol. 13, no. 1, April, pp. 159-184.

Wampler, B. (2007) *Participatory Budgeting in Brazil: Contestation, cooperation, and accountability.* Philadelphia: The Pennsylvania State University Press.

AN ETERNAL SPRING FOR THE "JASMINE" REVOLUTION? GOVERNANCE AND CORRUPTION IN TUNISIA AND THE DEMOCRATIC REVOLUTION IN MIDDLE EAST AND NORTH AFRICA (MENA)

Lim, Hui Ling[1]

Abstract

The protests throughout Middle East and North Africa (MENA) since the last quarter of 2010 and throughout 2011 have raised hopes that a more democratic agenda would be spreading through these countries. Why? How? By whom? Will it achieve its agenda? This paper will look into the case of Tunisia and seek to answer these questions, exploring the state of governance and democracy in the country and the more immediate triggers of the revolution, with the intention to illustrate the impacts of poor governance on society's welfare and highlight how such events present an opportunity for development and improvements to welfare in Tunisia. The arguments are formulated by availing of numerous sources, from institutional documents to international studies conducted by multilaterals, NGOs and researchers. Moreover, special attention is also accorded to testimonies found on Internet social media platforms, with the intention to give importance to the perception by Tunisians themselves of the impacts of poor governance on their society. Whilst it is still too early to forecast the impact of the revolution, the paper will conclude looking to the possibilities and challenges unlocked by the "Jasmine" Revolution.

Keywords: Governance, Corruption, Democracy, MENA

---

1 M.Sc. International Cooperation and Urban Development; specialisation in Development Economics. Technische Universität Darmstadt, Darmstadt, Germany/ Università degli studi di Roma Tor Vergata, Rome, Italy. B.A. in European Studies, National University of Singapore, Singapore. email: limhuiling.lim@gmail.com

Introduction

"The point is not whether America or France always, or ever, lived up to these ideas, any more than Russia was to do after 1917, but rather how ideas and aspirations that emerged from these revolutions retain their validity in subsequent epochs." (Halliday, 1999)

As Halliday stated eloquently, more significant than the immediate impact of the revolutions themselves are the legacies they leave behind. Many societies have adopted the agendas associated with the American and French revolutions throughout history, but the countries of the Middle East and North Africa (MENA) have seemingly proceeded on a separate trajectory. However, since the Tunisian uprising in December 2010 – termed the "Jasmine" revolution by the media – that deposed the long-standing kleptocracy of President Ben Ali, and the spread of the protests throughout MENA through 2011 - there are hints that the broad concepts of democracy can indeed be universal and the calls of the populace for a more egalitarian agenda are as valid in MENA as they were in 1789 in France and 1989 in Tiananmen Square.

Naturally, MENA is not a uniform entity. Its peoples and cultural values are as diverse as its plurality of political factions, colonial legacies and economic development strategies. Tunisia, the poster-child of the current upheavals in the region, will be put under the lens here. First, this paper highlights the institutional background and the quality of governance and democracy in the country. In the second section, the paper points out impacts of poor governance on Tunisian society's welfare, using complementary evidence from new media. This source is considered important not only because new media platforms have been a vehicle of the revolution, but because the prevalence of corruption should ultimately be measured from the citizens' perspectives; new media furnish significant amount of testimonies of these and serve as a good alternative source especially in a situation where traditional media has been heavily state-controlled. The paper then logically proceeds with an overview of the immediate triggers that contributed to the rupture in the status quo in December 2011. And finally, the paper will conclude with recommendations looking to the future. Where relevant, comparisons with neighbouring countries of the Maghreb[2] will be made, as these are closest to Tunisia in terms of history and institutions inherited from the French.

---

2   *A region of Northwest Africa, in this paper, referring to the former colonial territories of Tunisia, Morocco and Algeria.*

Institutional context and quality of democracy and governance prior to the Jasmine Revolution

First, a conceptual clarification is needed. Tunisia is a secular state, which means that the government has no religion. However, it does not mean that religious affairs were ignored. Under Mr. Ben Ali's leadership, religiosity was banned, female public officers were not allowed to be veiled at work and, just as in Egypt and Algeria, Islam-oriented parties were banned (UNDP, 2011: 70-71). The secularism was oppressive.

Interestingly, secularism has often been used to explain Tunisia's social and gender achievements, which, together with the other two Maghreb states, is relatively more progressive than the MENA average (UNDP, 2011: 58); for example, women have freedom of movement; the family code of 1956 bans polygamy and repudiation and institutes equal divorce proceedings (SIGI, 2011). The previous parliament under Mr. Ben Ali had the most women in the region (Aljazeera, 2011). These are facts and the accumulated gender capital bodes well for the future of governance and inclusive representation in Tunisia. But some media reports have mistaken correlation for causality between secular government and social achievements. *The New York Times* (Kirkpatrick, 2011) published a confused article suggesting that secularism and democracy were incompatible with Islam. This paper will not commit the same error of over-simplification. Instead, governance in Tunisia will be analysed without confounding the issues with whether the state is secular or religious.

Now, in contrast to social achievements, the political institutions in Tunisia had been under-performing or even regressing since the country's independence in 1956. Tunisia is not an electoral democracy; it is a well-known fact that Mr. Ben Ali seized power in 1987 by deposing his predecessor. Whilst in other neighbouring countries, reforms had been attempted – although amidst uncertain paths of advance and back-tracking – there had been no attempts or interest in reforms within Tunisia's ruling ranks. The President appointed members of the cabinet, the Prime Minister and even regional governors and the head of elections-monitoring; the Chamber of Deputies was directly elected (Freedomhouse, 2011). The system of checks-and-balances in Tunisia had been cannibalised by the executive. Oversight authorities had little independence; the executive was overseeing the judicial branch, controlling the appointment and assignment of judges, making the judicial system susceptible to political pressure and long delays, and resulting in poor enforcement of the rule of law (OECD, 2006: 10).

In terms of economic governance, there are also large gaps, as in other MENA countries. Financial markets are fragmented, with strong state-ownership of many companies (OECD, 2006: 7-11). The Doing Business Survey 2010 did however rank Tunisia a good 55 out of 183 economies, significantly better than the MENA average (IFC and WB, 2011). Not surprisingly, foreign investment inflows have always favoured Tunisia. However, macro-data fails to highlight the real business climate as experienced by Tunisians. In the blogosphere, accounts of the government's shady dealings are rife and leaders are indicted for failure to ensure equal opportunity to incentivise economic activities.

With widespread abuse of power, media and civil society organisations (CSOs) could not serve the usual watchdog functions. Throughout the MENA region, governments have restricted CSO activities, banning them, or tolerating them but making it infeasible for them to function, often scrutinizing their finances, especially if from foreign sources (UNDP, 2011: 71). In Tunisia, the situation had been similar under Mr. Ben Ali. Rights to freedom of association and assembly, whilst guaranteed *de jure*, were severely curbed (Freedomhouse, 2011). In 2010, Tunisia ranked 164 out of 178 in the Press Freedom Index (Reporters Without Borders, 2010). Freedom of expression is guaranteed constitutionally, but critical voices were regularly silenced with legal and regulatory instruments. Libel and defamation were criminalised and broadcast licences only approved for friendly media, which served as propaganda machines for the president and his cronies.

Consequences of poor governance and corruption on wellbeing

Clearly, governance, which should provide the basis for sustainable development and inclusive growth to take place, is in the case of Tunisia, instead, a hindrance to development In the previous section, it is shown that an ambiguous separation between the private and public sector had been perpetuated by the former first family, which can only suggest that many avenues were available for conflicts of interests, asset stripping and corruption to occur. In addition, private monopolies were created by Mr. Ben Ali's family in several sectors of the economy (Tunileaks, 2011), which economically speaking, represent decisions on a macro-scale that misallocate resources and work against society's welfare.

Amidst all this, fortunately, Tunisia does not exhibit traits of the classic "resource curse." 60 percent of the GDP comes from services, whilst oil and gas constitutes only a fraction of the 28 percent GDP contribution from industry and mining. Tourism and remittances are important sources of foreign receipts (WRI, 2003). The causes of welfare losses to society are however linked to corrupt public decision-making. Research has confirmed that whenever decision-making follows expediency of rent-seeking, resources are diverted towards high-rent sectors for private profit, leading to inefficiencies (Delavallade and de la Croix, 2007). This corruption curse is perhaps best embodied in Belhassen Trabelsi, the first lady Leila Ben Ali's brother, who had holdings that were rumoured to cover airlines, hotels, car assembly, radio stations, real estate and other high-rent sectors. Many online stories referred to other rent-seeking activities by the Trabelsis.

Further distortions in resource allocation can also be detected elsewhere. Nepotism – "by knowing the right people" — is popularly believed to influence scholarships and job awards in Tunisia (TuniLeaks, 2011). Ninety percent of all businesses are family-owned (CIPE, 2005: 13) and these companies carefully cultivate their ties with the political powers. This inefficient allocation of resources has generated vulnerabilities amongst those who are not well-connected to the crony capitalists. Youths are disproportionately affected. In 2005/06, youth unemployment in Tunisia was 27 percent, mid-way between a high of 46 percent in Algeria to a low of 6.3 percent in the UAE in MENA (UNDP, 2011: 109). However, these moderate figures have to be viewed critically as they hide the severity of unemployment. In certain cases, people accept any means of making a living, including non-permanent and unprotected jobs.

In addition, the delivery of public services is poor and rife with petty corruption. A TuniLeaks report sums up that "speeding tickets can be ignored, passports can be expedited, and customs can be bypassed - all for the right price (Tunileaks, 2011)." Again, this affects the poor disproportionately. Even worse, it is reported that torture is perpetrated within government facilities (Human Rights Council, 2008). So, instead of effectively protecting its citizens and delivering key services to them, the government represents a threat to human security. This underscores the tragic consequences of years of democratic deficit, poor governance and corruption on the wellbeing of Tunisian citizens.

Immediate triggers of the Jasmine Revolution

In December 2010, Mr. Mohamed Bouazizi burned himself to death to protest police harassment. This has now come to symbolise the Jasmine revolution and the "Arab Spring" as the revolution swept across MENA countries within a few months. Anti-government demonstrations erupted everywhere and finally forced the President to step down. The self-immolation represented the wider political despair and economic alienation that had been felt by the citizens of the MENA region for some time. In the UNDP/Arab HDR calculations, conducted across all Arab countries, there had been no improvements in governance from 1996 to 2007. In Tunisia during the same period, deterioration in component indicators, from voice and accountability, political stability and government effectiveness to regulatory quality, was observed. Improvements in the dimensions of rule of law and control of corruption were negligible as they started from low bases and recorded changes of only 0.52 and 0.18 respectively[3] (UNDP, 2011: 263).

The absence of coordinated demands for democracy and lack of organised mass demonstrations has for too long led leaders in the MENA region to think that merely aesthetic changes are needed. In Tunisia, throughout 2010, the authorities campaigned for amendments to lift the age limit on presidential candidates to allow Mr. Ben Ali to run for a sixth term. Applying the heavy-handed approach that had worked before, the government harassed and imprisoned political opponents, activists and bloggers who were against economic injustices, demanded increased transparency and rights to free and fair elections. But when the self-immolation act of Mr. Bouazizi sparked off a true revolution of the masses that superseded his individual cause, it was evident that people no longer wanted the patronage from the Tunisian elites. They demanded development and Mr. Bouazizi's suicide served to release all the built-up anger at the undemocratic status quo.

Much had been analysed in reports about the new tech-savvy generation using the tools of Wikileaks and Facebook to their advantage as well as the emergence of civil society in the MENA region, as if technology triggered the revolution. But these sensationalised reports do not give sufficient justice to how the mass protests had been incipient for a long time, stifled, re-emerged and finally gained momentum and burst into revolution. The Tunisian population was demanding their basic rights to a life of dignity. Civil society has always been present in Tunisian society, in spite of the authorities' best efforts in suppressing it. Indeed, technologically-literate youths were instrumental in spreading the message and building momentum for the cause. And true, millions of youths in MENA countries have been constructing alternative social spaces of resistance with the aid of communications technology; this was seen in Egypt where, before the

---

3 *From a range of -2.5 to 2.5, the higher the score the better.*

Arab Spring, they broke "through the rigid case of the state to mobilise — not in the streets but on the screens of computers" (Bayat, 2009: 135). But the revolution does not belong to this class alone; the Tunisian revolution included participation from every level of society. The uniting force was the call for democracy. The spread of the "Jasmine" revolution to the streets of Egypt, Algeria, Jordan, Yemen and Spain is evidence enough of this universal demand.

Conclusion and recommendations for the future

The challenges ahead for Tunisia are significant. The most urgent challenges to face include the quick introduction of good governance and real democracy, which is oxymoronic, as time is what's needed for these to develop organically, from the inside out, rather than being "introduced." Nevertheless, the grassroots-led revolution signals a good beginning and foundation. There are hints that there are sound leaders and a flourishing of citizen voices and active monitoring of the ongoing evolution of the governance processes at work. This is true bottom-up governance in the making. Already, in implementing the first item on the agenda, organizing free and fair elections, the Tunisians have done well with following the principles of democracy, unbanning political Islamist parties and ruling for gender parity in the electoral lists for the polls, an innovation in MENA (Aljazeera, 2011).

What role do international organisations have now? One can take inspiration from William Easterly's call to promote "searchers[4]", local people who can apply knowledge and innovations to local ground conditions. International organisations would do well to enable more local initiatives. A good example is the US Department of State's Middle East Partnership Initiative (USDOS, 2011), whose local grants help to "strengthen civic engagement and support electoral management," through supporting cooperation between two Moroccan- and Tunisian-based NGOs, Club UNESCO Bardo and young civil society activists (USDOS, 2011). The shape of any future governance structure should have more emphasis on local governance through decentralisation. This can proceed in small steps, for example, through participatory budget planning exercises, whose success and uptake has been proven in municipalities as geographically diverse as in South America and China.

---

4   In *The White Man's Burden* (New York: Penguin), William Easterly (2006) praised "searchers", the decentralised agents participating in open markets, in finding the development solutions that would work, over "planners", whose patronizing approach has been shown time and again to have failed.

In the same vein of supporting "searchers," the private sector can be enabled further. Tunisia has been cooperating quite actively internationally even under the previous regime to improve its corporate governance, such as being participant to the MENA-OECD-World Bank Initiative on Governance and Investment for Development. Going further, there should be a strategy for structural reforms and privatisation without necessarily suffering the shock therapy that many ex-Soviet Union states underwent. Divestiture through public offerings can be one of the most transparent and politically acceptable privatisation means. This can additionally stimulate the growth of a domestic investor base and financial markets, moving away from the classic state-financing model that had left many sectors vulnerable to rent-seeking behaviour.

For the gains in business and development to be shared out more, public governance, corporate governance and civic governance would all have to be improved. Rule of law has to be strengthened and enforced. More severe punishments have to be imposed on public office holders under anti-corruption laws.[5] As the new administrative system forms, taking into account the fact that citizen awareness of their role in governance is already heightened, participation and action in community-based monitoring can be promoted to good effect. Service users are already exchanging information with each other verbally and through online channels about the quality of public service they receive. This customer feedback loop can be integrated into the new administration. With such reforms, governance can serve its true role of citizen enablement, propelling the Tunisian population towards their own chosen future. It is critical that, during the transition period, one does not lose track of this final goal, that is, a goal of Tunisia's own choosing, and not one introduced by international organisations. It is true that many things need to proceed at once and that resources and time are short, but true democracy and good governance has to grow organically, taking decades before visible and measurable improvements can be observed. For this, the revolutionary fervour must necessarily calm down to a sensible patience for things to run their course.

---

5   This is the carrot-and-stick approach practiced in Singapore, where a mix of competitive salaries and heavy punishment for corruption within the public sector is coordinated with transparent public and corporate governance system to good outcomes.

References

Al-Dahdah, E. (2007) 'Gouvernance et développement dans les pays du Maghreb : constats et implications pratiques'. *La lettre d'information trimestrielle du Groupe de la Banque mondiale au Maghreb*, vol. 5.

Aljazeera (2011) 'Tunisian Gender-Party 'Revolution' Hailed'. Aljazeera, April, 26. [Online], Available: http://english.aljazeera.net/news/africa/2011/04/2011421161714335465.html [5 Jun 2011].

Bayat, A. (2009) *Life as Politics: How Ordinary People Change the Middle East*, Palo Alto: Stanford University.

Centre for International Private Enterprise (CIPE) (2005) *Regional Corporate Governance Forum: Private Sector Consultative Meeting*, Amman, [Online], Available: http://www.cipe.org/regional/mena/pdf/RCGFReport.pdf [4 Jun 2011].

Delavallade, C. and de la Croix, D. (2007) 'Growth, Public Investment and Corruption with Failing Institutions'. *Working Paper 61 ECINEQ, Society for the Study of Economic Inequality*.

Freedomhouse (2011) 'Tunisia', *Freedomhouse*. [Online], Available: http://www.freedomhouse.org/uploads/fiw11/Tunisia_FIW_2011.pdf [6 Jun 2011].

Halliday, F. (1999) *Revolutions and World Politics: The Rise and Fall of the Sixth Great Power*. Hampshire: Palgrave.

Human Rights Council Working Group of the Universal Periodic Review (2008) 'First Session', *Summary prepared according to paragraph 15(c) of the annex to Human Rights Council decision 1/5*. Geneva, 7-18 April. Geneva: UN High Commission on Human Rights.

International Finance Corporation (IFC) and World Bank (WB) (2011) 'Ease of Doing Business in Tunisia', *Doing Business*, [Online], Available : http://www.doingbusiness.org/data/exploreeconomies/tunisia/ [6 Jun 2011]

Kirkpatrick, D. D. (2011) 'Tunisia Leader Flees and Prime Minister Claims Power', *New York Times*, January 14. [Online], Available: http://www.nytimes.com/2011/01/15/world/africa/15tunis.html?_r=2&hp=&pagewanted=all [4 Jun 2011].

United States Department of States (USDOS) (2011). 'MEPI Local Grant Project Engaging Young Tunisian Civil Society Activists', *Middle East Partnership Initiative (MEPI)*, [Online], Available: http://www.mepi.state.gov/engaging-young-tunisian.html [10 Jun 2011].

Nawaat (2011) 'Nawaat', [Online] Available from: http://nawaat.org/portail/ [6 Jun 2011].

Organisation for Economic Cooperation and Development (OECD) (2006) 'Advancing the Corporate Governance Agenda in the Middle East and North Africa: A Survey of Legal and Institutional Frameworks', *OECD*, [Online], Available: http://www.oecd.org/dataoecd/43/59/38186933.pdf [8 Nov 2009].

Reporters Without Borders (2010) 'Press Freedom Index 2010', *Reporters Without Borders*, [Online], Available: http://en.rsf.org/press-freedom-index-2010,1034.html [7 Jun 2011].

Social Institutions and Gender Index (SIGI) (2011) 'Gender Equality and Social Institutions in Tunisia', *SIGI*, [Online], Available: http://genderindex.org/country/tunisia [5 Jun 2011].

TuniLeaks (2011) *TuniLeaks*, [Online]. Available: https://tunileaks.appspot.com/?p=33002 [7 Jun 2011].

United Nations Convention Against Corruption Civil Society Coalition (UNCAC Coalition) (2011) 'Uprisings in the Arab World: Time to Address Illicit Wealth',

UNCAC [Online], Available: www.uncaccoalition.org/en/home/167-uprisings-in-the-arab-world-time-to-deny-safe-haven-for-hiding-illicit-wealth.html [4 Jun 2011].

United Nations Development Programme (UNDP) (2011) 'Arab Human Development Report', [Online], Available: www.arab-hdr.org [14 Jun 2011].

World Bank (2011) 'World Governance Indicators' [Online] *World Bank*, Available from: www.govindicators.org [07.06.2011]

World Resources Institute (2003) 'Economic Indicators – Tunisia', *EarthTrends*, [Online], Available: http://earthtrends.wri.org/pdf_library/country_profiles/eco_cou_788.pdf [12 Jun 2011].

THE WALL, THE DOOR, AND THE KEY: RESILIENCE, EDUCATION AND PLANNING IN SEGREGATED URBAN COMMUNITIES

Smith, Kari[1]

Abstract

The concept of resilience has been increasingly used to understand and ameliorate a range of social challenges through examining how individuals, families and communities respond and adapt to stressful conditions. Resilience is appealing as a conceptual tool as it accommodates the complex, dynamic and multidisciplinary nature of the fields to which it has been applied, including urban planning and development.

This paper is an abbreviation of the author's Masters thesis (Smith 2011), which aimed to lay the foundation for the operationalisation of the concept of resilience in urban planning practice. To do this, this paper reviews education, urban planning, resilience and their possible configurations for the improvement of conditions commonly found in segregated urban communities. The motivation underpinning this analysis is an interest in how the concept of resilience has or could be used to design, implement and measure interventions made to improve the conditions of urban communities in distress.

Keywords: Resilience, Participatory Planning, Urban Segregation, Education, Non-Governmental Organisations (NGO), Urban Interventions

---

[1] M.Sc. International Cooperation and Urban Development; specialisation in Urbanism, Habitat and International Cooperation. Technische Universität Darmstadt, Darmstadt, Germany/ Université Pierre-Mendès-France, Grenoble, France. B.S. in Business Administration, Northern Arizona University, United States of America. email: kari.smith@yahoo.com

Introduction

Resilience in the social sciences refers to the ability of an individual or group to maintain their structure, cohesion and well-being despite difficult or trying situations, both traumatic incidents (i.e. a natural disaster, crime or other violent act) and long-term sustained stress (i.e. poverty, discrimination or oppression). The concept of resilience is increasingly being used to understand social problems and challenges; this paper explores its current and potential use by urban planners in the urban planning process. To do this, a review of the literature on resilience was conducted, a summary of which is provided to the reader. This will be followed by a presentation of the analytical framework developed for and employed within this thesis, a framework which is used to identify specific indicators and agents[2] of resilience. The agents identified for the purposes herein are planners and the planning process, education and non-governmental organisations (NGOs). Next, the identified definitions, indicators and agents of resilience are converged, producing a selection of potential scenarios that begin to test the practical applicability of resilience in planning. The paper will culminate with the author's conclusions and a summary of potential further research.

The concept of resilience

In terms of urban planning and development, resilience has largely been applied to disaster preparation and recovery, looking at how to minimise community vulnerability and improve response times and access to resources, with the overall goal of returning as quickly as possible to a previous state of well-being (Norris et al. 2008). Building on this work, persistent resilience looks at how communities survive and cope under conditions of long-term sustained stress, such as those resulting from segregation, poverty and oppression (Andres & Round 2011).

The flexibility and adaptability of the concept of resilience is perhaps both its strength and its weakness (Brown & Kulig 1996). In part due to its adoption from different disciplines, it has suffered from perhaps being too broad, flexible and adaptable; this can be seen in the number of ways in which the term is defined and interpreted. Although there are nearly as many interpretations of resilience as there are people who use it, we can identify common themes amongst them; some examples of this are the access and

---

2 Agent is defined as any entity or element that influences or has the potential to influence the resilience of another entity.

distribution of power and resources and the implicit and implied role of education in the development and demonstration of resilience.

In addition to the application of the concept of resilience to disaster preparation and recovery and in the study of communities living in conditions of sustained long-term stress, there has been some development of the concept that are applicable to, combine or supersede these two general categories. This includes 1) the concept of human agency, which is used to differentiate between mere survival and intentional action to improve one's situation and 2) social and institutional resilience which suggests that the presence or lack of resilience on the individual, family, community or other small scale may, in fact, be symptomatic of a lack of resilience at a larger scale.

As the concept of resilience has produced new insights and a deeper understanding and perhaps more innovative perspective towards social problems, the discourse has naturally led to the potential use of this understanding to prevent or minimise problems, mainly by reducing risk and vulnerability and increasing resilience and adaptation capacity. The application of resilience in the design and implementation of interventions is naturally more developed in those disciplines that were early adopters of the concept, namely in child development and psychology; other areas including urban planning are following suit, particularly in the fight against increasing environmental vulnerabilities due to climate change (Cinner et al. 2009). *Figure 1* offers a visual summary of the literature on resilience upon which this paper is based:

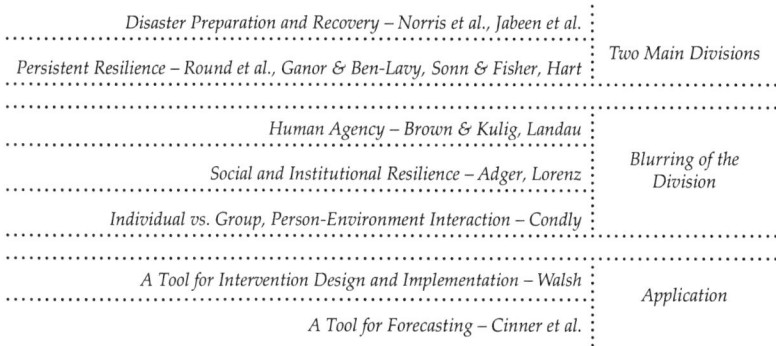

Figure 1: Summary of referenced resilience literature. Source: Smith, 2011

Moving forward from these definitions, how is the concept of resilience (or how could it be) translated into actual characteristics or features (herein referred to as indicators) and who or what influences or could influence the resilience of a given entity (herein referred to as agents)? Regarding measurement, *Figure 2*. "Summary of factors, criteria and indicators of resilience" was compiled from the aforementioned literature to provide a general sense of the indicators of resilience that can be found across and between research and disciplines.

Economics, Infrastructure & Resources
- *Employment rates – diversity, flexibility and stability of economic activity*
- *Infrastructure – spatial (i.e. housing), social (i.e. community) and services (water, electricity, etc.)*
- *Distribution of power, knowledge and resources*

Information, Communication, Skills & Competences
- *Distribution and accuracy of information*
- *Language, communication, literacy and levels / equity of formal education*
- *Critical thinking, problem-solving and decision-making*
- *Collective and self-efficacy, ability to organise and take action*

Social Capital, Social Networks & Relationships
- *Inclusivity, exclusivity and legitimacy of as well as linkages with institutions*
- *Political representation and political will*
- *Social networks and interpersonal relations*
- *Presence of mediating structures and alternative spaces*

History, Identity, Perspective & Other Psychosocial Factors
- *Narratives, cohesion, self- and group esteem*
- *Sense of belonging, attachment to place and macro-belonging*
- *Perception of and approach to adversity and change*

Figure 2: Summary of factors, criteria and indicators of resilience.[3] Source: Smith, 2011

Regarding agents of resilience, planners and the planning process, education and non-governmental organisations (NGOs) were identified as relevant agents of resilience for the purposes of this paper; *Table 1*. "Summary of

---

3 Based on Norris et al. 2008, Jabeen et al., 2010 Andres & Round 2011, Round et al. 2008 and 2010, Ganor & Ben-Lavy 2003, Hart 1973, Sonn & Fisher 1998, Brown & Kulig 1996, Adger 2000, Lorenz 2010, Cinner et al. 2009, Walsh 1996

Table 1 - Summary of resilience indicators by key agent

	Resilience Indicators		
Agents of Resilience — *Planners and those in the Planning Process*	Distribution of knowledge, power and resources	Participation, social networks and a sense of belonging	Distribution of power and resources
	Empowerment and creating points of entry for participation	Identity and esteem	Inclusivity/exclusivity of institutions and organisations
	Problem-solving and decision-making	Critical thinking, decision-making and problem-solving skills	Linkages with institutions and organisations
	Distribution and accuracy of information	Literacy, level/equity of formal education, training, language and effective communication	Relationships, social capital, trust and legitimacy
	Mediating structures and advocacy	Employment and economic diversity	NGOs as product or means of self-organisation and leadership
	Social capital, networks and relationships	Mediating structures and alternative spaces	Power (influence on public opinion) and distribution of information
		Education	*NGOs*

Source: Smith, 2011

resilience indicators by key agent" provides the results of a correlation between the sample of indicators (*Figure 2*) and the three selected agents (based on existing literature relevant to the three agents).

Analytical Framework

Figure 3 illustrates the analytical framework developed in order to explore both indicators and agents of resilience, specifically through the lens of the planner via the planning process.

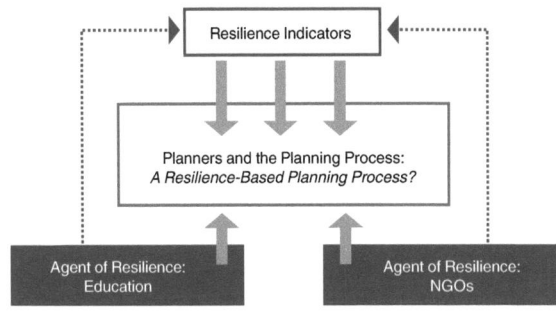

Figure 3: Analytical framework.
Source: Smith, 2011

The convergence of selected indicators and agents of resilience

As illustrated in the analytical framework, the chosen sphere of convergence is planning and the planning process, where the elements of analysis (the concept, indicators and agents of resilience) and their relationships (actual and potential) are considered. Forester's theories of participatory planning were used as a model for the planning process as they are particularly suitable (Forester 1996); equity, advocacy and collaborative planning theories are also strongly linked. Planning and the planning process is presented as the sphere of convergence (rather than education or NGOs) due to the limitations in scope of education and NGOs, the unique position of the planner and, according to Forester, the flexibility of the planning process (which depends on the planner's access to and use of energy, resources, networks, etc.).

Building upon the preceding correlation of definitions, indicators and agents of resilience, various scenarios were analysed to explore the potential practical use of resilience in planning practice. I will highlight here three notable results of these analyses. Firstly, the definitions of resilience identified were applied to Norris et al.'s "Model of stress resistance and resilience" (see *Figure 4*). This illustration positions an intervention as a form of disturbance, sharing characteristics and, to a degree, a similar trajectory as a disaster or crisis. This ultimately suggests that a combination of the two main divisions of resilience can be used in conjunction to understand and address social problems and/or an identified need for social change.

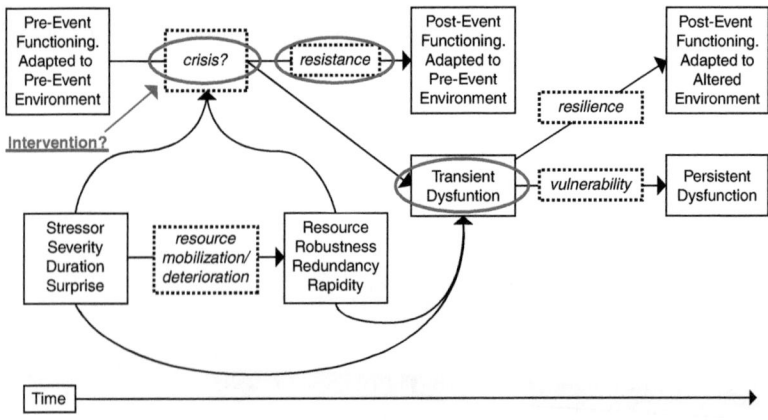

Figure 4: Source: Smith, 2011. Based on Norris et al.'s model of stress resilience and resistance. Highlights and added text (in red for coloured versions) are the author's.

The next two illustrations are used to explore the potential results of a planner's attempt to strengthen community resilience in an effort to increase citizen participation either directly or through the use of one or more other agents of resilience. The first of the two (see *Figure 5*) was generated from a scenario based on the planning theories of Forester regarding both the participation of citizens versus developers and on various strategies that Forester proposes as tools available to planners for managing conflicts in the planning process. Identifying a lack of power as a roadblock to participation, the following illustration was created to show the role an NGO could play as an agent of resilience in calibrating the balance of power in the planning process, thereby eliminating some barriers to citizen participation.

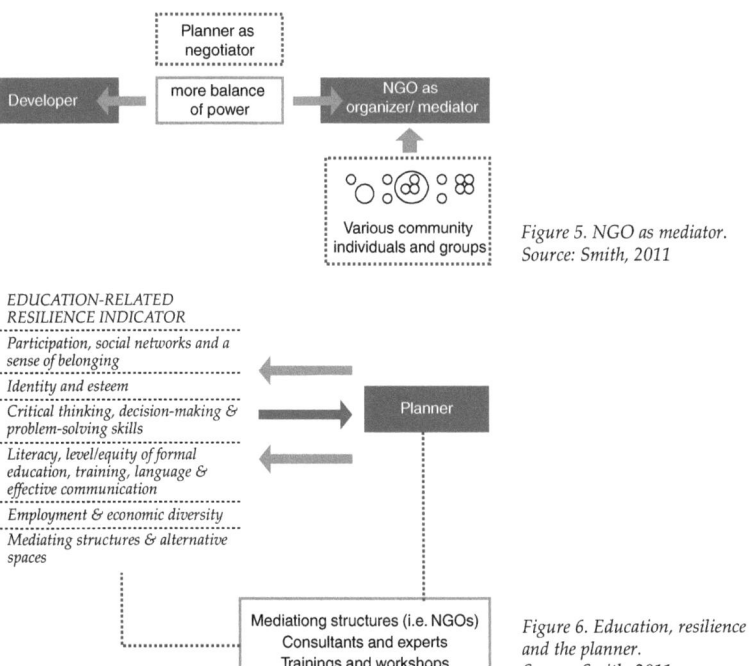

Figure 5. NGO as mediator.
Source: Smith, 2011

Figure 6. Education, resilience and the planner.
Source: Smith, 2011

Finally, the *Figure 6* was developed to summarise the relationship between education, resilience and the planner, illustrating the planner's influence on particular education-related resilience indicators as well as the planner's potential ability to employ external agents to influence education-related indicators that are potentially relevant to participation in the planning process.

Conclusions and potential further research

Overall, these analyses demonstrate that resilience is present in and has potential as a tool for urban interventions, particularly those delivered through the planning process, though to what degree should be further scrutinised. One key message is that a resilience-based planning process has potential to re-frame some elements of a problem or community that may at first appear to be negative or dysfunctional; taking context into consideration may reveal them as a manifestation of resilience or suggest their potential to promote resilience. In this regard, resilience and resilience-thinking on the part of planners and other practitioners may result in innovative problem-solving, decision-making, negotiating and mediating; a more efficient use of existing resources; and the prevention of undermining established systems that are valued, either consciously or subconsciously, by a community.

The complex and dynamic nature of resilience – the many contextual elements and the various groups and scales where resilience is subject to assessment (individuals, communities, institutions, society as a whole, etc.) – could easily become overwhelming and unwieldy to a practicing planner. However, if one takes a proactive or asset-focused approach, like that of Forester in discussing the management of conflict by planners, then resilience could be seen to offer a flexibility that is an appropriate fit to the complexity of urban planning.

Areas for further research would be based on the following three hypotheses: 1) a resilience perspective can act as a tool, framework and method for contextualizing urban problems and urban communities, 2) a resilience perspective can promote distinguishing between behaviours and context and, subsequently, a more complex consideration of the two in problem and solution identification and 3) a resilience perspective can help to forecast community and institutional responses to and capacity for change. The specific focus of further research could include further application of the analytical framework of this thesis, identifying additional indicators and agents of resilience (i.e. elected officials, policy, the community itself) and the relevance of the concept of resilience in planning education (i.e. resilience as a deliberate or innate approach to the planning process and the use of resilience in the development of the planner's instincts and judgment).

References

Adger, W.N., (2000) Social and ecological resilience: are they related? *Progress in Human Geography*, 24(3), pp.347-364.

Andres, L. & Round, J. (2011) The role of "persistent resilience" within everyday life: communities coping with marginality. *(PowerPoint presentation)*

Brown, D.D. & Kulig, J.C., (1996). The Concept of Resiliency - Theoretical Lessons from Community Research. *Health & Canadian Society*, 4(1), pp.29-50.

Cinner, J., Fuentes, M.M.P.B., Randriamahazo, H. (2009) Exploring Social Resilience in Madagascar's Marine Protected Areas. *Ecology And Society*, 14(1).

Condly, S.J. (2006) Resilience in Children: A Review of Literature With Implications for Education. Urban Education, 41(3), pp.211-236.

Davidoff, P. (1996) Advocacy and Pluralism in Planning. In R. T. LeGates & F. Stout, eds. *The City Reader*, 4th Edition. Abingdon, Oxon: Routledge, pp. 400-410.

Forester, J. (1996) Planning in the Face of Conflict. In R. T. LeGates, Frederic Stout, ed. *The City Reader*, 4th Edition. Abingdon, Oxon: Routledge, pp. 387-399.

Ganor, M. & Ben-Lavy, Y. (2003) Community resilience: Lessons derived from Gilo under fire. *Journal of Jewish Communal Service*, 79(2/3), p.105–108.

Healey, P. (2003) Collaborative Planning in Perspective. *Planning Theory*, 2(2), pp.101-123.

Hart, K. (1973) Informal Income Opportunities and Urban Employment in Ghana. *The Journal of Modern African Studies*, 11(1), pp.61-89.

Jabeen, H., Johnson, C. & Allen, A. (2010) Built-in resilience: learning from grassroots coping strategies for climate variability. *Environment and Urbanization*, 22(2), pp.415-431.

Landau, J. (2007) Enhancing resilience: families and communities as agents for change. *Family process*, 46(3), pp.351-65.

Lorenz, D.F. (2010) The diversity of resilience: contributions from a social science perspective. *Natural Hazards*.

Norris, F.H. et al. (2008) Community resilience as a metaphor, theory, set of capacities, and strategy for disaster readiness. *American journal of community psychology*, 41(1-2), pp.127-50.

Powell, W.W. ed. (1987) *The Nonprofit Sector: A Research Handbook*, New Haven and London: Yale University Press.

Round, J., Williams, C. & Rodgers, P. (2008) Everyday tactics and spaces of power: the role of informal economies in post-Soviet Ukraine. *Social & Cultural Geography*, 9(2), pp.171-185.

Round, J., Williams, C. & Rodgers, P. (2010) The Role of Domestic Food Production in Everyday Life in Post-Soviet Ukraine. *Annals of the Association of American Geographers*, 100(5), pp.1197-1211.

Smith, K., (2011). The wall, the door and the key: resilience, education and planning in segregated urban communities. *(unpublished Masters thesis)*

Sonn, C.C. & Fisher, A.T. (1998) Sense of community: Community resilient responses to oppression and change. *Journal of Community Psychology*, 26(5), pp.457-472.

Walsh, F. (1996) The Concept of Family Resilience: Crisis and Challenge. *Family Process*, 35, pp.261-281.

. penser le développment urbain . (ri) pensare lo sviluppo urbano . (re) thinking urban development . (re) pensar
Stadtentwicklung (um) denken . (re) pensando o desenvolvimento urbano . penilaian semula pembangunan
développment urbain . (ri) pensare lo sviluppo urbano . (re) thinking urban development . (re) pensando el desarrollo
ken . (re) pensando o desenvolvimento urbano . penilaian semula pembangunan bandar . (re) penser
pensare lo sviluppo urbano . (re) thinking urban development . (re) pensando el desarrollo urbano . Stadtentwick
pensando o desenvolvimento urbano . penilaian semula pembangunan bandar . (re) penser le développment
sviluppo urbano . (re) thinking urban development . (re) pensando el desarrollo urbano . Stadtentwicklung (um) de
desenvolvimento urbano . penilaian semula pembangunan bandar . (re) penser le développment urbain . (ri) pens
thinking urban development . (re) pensando el desarrollo urbano . Stadtentwicklung (um) denken . (re) pensa
. penilaian semula pembangunan bandar . (re) penser le développment urbain . (ri) pensare lo sviluppo urbano
development . (re) pensando el desarrollo urbano . Stadtentwicklung (um) denken . (re) pensando o desenvolvim
semula pembangunan bandar . (re) penser le développment urbain . (ri) pensare lo sviluppo urbano . (re) thinking u
pensando el desarrollo urbano . Stadtentwicklung (um) denken . (re) pensando o desenvolvimento urbano . penila
bandar . (re) penser le développment urbain . (ri) pensare lo sviluppo urbano . (re) thinking urban development .
desarrollo urbano . Stadtentwicklung (um) denken . (re) pensando o desenvolvimento urbano . penilaian semula peml
penser le développment urbain . (ri) pensare lo sviluppo urbano . (re) thinking urban development . (re) pensando
Stadtentwicklung (um) denken . (re) pensando o desenvolvimento urbano . penilaian semula pembangunan b
développment urbain . (ri) pensare lo sviluppo urbano . (re) thinking urban development . (re) pensando el desarrollo
ken . (re) pensando o desenvolvimento urbano . penilaian semula pembangunan bandar . (re) penser
pensare lo sviluppo urbano . (re) thinking urban development . (re) pensando el desarrollo urbano . Stadtentwick
pensando o desenvolvimento urbano . penilaian semula pembangunan bandar . (re) penser le développment
sviluppo urbano . (re) thinking urban development . (re) pensando el desarrollo urbano . Stadtentwicklung (um) de
desenvolvimento urbano . penilaian semula pembangunan bandar . (re) penser le développment urbain . (ri) pens
thinking urban development . (re) pensando el desarrollo urbano . Stadtentwicklung (um) denken . (re) pensa
. penilaian semula pembangunan bandar . (re) penser le développment urbain . (ri) pensare lo sviluppo urbano
development . (re) pensando el desarrollo urbano . Stadtentwicklung (um) denken . (re) pensando o desenvolvim
semula pembangunan bandar . (re) penser le développment urbain . (ri) pensare lo sviluppo urbano . (re) thinking u
pensando el desarrollo urbano . Stadtentwicklung (um) denken . (re) pensando o desenvolvimento urbano . penila
bandar . (re) penser le développment urbain . (ri) pensare lo sviluppo urbano . (re) thinking urban development .
desarrollo urbano . Stadtentwicklung (um) denken . (re) pensando o desenvolvimento urbano . penilaian semula peml
penser le développment urbain . (ri) pensare lo sviluppo urbano . (re) thinking urban development . (re) pensando
Stadtentwicklung (um) denken . (re) pensando o desenvolvimento urbano . penilaian semula pembangunan b
développment urbain . (ri) pensare lo sviluppo urbano . (re) thinking urban development . (re) pensando el desarrollo
ken . (re) pensando o desenvolvimento urbano . penilaian semula pembangunan bandar . (re) penser
pensare lo sviluppo urbano . (re) thinking urban development . (re) pensando el desarrollo urbano . Stadtentwick
pensando o desenvolvimento urbano . penilaian semula pembangunan bandar . (re) penser le développment
sviluppo urbano . (re) thinking urban development . (re) pensando el desarrollo urbano . Stadtentwicklung (um) de
desenvolvimento urbano . penilaian semula pembangunan bandar . (re) penser le développment urbain . (ri) pens
thinking urban development . (re) pensando el desarrollo urbano . Stadtentwicklung (um) denken . (re) pensar
. penilaian semula pembangunan bandar . (re) penser le développment urbain . (ri) pensare lo sviluppo urbano
development . (re) pensando el desarrollo urbano . Stadtentwicklung (um) denken . (re) pensando o desenvolvim
semula pembangunan bandar . (re) penser le développment urbain . (ri) pensare lo sviluppo urbano . (re) thinking u
pensando el desarrollo urbano . Stadtentwicklung (um) denken . (re) pensando o desenvolvimento urbano . penila
bandar . (re) penser le développment urbain . (ri) pensare lo sviluppo urbano . (re) thinking urban development .
desarrollo urbano . Stadtentwicklung (um) denken . (re) pensando o desenvolvimento urbano . penilaian semula peml
penser le développment urbain . (ri) pensare lo sviluppo urbano . (re) thinking urban development . (re) pensando
Stadtentwicklung (um) denken . (re) pensando o desenvolvimento urbano . penilaian semula pembangunan b
développment urbain . (ri) pensare lo sviluppo urbano . (re) thinking urban development . (re) pensando el desarrollo
ken . (re) pensando o desenvolvimento urbano . penilaian semula pembangunan bandar . (re) penser
pensare lo sviluppo urbano . (re) thinking urban development . (re) pensando el desarrollo urbano . Stadtentwick
pensando o desenvolvimento urbano . penilaian semula pembangunan bandar . (re) penser le développment
sviluppo urbano . (re) thinking urban development . (re) pensando el desarrollo urbano . Stadtentwicklung (um) de
desenvolvimento urbano . penilaian semula pembangunan bandar . (re) penser le développment urbain . (ri) pensa

CHAPTER III

CONTEMPORARY PLANNING AND COOPERATING IN THE SOUTH

Prof. Yang Guiqing
Greta Sanches Correa
Tara Saharan
Regina Orvañanos Murguía
AKM Fazlur Rahman

CONTEMPORARY PLANNING AND COOPERATING IN THE SOUTH: INTRODUCTION

Prof. Yang, Guiqing[1]

Today's globalisation has had an enormous impact on developing countries in the areas of economic and social development. In order to realise higher benefit, the capital in developed countries always seeks cheaper cost, including more low-cost raw materials and labour force, while simultaneously ensuring access to technology and quality products. The technology and quality of products can be controlled by sending technicians to developing countries or by acquiring technical training from developed countries. However, as a consequence, lower cost raw materials and labour force rely on those developing countries. Thus, globalisation produces capital flows from developed countries to developing countries, affecting the mode of production and the scale and type of land use in the latter through the establishment of industrial zones, thereby affecting the function and structure of local cities. This process of the globalisation of capital stimulates the process of urbanisation in developing countries.

The above-mentioned process of urbanisation in developing countries is both an opportunity and a serious challenge. Because on the one hand, the inflow of capital in developed countries is a shot in the arm to economic development for the recipient countries. It increases the city and the country's total economic output, improves local employment opportunities, and more or less increases the income of workers; on the other hand, the acquisition of such achievements has to pay the cost of the resources and environment. To some developing countries, this payment is heavy, through the excessive use of non-renewable resources, increased environmental pollution, and so forth.

Moreover, the benefit to developing countries from the process of the globalisation of capital is tiny because they do not retain the core technology of production, but rather cheap labour processing costs. The profit is mostly allocated to investors after the product enters the market. Further, for some products, the production process damages the local environment while the

---

1   Professor in urban planning, deputy head of Urban Planning Department, Tongji University. Urban Planning Department, College of Architecture & Urban Planning. Tongji University, 1234 Siping Road, Shanghai, 200092. P.R.China

convenience of the use of the product does not belong to these places. For example, during the production of some special quality paper, the paper making process causes serious pollution to local water environment in developing countries, while 100% of the paper products are sent back to the developed countries for use. For some other products, manufacture and sales markets are in developing countries, but because of not owning the value of technology, developing countries not only pay a contribution of low-cost labour, but also contribute the consumption of high-priced products.

From this point of view, capital is a neutral thing. Is it not malicious to destroy the objects that are involved in capital, a process that does not breed the care of any humanity either? When production cost is raised in a developing country, such as the cost of labour force and land, the global capital will relentlessly leave the country for more appropriate countries.

The opportunities and challenges brought about by the process of the globalisation of capital to developing countries are not only the physical aspects, but also the cultural and social. Along with global capital flows, relevant consumer culture and values conception invade developing countries along with production and products. The opportunity is to bring a modern sense of lifestyle and consumer attitudes, while the challenge is the impact on the culture and values of the local traditional culture and the conflicts that this causes. The dilemma is: lifestyle and culture of the modern sense of the international orientation is generally considered "right" but is it in reality?

In this process of the strong globalisation of capital, the opportunities and challenges of urbanisation that developing countries face is probably inevitable. The key question is: how can developing countries use planning tools better, in order to grasp the development opportunities and to avoid the negative impact of urbanisation as effectively as possible? This is probably the important task of the contemporary urban and rural planning.

In this scenario, contemporary urban and rural planning has the role of at least the following three aspects:

- **Planning as a policy tool** for the government of developing country to intervene in the process of urbanisation, such as: how to effectively use the globalisation of capital to stimulate economic growth and revitalisation in order to advance the transformation and upgrading of the local economic structure; through strategic planning and the overall urban planning ways to make reasonable arrangements to the scale, proportions and layout of the productive land; and making capital have a positive effect to urban land and space.

- **Planning as a social tool** for developing countries to realise urban social justice. In the face of strong capital strength, in addition to stimulating the growth of economic interests, planning an effective tool for the coordination of social and public interests in order to balance conflict caused by economic development to social, cultural and environmental conditions. The planning intervention can be used to balance great differences between the rich and the poor and to realise basic responsibilities to low-income families and the social poor, in order to achieve the sustainability of development. Specific implementation approaches in planning could be used such as: through the overall urban planning and development control planning, the local government can reasonably arrange land use type, size and layout of urban public facilities and municipal infrastructure, can formulate land use planning and housing development plans for low income families through public participation, and can effectively arrange the renovation of urban shantytowns, to meet the basic needs of life of urban low-income families.

- **Planning as a design tool** for environmental improvement. Through design control of urban land development, local governments can develop a series of planning efforts, such as zoning, structural planning or development control planning, so as to guide a rational urban structure during urban construction. This can foster the realisation of an effective urban function, order, and characteristics of urban space, thus achieving a compromise between urban modernity and urban traditional culture.

Cooperation among developing countries is also very important in the process of capital globalisation. In today's global scale, nearly 80% of the world's population is in developing countries. On the one hand, compared with developed countries, the level of economic development in developing countries is relatively backward. Serious environmental pollution, low levels of education and health care among the population, low standards of quality in urban construction are commonplace. However, on the other hand, these countries often hold a vast territory that rich in resources and a lot of products, and market potential is huge. Their urban history, cultural traditions and development models are diverse with characteristic features. In today's globalised process of development, through South-South cooperation and North-South dialogue, the developing countries together should learn from each other in order to better face the challenges of rapid urbanisation. Otherwise, developing countries will lose a golden opportunity for development.

In addition learning about experiences and taking lessons from each other, regional cooperation between developing countries and neighbouring cities in neighbouring countries is also crucial. This is because these areas share security factors such as water resources, river basins, the flow of factors of the regional commodity markets, and social and cultural exchanges between different countries and cities. International development cooperation and exchange among developing countries includes urban and rural areas, industrial and agriculture fields, technology and labour domains, and other aspects. Based on the principles of equality and seeking a win-win situation, the countries in the south can carry out effective cooperation in a variety of ways.

In short, the development opportunities in contemporary developing countries are unprecedented, but at the same time, the challenges are also very severe. Planning, served as an effective decision-making tool, will play an active role in selecting opportunities and avoiding risks. The key is how to choose a better development path with more wisdom according to its own national conditions. In this sense, planning itself is also facing the opportunities and challenges to innovative concepts and methods. The good news is that we see today that the urban and rural planning and construction in many developing countries has begun to learn not only the experience of developed countries, but also to their lessons in urbanisation and modernisation processes. The governments in developing countries can use planning tools to resolve conflicts through the ideas of smart growth and sustainable practices.

A TOOL FOR BRIDGING THE FORMAL-INFORMAL DIVIDE IN SÃO PAULO

Sanches Correa, Greta[1]

Abstract

Urban growth has often been accompanied by the escalation of informal settlements and socio-economic inequalities in many developing countries. Urban policies with the intention to integrate these settlements into the city fabric have been reinforced in Brazil after the City Statute approval (Brasil, 2001). This federal law gives local authorities a protagonist's role on urban management by providing them with a set of legal instruments to support land tenure regularisation programmes. However, although Brazilian legislation on urban planning is considered advanced worldwide, an effective policy formulation by municipalities is crucial. This paper explores the hypothesis that programmes awarding full ownership rights can lead to gentrification and socio-spatial segregation in the same way that slum upgrading without land tenure regularisation does. My purpose was to evaluate whether the establishment of Special Zones of Social Interest (ZEIS) can be a useful tool in protecting dwellers from gentrification processes. An analysis of the urban parameters defined to ZEIS by São Paulo law was made to discuss their applicability and effects. The case study of Paraisópolis shows that demarcating ZEIS minimizes development pressures and can promote low-income housing, but does not necessarily protect the poorest of the poor of being displaced by wealthier households.

Keywords: *Informal Settlements, Land Tenure Regularisation, Slum Upgrading, ZEIS, Gentrification*

---

[1] *M.Sc. International Cooperation and Urban Development; specialisation in Sustainable Emergency Architecture. Technische Universität Darmstadt, Germany/ Universitat Internacional de Catalunya, Barcelona, Spain. B.A. in Architecture and Urban Planning, Universidade Estadual de Campinas, Campinas, Sao Paulo, Brazil. email: gretasanches@gmail.com*

Discussion on urban informality

Recognised by their unplanned development patterns, most informal settlements are frequently located in public, environmentally vulnerable or disaster risk areas (i.e., the land where the formal market is not allowed or interested in occupying). The residents of these settlements are often lacking full security of tenure since there is no formal legal recognition of individual ownership or possession rights. This complex condition contributes substantially to the reinforcement of poverty and social exclusion and depends on the commitment and understanding of local authorities to be solved.

Besides the permanent fear of being evicted by local authorities and land owners, slum dwellers are permanently excluded from most of the economic and human development opportunities that cities can offer. In addition to suffering from prejudice and social discrimination, they often encounter difficulties in finding formal jobs and obtaining credit from shops or banks due the lack of an official address.

Common sense would promptly associate informality to poverty. However, although most slum dwellers are poor, poverty is not the only cause of informality. According to Fernandes (2011:14), who based his observations on IPEA data, while levels of absolute poverty have decreased in Brazil, informality has grown.

The role of urban policies

Urban legislation and policies greatly influence the ability of city dwellers to access land, services, housing and credit. When the needs and resources of city dwellers are not met, they are forced to occupy various forms of illegal settlements.

> *"Government neglect or indifference is one of the main reason slums are the only options for the poor. Moreover, policies that fix unrealistically high development standards and inappropriately costly building codes also create slums"* (Cities Alliance 2011).

Hence, the review of urban policies and legislation and their effective application by local governments is the first step to promoting further formal access to land and housing.

In Brazil, the approval of the law 10.257(2001), known as "City Statute" (Brasil, 2001), is acknowledged as a milestone in the urban reform agenda. It was formulated to regulate the chapter of the 1988 Federal Constitution on urban policy (Articles 182 and 183[2]), reinforcing and redefining the social function of property as the primary condition for recognizing individual property rights.

One of the most useful tools cities are given to regularize consolidated informal settlements is the possibility to demarcate them as "Special Zones of Social Interest" (ZEIS). These zones formally recognise the existence of informal settlements and make them eligible for social services, urban infrastructure, housing provision and property transfers by defining new parameters of occupation and building standards. The demarcation of ZEIS is intended, therefore, to scale-up social housing supply and is expected to minimize real estate market pressures by restraining property and land speculation.

It must be clarified that the City Statute as a federal law does not regulate in detail the ZEIS. It only lists it as one of the legal instruments available to support urban policies. The regulation of ZEIS is supposed to be provided at the municipal level through participatory master plans[3] and land use laws. The case of São Paulo presented in this paper provides more details on how a local government can make use of ZEIS in the local master plan and regulate them through municipal laws and decrees.

The responses to informality: scopes and challenges

the government response to the informality in Brazil was, during many years, through "eradication" or, in other words, forced eviction, removals and relocation to the peripheral, cheaper and sub-serviced land. These actions have mostly resulted in unsuccessful outcomes as relocated residents often left their new homes and moved back to slums close to job

---

2   It is worth mentioning that both articles were included in the 1988 Federal Constitution thanks to the popular pressure emerged from a national civil society movement, known as Movimento Nacional para Reforma Urbana (MNRU, National Movement for Urban Reform). This movement was framed in the sixties (when Brazil was politically under military dictatorship) and articulated social movements (housing, transport, sanitation), professional associations (architects, lawyers, engineers), labour unions, academic entities, NGOs, Catholic Church activists as well as progressive mayors and legislators.

3   By the end of 2006 all the municipalities with more than 20.000 inhabitants were requested to have a local master plan approved through a participatory process and that incorporated principles and tools introduced by the City Statute.

and services. However, since the 80s, there has been an important shift in the way policy makers have been addressing informality. This shift is the result of the popular pressure that will also influence the content of the texts of the 1988 Constitution on urban policies.

Within an enabling institutional and legal environment, policy makers were able to move towards a more balanced position through regularisation combined with upgrading programmes in order to integrate the *favela* into the city fabric.

However, political commitment and a deep understanding of land market dynamics (both formal and informal) by local governments is important for making an effective use of the new set of instruments available after the City Statute approval. One of the main questions being raised about informal settlement regularisation programmes are whether the beneficiary populations really remain in their communities after regularisation and upgrading and how to avoid gentrification knowing that regularisation and upgrading considerably increases the prices of land and housing (Abramo 2009, Gravois 2005, Durand-Lasserve and Selod 2007, Fernandes 2011).

The Peruvian and Brazilian paradigms

According to Fernandes (2011), regularisation programmes in Latin America usually follow two main paradigms. The first is exemplified by Peru, where the then-president Alberto Fujimori created in 1996 the Commission for the Formalisation of Informal Property (COFOPRI) which included the legalisation of tenure through the massive issuing of freehold titles. The second is exemplified by Brazil and combines legal titling with the upgrading of public infrastructure and services, job creation and community support structures.

The Peruvian experience was based on Hernando de Soto's idea that giving the urban poor property titles permits them to use property as collateral for accessing credit and, thus, achieve economic independence. However, according to Gravois (2005), there are some government studies on the Peruvian regularisation programme suggesting that titles did not really increase access to credit. In addition to property title, credit providers demand proof of repayment capacity through income statements. Thus, employed workers without property titles have had better access to official credit than unemployed people who have titles (Carderon, 2006).

Furthermore, banks are usually not interested in repossessing shanties in precarious locations where there is not yet a significant real estate value. On the other hand, the owners of newly regularised homes occupying high-value land are subject to development pressures and often end up selling cheap, thereby losing the fundamental geographic advantage that they once had (Gravois, 2005).

Unlike the highly centralised Peruvian programme, the Brazilian paradigm in land regularisation is shaped by various experiences led by local governments and financed by the Federal government or international development banks. Some of the most relevant experiences are the internationally acclaimed *Favela-Bairro* programme in Rio de Janeiro (1995), PREZEIS in Recife (1987), PROFAVELA in Belo Horizonte (1983) and the "Land regularisation programme" in Diadema (IBAM, 2002; Angel et al, 2006; Fernandes, 2011).

Although these programmes were developed in different contexts and had different priorities (more investment in upgrading than titling or vice versa), they have all contributed to establishing a new approach that is guiding the current activities delegated to municipalities by the Brazilian Ministry of Cities. This Ministry promotes the idea that security of tenure and socio-spatial integration are the two fundamental goals of a regularisation programme and must be pursued jointly in order to guarantee the permanence of communities in the land they have occupied and their full integration into the formal city.

It is indeed true that, so far, Brazilian local governments have been more successful in slum upgrading than in land legalisation as can be seen through the programme *Favela-Bairro*, initiated in 1995 by the city of Rio de Janeiro. This programme involved a massive investment in infrastructure, public spaces, services and community facilities but, initially, there was no emphasis on property-title regularisation. Only a few of the benefiting slums (five out of fifty-one) had formal property titles fully issued by another municipal programme[4] (IBAM, 2002), mainly through adverse possession and leasehold titles. Although the programme improved living conditions even before assuring the full legal tenure security, it caused a considerable increase in the land and property prices and rents, occasioning an important change in the socio-economic profile of the local community (Abramo, 2009).

---

4   After changes in the local political administration, the Favela-Bairro programme lost its
     intensity and was just recently replaced by the "Morar Carioca" programme.

Relying only on the strategy of implementing income generation projects for assuring the permanency of the original residents has been shown to be risky. Restricting the pressures of the informal real estate markets that exist inside the slums requires other land regularisation policies' strategies such as defining percentages of uses for social housing and restricting plot size.

ZEIS in São Paulo

São Paulo is a city of contrast. Although it is the richest and most populous city in Brazil, the economic and development model of the last decades left, and is still leaving, a considerable fraction of the population excluded from development opportunities. They are living in what the Brazilian Institute of Geography and Statistics (IBGE, 2011) denominates as *"assentamentos subnormais.*[5]*"* According to a report from Fundação SEADE (2008), 31.83% of São Paulo's population lives in slums or informal land subdivisions.

Table 1 - Urban parameters set for ZEIS

ZONE number	Floor Area Ratio			Dimensions and plot occupancy				Allowed uses
	Min.	Basic	Max	OR	Min. lot size (m2)	Min. Front	Height	
ZEIS 1	0.20	1.00	2.5	0.50	125 m2	5.00 m	no limit	80% HIS/HMP (50% HIS)
ZEIS 2	0.20	1.00	2.5	0.50	125 m2	5.00 m	no limit	80% HIS/HMP (40% HIS)
ZEIS 3	0.30	1.00	4	0.70	125 m2	5.00 m	no limit	80% HIS/HMP (40% HIS)
ZEIS 4	0.10	1.00	1.00	0.50	125 m2	5.00 m	9.00 m	70% HIS
ZER - 1	0.05	1.00	1.00	0.50	250 m2	10.00m	10.00	Residential

OR = Occupancy Rate (the percentage of land occupied by the building)
Min Front = Minimum front façade width

Source: adapted from the Table nº02/j attached to the Municipal Law 13.885 (LUOS), August 25 2004

---

5 The "assentamentos subnormais" are defined by IBGE as a group of at least 51 housing units that illegally occupies private or public land following a disorderly pattern of urbanisation and lacks basic public services.

The ZEIS were incorporated in the São Paulo Strategic Master Plan (Law nº13.430, Plano Diretor Estratégico) in 2002, followed by their regulation through the Zoning Law of 2004 (Law nº13.885, Zoneamento da Cidade de São Paulo), in which the ZEIS effectively obtain a spatial dimension as part of the city zoning and their parameters are set. In 2004, 964 perimeters were instituted as ZEIS, which corresponds to 9.23% of the municipal territory. They are distributed in four categories, based on specific local conditions:

- ZEIS 1: slums or precarious land subdivisions (67%)
- ZEIS 2: empty or underdeveloped areas (15%)
- ZEIS 3: land with infrastructure and services (15%)
- ZEIS 4: unbuilt lots and land in watershed protection and recovery areas (3%)

The urban interventions within these zones must be predominantly dedicated to the production of social housing, which are distinguished as either HIS *(Social Interest Housing)* and HMP *(Popular Market Housing)*. The Municipal Decree 44.667/04 determines that an HIS must be designated to households with revenue equal or below six minimum wages while an HPM should be designed to households with revenue equal or below sixteen times the minimum wage.

The land uses allowed in ZEIS are important factors to take into account when analyzing the gentrification potential for precarious settlements that are subject to land tenure regularisation. The Zoning Law determines the uses allowed by each ZEIS by setting proportions of HMP and HIS (last column in the *Table 1*) and urban parameters.

The last line of the table, ZER - 1, corresponds to "Residential zones of low density" and provides a reference for a "non-special zone." The neighbourhood of Morumbi in São Paulo is part of this zoning and borders the informal settlements of Paraisópolis, which is mostly classified as ZEIS 1 and the subject of an extensive urban upgrading programme.

The case study of Paraisópolis

The Paraisópolis complex is an informal settlement located in the southeast region of São Paulo (Vila Andrade) and it is considered to be the second largest slum conglomerate in the city. It is composed of three slums: Paraisópolis, Jardim Colombo and Porto Seguro. According to official data from SEHAB (the Municipality of São Paulo's Housing Department), based on a survey made in 2005 by the consultancy firm Hagaplan / Sondotécnica, it has a population of approximately 55.590 inhabitants, distributed throughout 17.141 housing units. The Zoning Law demarcated a large section of Paraisópolis as ZEIS 1 and smaller sections as ZEIS 2 and ZEIS 3 *(Figure 1)*. Furthermore, Plans of Urbanisation (PU) for some of them were approved in 2004 by the ZEIS Management Council and the Mayor through the Municipal Decrees 46.018/05, 46.117/05 and 46.345/05.

One of the richest neighbourhoods in the city, Morumbi, is located within Paraisópolis' boundaries as illustrated by *Figure 2* and *Figure 3* and belongs to a ZER 1 (exclusively residential zone of low density), whose parameters are listed in the *Table 1*.

Figure 1 (left): ZEIS in Paraisópolis. Source: HABISP 2011
Figure 2 (right): Paraisópolis and Morumbi. Source: Google maps

The Paraisópolis complex is currently the subject of major investment by the municipality of São Paulo through a programme aiming to integrate precarious communities and the formal city through urban and land tenure regularisation. However, due to its desirable location and the fact that the land is mostly private, the Paraisópolis complex has great potential to be gentrified. It is still not possible to prove that Paraisópolis is going through a gentrification process, as the programme is ongoing. The land regularisation has just benefited a small proportion of households whose units, with no legal value before, are acquiring regular neighbourhood prices. However, some data on the socio-economic profile of this community and the urban parameters and uses defined by the Zoning Law of São Paulo can give an indication of what could happen once the land regularisation processes are over.

According to the survey delegated by the Housing Secretariat of Sao Paulo municipality to the private consultancy firm, HAGAPLAN(2005), more than 50% of the households in the Paraisópolis Complex earn between one and three minimum wages (*Table 2*) and the average income is equal to 2,58 minimum wages. If the ZEIS are being used as a mechanism to encourage the production of new housing units by the private sector, we can expect that the uses stipulated by ZEIS (at least 50% of HIS according to *Table 1*) do not necessarily protect this population from being evicted by the market, since HIS serves households with an income of up to six minimum wages. This population will most likely be displaced by a slightly wealthier group in the medium or long-term.

Table 2 – Socio-economic profile of Paraisópolis in 2005

Revenue	Number of members in the family				TOTAL	
	1	2-4	5-8	+8	Quantity	%
no revenue	175	242	61	4	482	2,93%
-1 MW	417	881	231	7	1.536	9,34%
1-2 MW.	950	2.893	745	17	4.605	28,00%
2-3 MW	376	2.099	668	24	3.167	19,25%
3-4 MW	135	1.672	504	26	2.337	14,21%
4-5 MW	26	742	315	9	1.092	6,64%
+5 MW.	23	568	428	39	1.058	6,43%
No information	1.462	663	46	0	2.171	13,20%
TOTAL	3.564	9.760	2.998	126	16.448	100,00%

Source: SEHAB - Hagaplan / Sondotécnica, 2005
MW = Minimum Wage (560 BRL in 2011, which corresponds to approximately 280 USD)

Figure 3: Paraisópolis and Morumbi. Source: Thiago Soares Barbizan

Conclusion

It is known that several Master Plans created for the city of São Paulo in the past, by defining idealistically a very rigid zoning, do not match the urban dynamics of Brazilian cities. There is no *favela* that meets or even gets close to the urban scheme defined for its occupied area. Undoubtedly, the introduction of ZEIS in the 2004 Master Plan was a great effort to adapt the urban legislation that has historically been elitist and inclined to the consolidation of socio-spatial segregation.

The case study of São Paulo shows that, even though the ZEIS contribute to keeping the low-income uses within their perimeters by allowing smaller plot sizes and establishing that 50% of the area should be occupied by HIS, this typology was not accessible to the majority of Paraisópolis' residents in 2005. However, gentrification will be more effectively measured when basic data of HIS occupants is collected and compared with the original residents who had eventually moved. Furthermore, this is only one example and further research should be done to elucidate if this finding is recurrent in other areas of the city.

At this point of the analysis, it becomes evident that preventing informal settlements from emerging is easier than integrate them once it is consolidated. Mechanisms for facilitating the access of the poorest of the poor to housing and land are extremely necessary and this currently constitutes a major challenge for the city of São Paulo. The current government strategy of involving the private sector in the production of low income housing through fiscal and financial incentives is working for the population earning between three and ten times the minimum wage, but this is still not attractive enough to address those earning between zero and three times the minimum wage (where the deficit is concentrated), especially in big cities where the land prices are very high.

References

Abramo, P. (2009) *Favela e mercado informal: A nova porta de entrada dos pobres nas cidades brasileiras*. Porto Alegre: IPPUR.

Angel S., Brown E., Dimitrova, D., Ehrenberg D., Heyes J., Kusek P.,Marchesi G., Orozco V.,Smith L.,Vilchis E. (2006) *Secure tenure in Latin America and the Caribbean: Regularization of informal urban settlements in Peru, Mexico and Brazil*. Princeton, NJ: Woodrow Wilson School of Public and International Affairs, Princeton University

Brasil. Lei nº 10.257 (2001) *Estatuto da Cidade e Legislação Correlata*. Brasília: Senado Federal, Subsecretaria de Edições Técnicas.

Brasil. Medida Provisória nº2.220 (2001) 'Provisions about titling municipal public lands'. In: *Estatuto da Cidade: guia para implementação pelos municípios e cidadãos*. Brasília: Instituto Pólis/CEF.

Calderon J.C. (2006) *Considerations on illegal and informal urban land markets in Latin America*. Working Paper. Cambridge, MA: Lincoln Institute of Land Policy.

Cities Alliance and Prefeitura de São Paulo (2008) *Social Housing in São Paulo: Challenges and New Management Tools*. Washington: The Cities Alliance.

Cities Alliance (2011) *'Some Myths and Realities about Slum Upgrading'*, [Online], Available: www.citiesalliance.org/ca/myths [22 Nov 2011].

Durand-Lasserve, A. and Selod, H. (2007) 'The Formalisation of Urban Land Tenure in Developing Countries', [CD ROM] *Fourth World Bank Urban Research Symposium*, 14-16 May, Washington

Fernandes, E. (2011) *Regularization of Informal settlements in Latin America:* Policy Focus Report, London: Lincoln Institute of Land Policy.

Fundação SEADE (2008) *Updating of census data on population in Favelas and Informal land subdivision in the MSP:* final report, São Paulo.

Gravois J. (2005) 'The De Soto Delusion' [online]. *The Slate Group*. Available from: www.slate.com/id/2112792/ [22 Nov 2011]

IBAM (2002) *Estudo de avaliação da experiência brasileira em urbanização de favelas e regularização fundiária*. Rio de Janeiro: IBAM.

Ministério Das Cidades (2006) 'Regularização Fundiária de Assentamentos Informais', *Aliança das Cidades*, [Online], Available: http://www.cidades.gov.br/images/stories/ArquivosSNPU/Biblioteca/RegularizacaoFundiaria/Regularizacao_Fundiaria_Assentamentos_Informais_Urbanos.pdf [22 Nov 2011] .

Ministério Das Cidades (2007) 'Regularização Fundiária Plena: Referências Conceituais'. *Ministério das cidades*, [Online], Available: www.cidades.gov.br/images/stories/ArquivosSNPU/Biblioteca/RegularizacaoFundiaria/Livro_Regularizacao_Fundiaria_Plena_Referencias_Conceituais.pdf [22 nov 2011]

Rolnik, R. (2006) 'A construção de uma política fundiária e de planejamento urbano para o país – avanços e desafios'. *IPEA, Políticas Sociais – Acompanhamento e Análise*, 12, 199-210

São Paulo (2002) *Plano Diretor Estratégico*. Lei nº 13.430 de 13 de setembro de 2002. São Paulo: Secretaria Municipal de Desenvolvimento Urbano.

São Paulo (2004) *Zoneamento da Cidade de São Paulo*. Lei nº 13.885, de 25 de agosto de 2004. São Paulo: Secretaria Municipal de Desenvolvimento Urbano.

UNDERSTANDING THE NEEDS OF URBAN POOR: CASE STUDY OF VP SINGH CAMP, A SLUM SETTLEMENT IN DELHI, INDIA

Saharan, Tara[1]

Abstract

With the world urbanising at a rapid rate, the future lies in the cities of the globe. Urban centres are marked by concentrations of people and serve as the growth centres of nation states. However, urban landscapes in emerging economies are characterised by rampant inequality and slums and their histories are full of paternalistic endeavours to improve living conditions for people living in these settlements.

This paper aims to understand the key areas of development for slum populations, as stated by them. A survey was conducted in the selected case study of VP Singh Camp in 2011 to understand the needs of the urban poor. The paper argues that the people living in the urban slums have clear responses to improve their own situation and therefore should be made integral to the decision-making process of their development which at present bypasses them.

Keywords: Urban Slum, India, Delhi, Development and Needs.

---

1   PhD student, Amsterdam Institute of Social Science Research, University of Amsterdam, Amsterdam, The Netherlands. M.Sc. International Cooperation and Urban Development; specialisation in Urbanism, Habitat and International Cooperation. Technische Universität Darmstadt, Germany/ Université Pierre-Mendès-France, Grenoble, France. M.U.R.P. Masters in Urban and Rural Planning, Indian Institute of Technology, Roorkee, India. B.A. of Architecture, Manipal Academy of Higher Education, Manipal, India. email: tsaharan@gmail.com

Introduction

Cities in the developing economies are increasingly becoming growth centres with concentrated wealth and poverty co-existing parallel to each other. Nearly half of the 55 billionaires in India, as listed by the Forbes ranking of 2011[2], reside in Bombay. Contrastingly, as per the slum population enumerated by the 2001 Census, the Indian Government estimates that more than half the population of the Bombay lives in slums (Government of India, 2001). These disparities mark the urban landscapes of contemporary cities of developing nations.

The United Nations projects that the world's population will reach 8.27 billion by 2030, an addition of over 2 billion people to the current population. Virtually most of this increase will take place in developing countries, and the cities will absorb the vast majority (UN Habitat, 2010). This increase in population would demand increased need for shelter and lack of affordable housing would result in expansion of slum settlements in the urban areas of developing countries. Slums have existed for decades as the "invisible" city, often omitted from the official maps and documents and are frequently physically hidden by the local authorities by colourful walls and fences (Sinha, 1985). However, now there is urgent need not only to cater to the present demand but make adequate planning for the future needs.

According to the World Bank estimates, slums account for one-fourth of all urban housing in India[3]. 640 cities/towns in 26 States/Union territories in 2001 have reported slum population (Government of India, 2001). As per the Slum Census of 2001, about 42.6 million people live in slums in India[4]; they constitute one-seventh of India's entire urban population or about one-twentieth of the total population of the country. Concentrated poverty, evident in the form of slums, has become a reality for the country's large metropolitan areas.

---

2 Based on data at the Forbes website: http://www.forbes.com/wealth/billionaires#p_1_s_arank_-1__66

3 Based on the data indicated in the World Bank website, refer the section which focuses on urbanisation in India.

4 The Slum Population for the Census of India 2001 has covered only towns and cities with 50,000 populations and above. So the estimates presented here by the India Census 2001 are exclusionary as they do not take into consideration all the towns in the whole country.

As slum dwellers are the most intimate witness of their reality, this research involved people living in slums by means of survey and they were asked what they need for their development. The focus of the study is on India, which contains one-sixth of the world population and is urbanizing rapidly. The following research focuses on the needs of the urban poor in India, with a case study of V.P. Singh Camp, a slum settlement in Delhi. Firstly, the research methodology adopted for the study is explained and then the case of Delhi and its slum population is analysed. This is followed by a description of the settlement profile of VP Singh camp, forming the background of the research[5]. Finally the needs, as reported by the people, are discussed.

Research methodology

The case study research methodology was adopted by using qualitative analysis for the study. The research consisted of household surveys conducted in April 2011 among a sample of 30 respondents in a slum settlement of Delhi called "V.P. Singh Camp". Enumerating needs poses great difficulty for any person, yet care was taken not to undertake the field visit with any preconceived list to adhere to. Therefore, the survey was composed of open ended queries related to the needs that people value for their development.

Purpose sampling by reasoned choice method was undertaken in the survey. A list was drawn based on caste, place of origin, religious affiliation, gender, profession and location of the house in the settlement. An attempt was made to include all the different categories of the people living within the heterogeneity of the settlement. Before finalising the questions, the questionnaire was pre-tested in the field.

Delhi and the slums in the city

Delhi is located on the edge of Gangetic plains in the north of India and has seen many rulers; the site of no less than seven capital cities, all but two of which are in ruins (Mitra, 1970 and Baquer, 1993). Delhi has grown over the years to prove its economic potential as a production centre of the country; be it economics, trade, banking, news, culture, research – Delhi is at the forefront (Cadene, 2000). Presently, Delhi is the seat of power and politics

---

5   The settlement profile presented in the paper is the result of field investigation by M.M. Shankare Gowda coupled with information collected by the author during the field work in March April 2011.

in the map of democratic India, a metropolitan city bustling with people from all over the country, albeit mostly from northern states. From half a million residents in 1901 to about 16 million inhabitants[6] in 2011, Delhi is designated as a class 1 city as well as mega city of India[7]. Delhi, in its master plans, has aims to be a "global metropolis" and "world class city" and, in line to achieve its global image, Delhi hosted the Commonwealth Games in 2010.

For the purpose of beautification and infrastructure, the city has been witness to many slum demolitions (Dupont, 2011). According to the 2001 census of India, about 1.9 million people resided in slum settlements in the Municipal Corporation of Delhi[8]. In its last two master plans, the Delhi government has followed a three-fold strategy with respect to urban slums: in-site up-gradation, relocation and environmental improvement. Among the three approaches environmental improvement was a complementary approach, in-situ up-gradation was limited to a few number of cases and relocation was the most common practice (Dupont, 2008). Relocation as its primary objective, the Delhi Government has been pushing the urban poor out of the city limits in the name of development.

Profile of Vp Singh camp

VP Singh Camp is located in the southern periphery of the city in close proximity to the Mehrauli-Badarpur Highway on the southern side and Ma Anand Mayee Marg on its western edge. The settlement is surrounded by the Indian Container Depot, a closed cement factory and landfill area on the north and the Railway Colony on the east. The industrial area of Okhla and the business district of Nehru Place are located within a radius of 8kms from the case study area.

---

6   As stated in the Census of India 2011 Provisional Population Trends.

7   Cities with a population of over 100,000 qualify as "Class 1" cities in India. Numbering roughly 393 in total, in 2001, they accounted for 69 per cent of the total urban population of the country. Delhi is also one of the thirty-five metropolitan or mega-cities, each with a population of over 1 million, and accounting, in 2001, for thirty-eight per cent of the total urban population of India. Alongside Bombay, Calcutta, Madras, Bangalore, and Hyderabad, Delhi is one of the biggest urban agglomerations in the country.

8   This data is based on official definition of slums as provided by the Census of India. According to the Slum and JJ Department of Delhi Government, about an estimated population of 3 million slum dwellers were living in the city in 1998.

The origin of the settlement dates back to the seventies. Migrant populations from neighbouring states of Delhi, such as Uttar Pradesh and Bihar were the first settlers of the area. They primarily served in the Indian railways as informal porters and track maintenance workers.

Due to the precarious nature of the settlement, it was very challenging to determine the exact population, however, it was roughly estimated that there were approximately 6000-7000 residents, of which 3992 were registered on the 2009 voters' list. The majority of the population residing in the settlement were Hindus followed by Muslims with a few Christian families also living in the area. Among the Hindus, the majority of the population belonged to the Schedule caste and Scheduled tribes with a few exceptions of Brahmins and Rajput households.

In terms of work, the residents were employed in informal as well formal sectors of the economy. The settlement was primarily residential in nature with scattered commercial activity by means of small-scale utility shops. The area was designated as a 'Slum Squatter' settlement under the category of 'jhuggi jhopari'[9] clusters and no residents had any formal or legal tenure. The typology of housing in the settlement ranged from permanent, semi-permanent to temporary in nature.

The majority of houses were for individual households without any toilet facility, although in some parts housing with courtyards as well as attached toilets could be seen. Most of the people in the V.P. Singh Camp lived in a structure which was self-made but some families lived as tenants paying rents to the owner of the structure.

In the majority of the cases, a single room served as a living room, bedroom, kitchen, dining room etc. The rooms were very dark and mostly artificial lights were needed even during the bright daylight. Fresh air was lacking in the houses as the rooms were built back to back, with only a small ventilator as a source of air circulation.

---

9   As per the *Delhi Urban Shelter Improvement board (official board for slum development of the city)* the slum areas are those that are notified under the *Slum Improvement and Clearance Areas Act of 1956* – *"Buildings and/or areas that are considered to be unfit for human habitation were declared as the slum areas under Section 3 of the Act. As such, they are considered to be legal structures and are eligible for benefits under the Act. The squatter of Jhuggi Jhopari Clusters settlements on the other hand are considered as an encroachment on public or private lands"*. Here *"Jhuggi Jhopari"* is the local terminology for the slum settlement in the city of Delhi.

There was limited open space in the settlement except for the Public Square, the Community Park and narrow passages with dwellings on either side. These spaces served as the recreation space for the residents of the settlement. There were no formal health or education facilities in the settlement and, in terms of infrastructure the settlement was well facilitated with water supply and electricity but had serious deficits in the areas of sanitation; accessibility to sewage and waste disposal in particular.

The needs of the urban poor

Based on the primary survey, needs were analysed and categorised into five sections: subsistence, material, infrastructural, identity, lack of needs and others. The anonymous quotes presented in the text are from persons residing in the slum who were interviewed during the survey of the area[10].

Subsistence needs: The subsistence need of food, housing and work was reported by many respondents. Food is central to life and human existence. Proper food intake would help the person to live a healthier and more productive life and also ensure utility in terms of pleasure generated by a tasty meal. Beyond the notion of existence, good food can also play an important role in social relations.

Housing was raised by the majority of the respondents as one of the most critical need on the individual, household as well community levels as the lack of adequate housing is a common characteristic of the settlement. Housing satisfies the need of shelter in physical terms and provides a sense of self-respect, safety and satisfaction in life for the dwellers. In addition, for many, housing exhibits social status with home ownership putting, predominantly, a man, and his family, on a higher stratum of society.

Education has been stated as an important need for the household, as well as the individual, by many it is an essential tool for attaining knowledge and acquiring skills for better employment opportunities.

Unemployment of youths has been stated as one of the most urgent problems fostering delinquencies in the area. Employment provides monetary as well as social benefits to the population. Better employment opportunity would be a key to fight poverty as one of its most apparent characteristics

---

10 Initials are used in the quotes. TS is reference to the author whereas R1, R2, till R30 has been used to maintain the anonymity of the thirty respondents who participated in the survey for the collection of primary data.

is "income deprivation". Better health has been pointed also as a priority by many and an environment with a lower disease burden would lead to better health, fewer days of absence from work, more income and better lives.

Material needs: Several young men living in V.P. Singh Camp mentioned the need of mobile phones and nice clothes. For them material benefits include higher social status along with the regular functional role that it serves. Owning a car was also mentioned by some who explained that it would enable them to travel more quickly and efficiently. Also, having a car helps to realise a desire and also gain status and respect among peers.

Several respondents reported suffering from disease for a long period of time; therefore regular access to medicines had become a daily need for them.

Consumption of alcohol is seen as a vice in the Indian society and its use has an anti-social and class element, particularly due to its causational involvement with domestic violence. However, some respondents reported both alcohol as well as tobacco as an important need because it takes away the pain of the hard labour they undertake daily; and in return provided relaxation and pleasure.

A gas connection to one's house was stated as a need by a couple of respondents who saw it as a step towards formalisation. It is also considered a formal utility in India and serves as a proof of address while facilitating cooking and relieving the cooks, and other parties, from pollution generated by alternative cooking fuels.

The scorching summer of Delhi is unbearable under ordinary circumstances and living in a slum, devoid of many basic facilities, the situation can get worse. A mother of two children stated that she needed a 'cooler' as her children suffer a lot in the heat. From the above finding, it can be concluded that many people mentioned the need of material objects not as an end to itself but as a means to realise another purpose including, for many, an increased social status. For the people living in this settlement, owning a car or having a gas connection is an important part of development as these materials set an image in society of a certain class. People want to break away from the image that is associated with them, their settlement and their state.

Infrastructure needs: Deficits in infrastructure - as related to waste disposal, water, drainage, roads and park areas - were stated by many respondents as household as well as settlement needs. Open drains, or merely wastewater running through natural channels, were stated as the most common reason for all types of disease in the area. The need for regular waste disposal coupled with a covered drainage network was regarded as important to achieving better health in the area. Sewer, water, road and drainage networks in the area would provide a set of basic infrastructure to the settlement, the absence of which is an important characteristic of a "jhuggi jhopari", or slum settlement. Therefore, the expression of this need can also be translated into the aspirations of people to see their settlement as any formal residential locality in Delhi.

> [R25]: "There are many common facilities that the colony needs such as better toilet facility, community centre for the weddings and school for children."

Several other respondents also felt the need for a park as well as a community centre for the facilitation of recreation and social activity among the people.

Identity: The needs for good self-esteem and a feeling of inclusion are more complex than the ones presented earlier and were mentioned by two different respondents. These needs illustrate lack of self-belief and rights with slum settlements not only being erased from the formal maps of the city but also facing widespread social exclusion in terms of harassment by police, etc. The need for inclusion, which characterises equal rights and removal of social stigma, are central to development. Provision of services does improve the lives of people, but the image that they, and others who live in the city, have of them is equally important if not more as shown below:

> [R6]: "One day I and my friends were coming back from a temple when one police-man asked us where we live. As soon as we told him VP Singh Camp he started swearing at us and hitting us with his stick. Then he told us to leave from there. It seems like we feel Delhi is our city but the city does not treat us equal as the rest of the citizens."

Other needs: Many of the people residing in the slums are aware of the power that they have in the democratic set up of India; however, most of them use their voting rights for short-term personal gains. Political awareness, in terms of their rights as well as responsibilities, was stated by a respondent as an important settlement need.

Lack of needs: Almost half of the respondents stated a lack of needs for the question of individual needs. This may not illustrate that, even in the absence of many basic services, people do not feel the need for anything; rather, it may highlight the helplessness of people, as they do not believe that their situation is going to change. The hope for anything more would leave them frustrated and angry and in no way improve their existing scenario. It is important to note that lack of needs was a common reply to the question of individual needs. It can also be understood that, by keeping their family and settlement ahead of their individual interest, people feel a sense of satisfaction. The group needs seems to have greater importance in comparison to personal or individual needs as illustrated below:

[TS]: *"What are your needs on an individual level?"*

[R25]: *"Expenditure on food and education for children."*

[TS]: *"But that is your family need and I want to know your needs please."*

[R25] *"Mine? Well there are no needs of my own. What can I tell you? I have no needs. I am what my family is."*

Conclusion

Although the study is based on a small sample which is not representative of the entire settlement, the findings of the research clearly indicate a wide array of needs shedding light at the fact that the people are well aware of their challenges as well as the solutions that they need to overcome them. It can also be concluded that needs of the slum dwellers are diverse in nature at personal, household as well as the settlement levels. Housing can be regarded as one of the most important needs as it is stated by many on all three accounts but infrastructure, food, employment and health are other concerns stated by many. Material needs, including having a mobile phone, good clothes, alcohol, tobacco, car, etc. have also surfaced yet 'a lack of needs' entirely was also a very common answer at the level of individual response. Interestingly, community awareness and political empowerment was also highlighted as critical to the development of the area along with the complex needs of greater self-esteem and inclusion.

Policies related to slum populations generally concentrate on more tangible goals involving infrastructure and housing provision, missing many of the issues raised in this survey such as need for identity, social inclusion, etc. Therefore, both researchers and policymakers must be careful that efforts to improve the condition of slum dwellers not be a paternalistic endeavour.

This study clearly depicts, that the people are well aware of what they need for their own development. They have demonstrated their entrepreneurialism in creating the settlement and have continued to exist, devoid of basic services, for decades. They have shown the strength of their community in the social networks that have supported them through these efforts and, furthermore, they have demonstrated a strong will to survive in conditions that often make researchers and policymakers cringe, but which these people have made into lasting homes. Based on this study it can be clearly concluded that it is not only important but also imperative that the best initiative for the development of slums would involve the residents in the creation of knowledge and policy regarding their situation.

References

Baquer, A. (1993) 'Delhi- The journey of a Legend'. In A. Baquer, Delhi. *A Tale of Two Cities*. New Delhi: A Vhai Publication, pp. 11-34.

Cadene, P. (2000) 'Delhi's Place in India's Urban Structure'. In V. Dupont, E. Tarlo, & V. Denis, *Delhi - Urban Space and Human Destinies*. New Delhi : Manoher Publisher and Distributer, pp. 241-250.

Census of India. (2001) [Online], Available: http://www.censusindia.net/ [31 Jul 2011].

Census of India. (2011) [Online], Available: http://censusindia.gov.in/ [1 August 2011].

Delhi Development Authority. (2009) *Draft Master Plan of Delhi 2021* [Online], Available: http://dda.org.in/planning/master_plans.htm [5 Jul 2011].

Devadas, V.,Saharan, T., and A.L., Venkata Narayanan. (2010) 'Slum as an integral part of urban system – a case study of Kolkata city, India'. In: *Institute of Town Planners India*, 58th National Town and Country Planners Congress – Inclusive Planning for Empowering Urban Poor, Nagpur, India 4-6 January. New Delhi: Institute of Town Planners.

Dupont, V. (2011) 'Access to land and housing for slum dwellers in Delhi - the impact of infrastructure projects and real estate developments'. Paper presented in conference at Yale University, titled - *URBAN INDIA - Historical Processes and Contemporary Experience*.

Dupont, V. (2008) 'Slum demolition in Delhi since the 1990s: An Appraisal'. *Mumbai: Economic and Political Weekly*, pp. 79-87.

Government of India (2001) *Census of India 2001 - Slum Population*. New Delhi: Directorate of Census operation.

Mitra, A. (1970) *Delhi - Capital City*. New Delhi: Thomson Press India Limited.

Sinha, S. (1985) *Slum Eradication and Urban Renewal*: Patna. New Delhi: Inter-India Publication.

UN-Habitat (2010) *State of the World's Cities 2010/2011*. Nairobi: UN-Habitat.

World Bank (2011) *Urbanization in India* [Online], Available: http://www.worldbank.org.in/WBSITE/EXTERNAL/COUNTRIES/SOUTHASIAEXT/INDIAEXTN/0,,contentMDK:23008811~pagePK:141137~piPK:141127~theSitePK:295584,00.html#ui [3 August 2011]

DISAPPEARING CITIES: THE CASE OF THE REFUGEE SETTLEMENTS

Orvañanos Murguía, Regina[1]

Abstract

To disappear means to cease to exist, but also to cease to be visible.

The following article explores to what extent human settlements, such as refugee camps, can plan their own contraction and eventual disappearance. Refugee camps are a neglected typology of human settlements and an example that reminds us of temporariness, being settlements that foresee their own disappearance. The concept of camp closure is examined in the convergence of refugee solutions and the de-urbanisation of camps themselves. The article looks at possible lessons from the refugee settlements, as a specific settlement typology. All these, from the context of shrinking cities becoming more frequent in the western world; while human displacements are feared to become a part of everyday in some other parts of the world.

Keywords: *De-urbanisation, Refugee Camps, Informal Urbanism, UNHCR, Shrinking Cities*

---

[1] M.Sc. International Cooperation and Urban Development; specialisation in Urbanism, Habitat and International Cooperation. Technische Universität Darmstadt, Germany/ Université Pierre-Mendès-France, Grenoble, France. Lic. in Architecture, Instituto Tecnológico y de Estudios Superiores de Occidente, Guadalajara, Mexico. Consultant, Share the Road Programme: Non-Motorised Transport for East Africa. United Nations Environment Programme. Nairobi, Kenya. email: reginaorvananos@gmail.org

Introduction

Cities can die. In most cases their death is either related to a long term disease or mal-function: economic stagnation, depopulation, abandon and decay. Sometimes, death comes unexpectedly in the shape of a natural disaster, a change in the access to resources or wealth, to which it cannot adapt, or man made destruction of the built environment. Prior to the accelerated urbanisation caused by the industrial revolution, cities did not experience such rates of growth as we know today. Cycles of urban decay or growth would alternate throughout history, and sometimes cities would simply disappear. Today, after centuries of sustained economic and population growth, we have forgotten this phase of urban development (Oswalt 2005, Oswalt and Rieniets 2006).

The concept of *The Disappearing City*, was first used by Frank Lloyd Wright (1932) to "recreate a post-urban model that would not be recognised as a city" (Frampton 1993, 192). This model referred to the loss of urban character of a human settlement and originated as a critique of early modernism to the urban way of living, leading to the adoption of anti-urban features.

The second meaning of disappearing cities, the physical disappearance, came back into scene in recent times. Urban planning as a discipline had never before encounter the problem of planning cities to contract. According to Oswalt (2005), three main phenomena brought the concept of planned de-urbanisation into the agenda: 1) the fall of communism in Eastern Europe that brought a rapid depopulation of East Germany and former Soviet Union, 2) the deindustrialisation of cities, and 3) demographic aging.

The new discussion has been enclosed under the concept of shrinking cities. The term *shrinking city*, "describes a symptom of population loss, however, a wide variety of processes and causes can be hidden behind this symptom" (Oswalt and Rieniets 2006). City shrinkage, in its wider connotation can be due to destruction, loss of resources, migration and socio-political change. Another set of considerations related to the concern for environmental sustainability and its impacts on human settlements has developed since the 1980s. Crises, both natural and human-caused, are considerable factors provoking mass displacements of population. They are becoming more recurrent and are expected to increase during the twenty first century. The imminence of increased numbers of disasters caused by climate change has revived the idea of disappearing cities. The materialisation of any of these threats would cause millions of people to be displaced and the incorporation of the environmental refugee into an everyday reality.

Figure 1: Djabal Camp overview in Chad, hosting over 15,000 refugees.
Source: UNHCR/H.Caux © 2004

The refugee situation

In this context, the United Nations High Commissioner for Refugees (UNHCR) is the agency of the United Nations for refugees that coordinates international action for the worldwide protection of refugees; the stateless, internally displaced and returnees that fall into its concern. Its primary purpose is to safeguard their rights, well-being and physical protection. Around the world there are already over 35 million refugees and other people of concern[2] to UNHCR (UNHCR 2011). A refugee is a person who "owing to well founded fear of being persecuted for reasons of race, religion, nationality, membership of a particular social group or political opinion, (…) is outside the country of his (or her) nationality and is unable or unwilling to return to it" (United Nations 1951).

A refugee camp is a common settlement response to a mass influx of population crossing international borders in the quest of a safer environment. It is a temporary solution to give immediate shelter in the context of a large-scale emergency; a human settlement conceived to give protection, granted by international law, to the people that have been displaced.

---

2 *Including stateless, returnees and internally displaced population that fall into the category of Population of Concern to UNHCR.*

It can take a variety of shapes and configurations. It can be planned by the host government or aid organisations; or it may be spontaneous, similar to the thousands of informal settlements all over the world; or a mixture of both. The catalogue of refugee settlements varies into the official division of: dispersed settlements, mass shelters and camps.

A planned camp is, by definition, a "purpose-built site where a full range of services, within possible means, are provided" (UNHCR, 2007:208). The principles of camp planning, based on "structured organisation, low density, and clear separation of functions and uses, suggests an idealised city reminiscent of those of early modernist urban planning of the 1920s. It is marked by a notion of modernist optimism and trust in order and hygiene" (Herz, 2007:7).

Figure 2: Built extension of three refugee camps conforming Dadaab complex.
Source: UNITAR/ UNOSAT © 2009

As seen in *Figure 1*, the strict principle of modular planning defines its layout. A camp module comprises of 90 hectares to give shelter to 20,000 people. The planning units are progressively conformed by the family, a community (16 families); a block (16 communities); a sector (4 blocks), and camp module (4 sectors). When this number is reached, a new camp should be planned (UNHCR, 2007:211). It is a static urban entity that has neither past nor future vision. It becomes what George Orwell defined as the "endless present" (Weizman, 2008:267).

Due to the scale and magnitude of some refugee camps, they can be considered new typologies of human settlements. They remain under oblivion to the urban discipline despite their size and urban resemblances.

Dadaab refugee complex in Kenya *(Figure 2)* - the largest in the world - counted over 380,000 inhabitants in July 2011 (Loewenberg 2011). The particularities of refugee camps create a particular settlement model: planned under military principles and managed by humanitarian agencies. Their fate is designated by international politics; they have the logistics of any global city but the urban shape of a slum.

The invisible city: camp urbanisation

Refugee camps are dynamic entities that go through an evolutionary process. Unlike most human settlements, their evolution is not linear. They follow a diversity of patterns that confront the rigid institutional classifications. Both the political situation and its population may vary dramatically over a short period of time. The patterns of camp evolution rather reflect a sequence of lateral population movements shifted from one place to another through a series of spontaneous or forced displacements.

The natural population growth, in contrast, is not detached from the global tendencies of fast urbanisation found in developing regions. The major refugee situations are in countries among the highest birth rates in the world: Uganda 3.58%, Burundi, 3.46%, Western Sahara, 3.10%, Liberia 2.66%, Guinea 2.65%, Sudan, 2.48%, Eritrea 2.47% (CIA 2011). Such distinct conditions can steer the development of the camp into divergent processes of urbanisation or de-urbanisation.

Within the coexistent potential of urban growth or decay, refugee camps experience an unrecognised urbanisation: "dwellings and neighbourhoods in refugee camps become denser, commerce, barter and cultural exchange develop and camps acquire a proto-urban complexity" (Weizman, 2008:267). Consolidation leads refugee camps into a state where they are neither a permanent city nor a camp: they become *invisible cities*.

The obtained urban characteristics of camps go beyond the concentration of people; the process of camp urbanisation is also a process of acquiring urbanity for the population. Urbanised refugee camps, as Perouse de Montclos describes (2000:206), "not only are urban like settlements, but have the cosmopolitan surrounding of a global settlement." Through their concentration, they become trading centres as well as labour markets and gain the benefits of urbanity (Perouse de Montclos and Kagwanja 2000). In other words, a refugee camp can become a city following the Latin concept of an *urbs:* a space of urban sociability and human congregation (Agier, 2010:337).

Non-urban features of camps

Despite all the similarities that urbanised refugee camps may share with cities, there are substantial differences that have a profound impact on the way they operate. In their legal framework, camps remain under the dominion of international humanitarian organisations and therefore do not have a similar juridical status as most ordinary urban entities in which some form of participation is inscribed (Misselwitz, 2009:85). They remain as extra-territorial enclaves ruled by the humanitarian regime. In the same sense, as the camps are not recognised as cities, they do not fall into the national legislation of the host country, thus services and infrastructures are run in parallel with ad hoc created institutions run by Non-Governmental Organisations (NGO).

Refugees are not citizens. Regardless of international laws, host governments deny refugees the right to work and earn a livelihood, the right of move - to choose their place to live - and the right to buy property, among others (Pacione, 2009:184). These restrictions and misrecognitions of refugees' rights, in comparison to full-righted citizens, throw the refugees to cope with survival strategies similar to the ones of inhabitants in informal settlements. In conclusion, Michel Agier (2002:36) expresses that "the camp is comparable to the city, and yet it cannot reach it". In other words, urbanised camps are not polis - the Greek concept of a city - as their inhabitants are not politicised[3].

The disappearing city: camp de-urbanisation

Camps are meant to disappear after the purpose for which they were created ceases to exist. Camp closure should ideally be linked with a durable solution, implying that the displacement problem has been solved and refugees are no longer in need of international protection. The aid can be therefore withdrawn and the camps may be closed down, dismantled, or handed over to the local communities.

---

3 The definition of urban can be traced down to the ancient concepts of *urbs* and to the *polis*. A *polis*, from the ancient Greek city, in the original sense refers of a self-governing city or state with its dependencies; in its extended use, it has been affirmed that inhabitants of the *polis* must be politicised. In comparison *urbs*, its Latin version refers to the city as a technical entity, or in contrast to a suburb (*Oxford English Dictionary* 2006).

Mundus Urbano: (re) thinking urban development

Figure 3: Former Kacha Garhi Camp in Peshawar, Pakistan. Source: Google Earth, 2011

UNHCR recognises three official durable solutions to the refugee problem: 1) voluntary repatriation and reintegration, 2) resettlement in a third country and 3) local integration.

Voluntary Repatriation and Reintegration are often seen as the most desired durable solution by the international community. The conditions in the country that originated the conflict must be favourable for the return of thousands of exiled people. Usually, it requires the home country to be declared in a *post-conflict* stage, along with a possible cessation[4] of the refugee status. In Afghanistan, this state was declared as soon as the Taliban regime was overthrown, triggering the largest UNHCR-assisted repatriation programme, involving the return of about five million refugees between 2002 and 2009 (Schmeidl, 2009:20). The former camps, such as Kacha Garhi in Peshawar, Pakistan (*Figure 3*) were subsequently closed and dismantled.

Third Country Resettlement. Whenever refugees cannot go home or their needs cannot be addressed in the country where they first sought protection; a third country resettlement is considered the safe and durable solution. Less than one per cent of refugees were submitted for this option to the twenty-five countries that admitted refugees regularly in 2010 (UNHCR,

---

4   The Cessation Clause of the '1951 Convention' relating to the status of refugees allows the States to withdraw refugee status in five circumstances. One of them is based on the premise that when the circumstances causing the refugee to flee have ceased to exist, a refugee is required to return to his country of origin (Siddiqui 2011).

2010:61). Meanwhile, eighty per cent of the 10.5 million refugees worldwide are hosted in developing countries, in which encompasses the 25 countries most affected by a prolonged refugee presence (Guterres 2010).

Local integration, the third durable solution; implies the naturalisation of refugees to the host country with the provision of rights as the rest of their citizens. In particular, it means the right to move freely, to have complete personal documentation, the entitlement to find a job and to own property. It often implies a second resettlement if the initial camps, meant to be temporal responses, are closed.

Table 1 - Matrix of permanent solutions and their side consequences

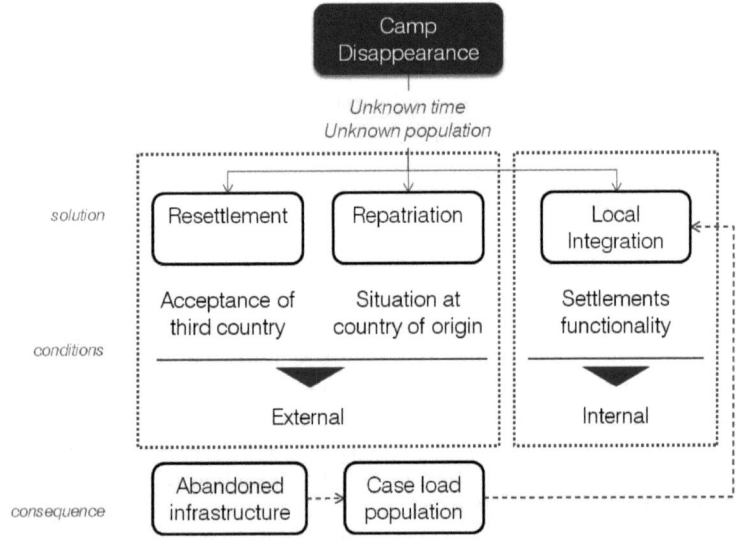

As shown in *Table 1*, the multiplicity of causes for camp closure can be motivated by external or internal factors to which the three official solutions may not be flexible enough to adapt. Repatriation and third-country resettlement imply favourable conditions at the country of origin that go beyond the control of the refugee settlement level. In opposition, local integration relates closely with the living conditions at the settlement. This relation can be in two directions: 1) good living conditions at the camp that allow refugees' self-reliance and therefore a lack of need for further assistance or 2) worsening living conditions with the expectation of forcing refugees back to their home countries.

Following a more restrictive asylum climate, countries in many parts of the world are disinclined to promote settlements which might imply the permanent or long-term presence of people on their territory (Crisp, 2004). Instead, governments deny refugees the right to work, to be involved in economic activities or to practice a determined profession; the right to move from the camp, to choose their residence or buy property or land; the right to access resources such as firewood for cooking, land for grazing or for agriculture.

The fear of refugees competing for scarce resources has promoted such hardship conditions that may cause a camp to close. Other reasons for camp closure without a solution for the refugees may include: a diminution of the population by spontaneous returns, due to improved conditions at the country of origin; becoming a viable permanent settlement, town or site of economic or social activity, where assistance and service provision is phased-out; dwindling donor support and withdraw of humanitarian presence; or abrupt and chaotic closure due to security threats, government coercion or fears of eviction (NRC 2008).

The terminology *camp closure* is used by relief organisations to refer to a complex process implying multiple actions. In some cases, camps disappear without a trace; their process of de-urbanisation implies the deconstruction, dismantling and recovery of useful material, followed by an environmental rehabilitation to recover previous conditions of the site. A second case will leave behind new infrastructure such as roads, canalisations or public buildings that may or may not be used by remaining communities. In other cases, assistance and service provision is phased out, but the settlements stay put and continue to grow.

In a last case, camps do not disappear and remain for years. In fact, nearly two thirds of refugees in the world are in a protracted situation. For UNHCR a *Protracted Refugee Situation (PRS)* is defined when a population of more than 25,000 refugees lives in exile over five years and do not have a visible durable solution in the short term (Guterres 2010).

Conclusions: consequences of disappearance

Under these circumstances, which are the consequences of camp disappearance? What does their announced fate represent? Recalling, the *disappearing city* in the urban context has evolved from Frank Lloyd Wright's loss of urban quality, into the physical contraction of human settlements. In opposition, disappearance in the refugee context developed from the expectation of de-urbanisation, depopulation and deconstruction; into to the loss of its own character as temporal settlements.

Despite the fact that the refugee settlements are *intended* to be temporal urban structures, the consequences of their disappearance- with or without a solution, often results in a process of urbanisation rather than one of de-urbanisation. In other words, camp disappearance can also mean the birth of a permanent settlement. Yet, camps evolve under the uncertainty of their fate, and planning becomes the management of their unpredictable future without knowing if the *urbs* will be dismantled, or if the *polis* will ever be reached.

We can therefore presume that, the management of a camp's evolution is both an opportunity for urbanising the *polis* while planning the deurbanising of the *urbs*. In conclusion, both urbanisation and de-urbanisation processes of refugee camps imply a coexistent management of change; paradoxically, they are planned as a state of a permanent present.

References

Agier, M. (2002) 'Between War and City: Towards an Urban Anthropology of Refugee Camps.' *Ethnography*, 3 pp. 317.

Agier, M. (2010) *Managing the Undesirables*. Oxford: John Wiley and Sons Ltd,

CIA. (2011)*The World Factbook*. Central Intelligence Agency. United States of America.

Crisp, J. (2004) 'The local integration and local settlement of refugees: a conceptual and historical analysis.' *New Issues in Refugee Research*, Geneva. April: 11. pp. 11.

Frampton, K. (1993) *Historia crítica de la arquitectura moderna*. Third edition. Translated by Jorge Sainz, Barcelona: Gustavo Gili.

Guterres, A. (2010) *Restoring rights: forced displacement, protection and humanitarian action*. Harrell-Bond Human Rights Lecture. University of Oxford: Refugee Studies Centre, 13 Oct.

Loewenberg, S. (2011) 'Kenya´s Latest Crisis: The Refugee Camp around the

Refugee Camp'. *Time magazine*, 19 July.

Misselwitz, P. (2009) *Rehabilitating Camp Cities: Community-Driven Planning for Urbanised Refugee Camps*. Stuttgart: Universität Stuttgart.

NRC. (2008) *The Camp Management Toolkit*. 2nd Edition. Norwegian Refugee Council.

Orvañanos, R. (2011) *Disappearing Cities: The Refugee Settlement's Perspective*, Master Thesis. Université Pierre-Mendès-France. Grenoble

Orwell, G. (1950) *1984: A Novel*. New American Library. pp. 268

Oswalt, P. (2005) *Shrinking Cities, Volume 1. International Research*. Ostfildern-Ruit, Germany: Hatje Cantz Verlag.

Oswalt, P., Rieniets, T. (2006) *Atlas of Shrinking Cities*. Hatje Cantz Publishers.

Oxford English Dictionary (2006) Third Edition. Oxford University Press.

Pacione, M. (2009) *Urban Geography. A global perspective.* 3rd. New York: Routledge.

Perouse de Montclos, M.A., Mwangi Kagwanja, P. (2000) 'Refugee Camps or Cities? The Socioeconomic Dynamics of Dadaab and Kakuma Camps in Northern Kenya'. *Journal of Refugee Studies:* pp. 205-222.

Schmeidl, S. (2009) 'Repatriation to Afghanistan: durable solution or responsibility shifting?' *Forced Migration Review: Protracted displacement,* September 2009: pp. 20-22.

Siddiqui, Y. (2011) 'Reviewing the application of the Cessation Clause of the 1951 Convention relating to the status of refugees in Africa'. *RSC Working Paper Series*: pp. 52.

UNHCR (2010) *Global Report 2010.* Geneva: United Nations High Commissioner for Refugees

UNHCR (2007) *Handbook for Emergencies,* 3rd Edition, Geneva: United Nations High Commissioner for Refugees.

UNHCR (2011) *Global Appeal.* Appeal, Geneva: United Nations High Commissioner for Refugees.

Weizman, E. (2008) 'Between Permanent and Transitory. The Endless Present' in Ruby I., Ruby A (ed.) *Urban Transformation* pp. 266-257. Berlin: Ruby Press.

Wright, F.L. (1932) *The Disappearing city.* New York: W.F. Payson

Mundus Urbano: (re) thinking urban development

THE POLITICAL ECONOMY AND STRATEGIES OF INTERNATIONAL DEVELOPMENT COOPERATION. A CASE OF AGRICULTURAL SECTOR IN BANGLADESH

Rahman, AKM Fazlur[1]

Abstract

Bangladesh, which is categorised as one of the Least Developed Countries (LDCS) by Organisation for Economic Co-operation and Development (OECD), received on an average seven percent of total Official Development Assistance (ODA) given to LDCS during the 2000 to 2008 period. Further, the share of agricultural aid in Bangladesh is very low compared to the total aid it has received. Agriculture is a key economic driver in Bangladesh, accounting for nearly 21 percent of the Gross Domestic Product (GDP) and 65 percent of the labour force. In this paper, ODA flow from Japan as a donor country to Bangladesh as a recipient country is analysed. The strategies to promote agricultural investment and development as outlined in National Strategy for Accelerated Poverty Reduction II[2] (NSAPRII) of Bangladesh is compared to a document prepared by United Nations Economic and Social Commission for Asia and the Pacific (UNESCAP). The country strategy of Japan for development cooperation in agriculture in Bangladesh is reviewed using the World Bank's Priorities for Agriculture Development in Bangladesh. Then, an agricultural synthetic index is developed for 188 countries using three indicators (three variables related to agriculture). Lastly, ODA dataset is analysed focusing on trend of ODA flows, sectoral priorities, type of aid, and channels of aid.

Keywords: Official Development Assistance, National Strategy for Accelerated Poverty Reduction, Climate Change

---

1 *M.Sc. International Cooperation and Urban Development; specialisation in Development Economics. Technische Universität Darmstadt, Darmstadt, Germany/ Università degli studi di Roma Tor Vergata, Rome, Italy. B.A. of Urban and Rural Planning, Khulna University, Pakistan. email: russel82@gmail.com.*

2 *National Strategy for Accelerated Poverty Reduction II is the second Poverty Reduction Strategy Paper (PRSP) which has been prepared by the Government of Bangladesh for achieving accelerated growth and poverty reduction during Financial Year 2009-2011.*

Introduction

ODA refers to flows of official financing administered with the promotion of the economic development and welfare of developing countries as the main objective and which are concessional in character with a grant element of at least 25 percent (using a fixed 10 percent rate of discount) (OECD, 2003a). According to OECD, Net ODA[3] in 2008 amounted to USD 119.60 billion. Bangladesh received USD 2.06 billion in 2008 which is 1.72 percent of net ODA.

Bangladesh is a small South Asian country (area 143,998 km²) with one of the highest population densities in the world (1,099 people/km²). It has a low GDP per capita (PPP[4]) of USD 1420 (World Bank, 2011a). In last 20 years, Bangladesh has about five percent annual growth of GDP. In 2008, it received 2061 million USD worth of ODA, which makes it one of the highest recipients of aid in South Asia with an ODA equated to 2.4 percent of Gross National Income (GNI) (World Bank, 2011a). Agriculture is a key economic driver in Bangladesh, accounting for nearly 21 percent of the GDP and 65 percent of the labour force.

The agricultural sector in Bangladesh is undergoing rapid change; it faces problems such as low agricultural productivity, poorly functioning agricultural markets, vulnerability to natural disasters, inefficient land administration, limited access to rural finance, inadequate rural infrastructure and irrigation and drainage problems, especially in the coastal regions. At present, the impact of Climate Change (CC) is the one of the key agricultural challenge for Bangladesh.

The performance of the agriculture sector has considerable influence on overall growth, the trade balance and the level and structure of poverty and malnutrition (World Bank, 2011b). In 2008, Bangladesh faced a shortage of at least three million tons of rice (a staple food for the country) after two waves of floods and a cyclone. Three natural disasters within four months have ruined the late-monsoon Aman paddy, the second major

---

3 Net official development assistance is disbursement flows (net of repayment of principal) that meet the DAC definition of ODA and are made to countries and territories on the DAC list of aid recipients.

4 Purchasing Power Parities (PPPs) are currency conversion rates that both convert to a common currency and equalise the purchasing power of different currencies. In other words, they eliminate the differences in price levels between countries in the process of conversion.

cereal crop in the country. The higher temperatures and changing rainfall patterns, coupled with increased flooding, rising salinity in the coastal belt and droughts are likely to reduce crop yields and crop production in Bangladesh (Government of Bangladesh, 2008). The Intergovernmental Panel for Climate Change (IPCC) estimates that, by 2050, rice production in Bangladesh could decline by eight percent and wheat by 32 percent (against a base year of 1990).

Japan is one of the major donor countries for Bangladesh and their country strategy for agriculture development in Bangladesh is examined in this paper. To understand the national strategy of Bangladesh to promote agricultural investment and development, NSAPRII is reviewed and compared to the document prepared by UNESCAP. The country strategy of Japan is examined using the World Bank's Priorities for Agriculture Development in Bangladesh to figure out the coherence of policies among donors. An agricultural synthetic index is developed for 188 countries using three indicators. To determine the ODA flows, sectoral priorities, type of aid and channels of aid, the ODA dataset is analysed.

Strategy to promote agricultural investment and development

In the NSAPRII, the supply of modern seeds; introduction of crops suitable for particular regions as well as fruits, spices and medicinal plants in hilly districts; promotion of livestock and fisheries sub-sectors through the provision of research and extension services; and the promotion of the cultivation of local fruits and spices were identified as the key areas of intervention for the agriculture sector. To tackle epidemics such as bird flu, the strategy includes awareness building among the farmers. In addition, the use of more organic fertilisers and compost and less chemical fertilisers, effective marketing mechanisms to ensure fair prices for the farmers and crop intensity increases in coastal districts are also included. In this strategy, the emphasis on adaptation to CC is given; however, the programmes and projects are not spelled out appropriately.

To compare the strategies outlined in NSAPRII, a report of UNESCAP on Bangladesh agriculture is considered. The NSAPRII document extensively covers all the challenges faced by the agriculture sector in the country. However, the UNESCAP document adds several important issues which include an introduction to crop insurance policies, homestead gardening, the protection of agricultural land from industrial usage, the construction of cold-storage facilities by the public sector, creating a buffer stock of fertiliser in the public sector for meeting unexpected demand and distribution to inaccessible areas and cautious use of marine resources. In addition to these, other important issues not included in these two documents are agriculture governance and policy implementation and monitoring, strategies towards shrimp and prawn cultivation, revival of the jute industry and the impact of construction of embankments by upstream countries.

Japan's assistance policy towards the agricultural development of Bangladesh

Japan considers Bangladesh a model recipient of ODA. Within the agricultural development of Bangladesh, the Government of Japan (GOJ) focuses on the enhancement of income and productivity and the improvement of rural infrastructure in order to alleviate poverty in rural areas and to assure food security for the nation. Taking into consideration the ongoing assistance for the enhancement of productivity through technical assistance for poultry and the development of irrigation and drainage facilities, GOJ carefully studies the types of assistance that are appropriate in the sub-sector of diversification or advancement of high-value-added products (Japan Ministry of Foreign Affairs, 2011).

Table 1 - Top Ten Donors in the Agriculture Sector of Bangladesh (Disbursements: 2006-2008 AVERAGE, USD Million, constant 2007)

Donor	Amount (US$ Million)	Share of total aid to agriculture (%)	Share of total aid given (%)
IDA	22.72	47.67	3.66
Denmark	7.22	15.16	23.61
Netherlands	3.37	7.08	4.00
United Kingdom	2.33	4.89	0.97
United States	2.29	4.80	2.35
Canada	2.28	4.79	3.51
Japan	2.28	4.78	0.54
EC	1.42	2.99	1.08
Germany	0.87	1.83	1.91
Ireland	0.86	1.81	22.19
All Donors	47.66	95.78	

Source: OECD, 2011

To compare Japan's Assistance Policy for agricultural development in Bangladesh, the World Bank's priority areas for agricultural development of Bangladesh are examined. The World Bank has taken a wide range of areas as priority areas for its support in Bangladesh, which includes increasing agricultural productivity, diversification and value addition, improving factor markets, access to assets and natural resource management and strengthening rural institutions and livelihood support (World Bank, 2011c). Japan's Assistance Policy and the World Bank's priority areas for support merge in increasing agricultural productivity, water resource management and providing infrastructure to improve access for agricultural inputs and outputs.

Agricultural synthetic index

In this paper, Agricultural Synthetic Index (ASI) is prepared by the author to compare the situation of agricultural sector in respect of other countries in the world. This is an index similar to the Human Development Index (HDI) of UNDP where ranking of countries are done by level of human development. To develop the agricultural synthetic index, three indicators are taken from the World Bank Development Indicator[5] for 213 countries.

However, information for all the indicators is not available. In order to obtain information for most of the countries, the year 2005 was selected. The indicators are aligned with the country strategies of both donors and the Government of Bangladesh. Cereal yield (kg per hectare) defines

Table 2 - Agricultural Synthetic Index

Country Name	Indicator 1: Cereal yield (kg per hectare)	Indicator 2: Agriculture value added per worker (constant 2000 US$)	Indicator 3: Improved water source, rural (% of rural population with access)	Standardisation of Indicator 1	Standardisation of Indicator 2	Standardisation of Indicator 3	Index 1 (Arithmetic Mean)	Index 2 (Weighted Average)
Malaysia	3407	550	99	0.38	0.01	0.99	0.46	0.44
Bangladesh	3682	369	78	0.41	0.00	0.75	0.39	0.39
Nepal	2317	245	85	0.25	0.00	0.83	0.36	0.33

Source: World Bank, 2011

5 *The primary World Bank collection of development indicators, compiled from officially-recognised international sources. It presents the most current and accurate global development data available and includes national, regional and global estimates (World Bank, 2011).*

agricultural productivity; here Bangladesh is ranked 41 among 175 countries. For the agriculture value added per worker indicator, Bangladesh is ranked 133 among 157 countries. In the strategies for agricultural development of Bangladesh, improvement of water sources is an important issue. Bangladesh is ranked 113 among 180 countries in this indicator. The final index is calculated using two methods namely arithmetic mean and weighted average. For the weighted average method, the first indicator is given a weight of one (1) and other two indicators are given a weight of 0.5. For Bangladesh, both methods produce the same result; however, for most of the countries the result is different. Bangladesh is ranked 71 in 188 countries using the arithmetic mean method and 60 in the weighted average method (*Table 2*).

Agriculture aid statistics

In the trend of ODA flow in agriculture, the forestry and fisheries sectors in Bangladesh show that most donors are granting aid on a steady basis except for the Islamic Development Bank, who increased their aid from 6.4 to 51.9 million USD between the years 2007 and 2008. Again in 2009 it dropped to 15.1 million USD *(Figure 1).*

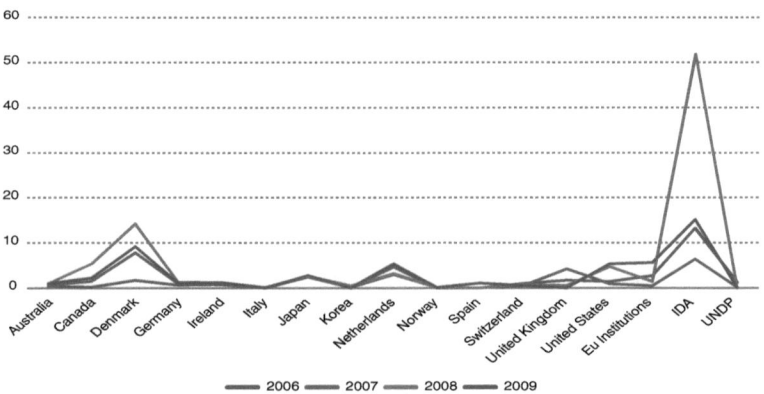

Figure 1: Trend of ODA Flows in the Agriculture Sector of Bangladesh (Disbursements gross constant 2008 USD Millions), Source: OECD, 2011

The share of agricultural aid in Bangladesh is very low compared to the total aid Bangladesh has received. In 2009, total aid for Bangladesh dropped by 45 percent and agriculture aid by 56 percent from the previous year *(Figure 2).* Among the three sectors, agriculture is the highest priority and fisheries are the most neglected in terms of aid given *(Figure 3).*

Mundus Urbano: (re) thinking urban development

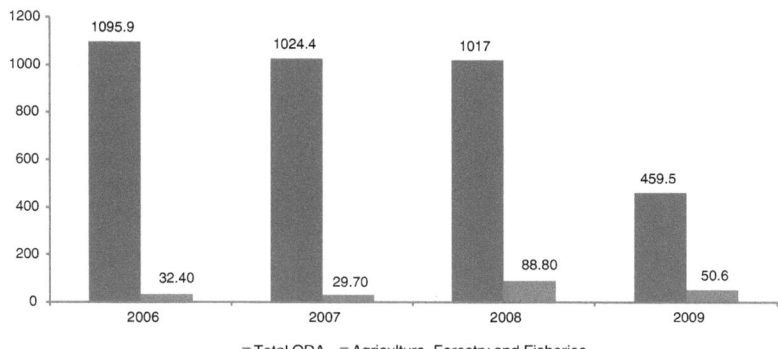

Figure 2: Total ODA and ODA in Agriculture, Forestry and Fisheries (Disbursements gross constant 2008 USD Millions), Source: OECD, 2011

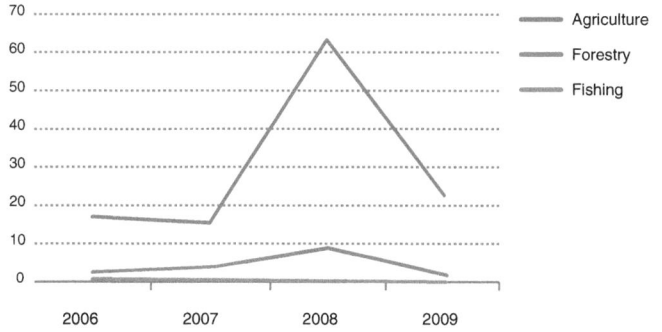

Figure 3: ODA Flow in Agriculture, Forestry and Fisheries Sectors (Disbursements gross constant 2008 USD Millions). Source: OECD, 2011

According to donor strategies, agricultural productivity is one of the major areas of concern for Bangladesh. In this respect, 52 percent of ODA went to agricultural production *(Figure 4)*. The amount of ODA in the agricultural research sector is also very encouraging. Agricultural water resources management is an important aspect of agriculture in Bangladesh; however, the amount of aid in this sector is very low.

Seventeen percent of aid in the agriculture sector is disbursed by the government and eleven percent is disbursed by NGOs and civil society *(Figure 5)*. Investment projects are predominant among the type of aid in the agriculture sector of Bangladesh *(Figure 6)*.

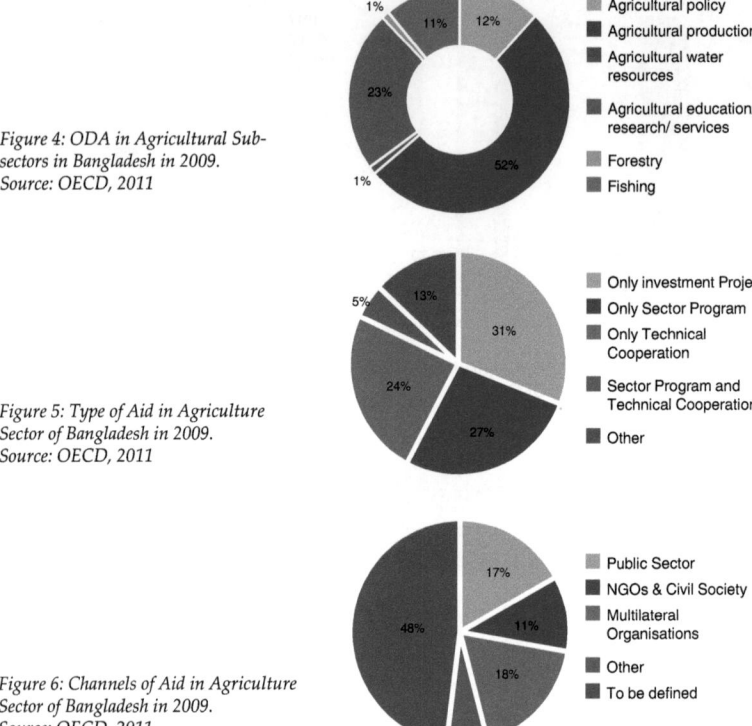

Figure 4: ODA in Agricultural Sub-sectors in Bangladesh in 2009.
Source: OECD, 2011

Figure 5: Type of Aid in Agriculture Sector of Bangladesh in 2009.
Source: OECD, 2011

Figure 6: Channels of Aid in Agriculture Sector of Bangladesh in 2009.
Source: OECD, 2011

Conclusion

Although agriculture sector contributing 21 percent of GDP in Bangladesh, it receives only 6 percent of total ODA for this country. The priority areas that are identified by donor community including World Bank and Japan clearly reflect the current challenges in this sector. The strategies outlined by Government of Bangladesh for agricultural development are in line with the donor community. However, the programmes and projects are not spelled out correctly in NSAPRII. As discussed in section 2, CC impacts will be a very big challenge for the agriculture sector. According to the Global Climate Risk Index 2010, Bangladesh is the most vulnerable country regarding CC impacts. The food security situation in Bangladesh will not improve without the appropriate agricultural adaptation technology to CC impacts. The amount of aid in agricultural research is encouraging for developing adaptation technology for CC impact; however, more aid is needed to tackle CC impacts.

References

Bangladesh Ministry of Finance (2011) *Bangladesh Economic Review*. [Online], Available: http://www.mof.gov.bd/en/index.php [20 Feb 2011].

Department of International Development (UK) (2005) [Online], Available: www.dfid.gov.uk/mdg/aid-effectiveness/newsletters/js-policynotes.pdf [23 Feb 2011].

Government of Bangladesh (2008) *Bangladesh Climate Change Strategy and Action Plan*. National Strategy. Dhaka: Government of Bangladesh.

Government of Bangladesh (2009) *National Strategy for Accelerated Poverty Reduction II*. National Strategy. Dhaka: Government of Bangladesh.

Japan Ministry of Foreign Affairs (2011) *ODA Policies: Rolling Plans*, [Online] Available: http://www.mofa.go.jp/policy/oda/rolling_plans/region/bangladesh.pdf [19 Feb 2011].

Mandal, M.A.S. (2005) *Agriculture e-Resources: Reports*. [Online], Available: http://www.lcgbangladesh.org/Agriculture/reports/vol-3.pdf [20 Feb 2011].

OECD, (2003a) *Glossary of Statistical Terms*. [Online], Available: http://stats.oecd.org/glossary/detail.asp?ID=6043 [17 Oct 2011].

OECD (2003b) Glossary of Statistical Terms. [Online], Available: http://stats.oecd.org/glossary/detail.asp?ID=6043 [Accessed 23 Feb 2011].

OECD (2011) *Creditor Reporting System*. [Online], Available: http://stats.oecd.org/Index.aspx?DataSetCode=CRSNEW [25 Feb 2011].

OECD (2011) *Focus on aid to agriculture*. [Online], Available: http://www.oecd.org/document/44/0,3746,en_2649_34447_43817324_1_1_1_1,00.html [22 Feb 2011].

Planning Commission Bangladesh (2005) *National Strategy for Accelerated Poverty Reduction*. National Strategy. Dhaka: Government of the People's Republic of Bangladesh.

Wikipedia (2011) *Official Development Assistance*. [Online], Available: http://en.wikipedia.org/wiki/Official_development_assistance [24 Feb 2011].

World Bank (2011a) *Data by Country*. [Online], Available: http://data.worldbank.org/country/bangladesh [20 Feb 2011].

World Bank (2011b) *Climate Change: Bangladesh Facing the Challenge*. [Online], Available: http://web.worldbank.org/WBSITE/EXTERNAL/COUNTRIES/SOUTHASIAEXT/0,contentMDK:21893554~menuPK:158937~pagePK:2865106~piPK:2865128~theSitePK:223547,00.html [20 Feb 2011].

World Bank (2011c) *Bangladesh: Priorities for Agriculture and Rural Development*. [Online], Available: http://web.worldbank.org/WBSITE/EXTERNAL/COUNTRIES/SOUTHASIAEXT/EXTSAREGTOPAGRI/0,contentMDK:20273763~menuPK:548213~pagePK:34004173~piPK:34003707~theSitePK:452766,00.html [23 Feb 2011].

World Bank (2011d) *World Development Indicators*. [Online], Available: http://data.worldbank.org/data-catalog/world-development-indicators [17 Oct 2011].

nser le développment urbain . (ri) pensare lo sviluppo urbano . (re) thinking urban development . (re) pensando
entwicklung (um) denken . (re) pensando o desenvolvimento urbano . penilaian semula pembangunan b
oppment urbain . (ri) pensare lo sviluppo urbano . (re) thinking urban development . (re) pensando el desarrollo
m) denken . (re) pensando o desenvolvimento urbano . penilaian semula pembangunan bandar . (re) penser le
ensare lo sviluppo urbano . (re) thinking urban development . (re) pensando el desarrollo urbano . Stadtentwick
ndo o desenvolvimento urbano . penilaian semula pembangunan bandar . (re) penser le développment u
oo urbano . (re) thinking urban development . (re) pensando el desarrollo urbano . Stadtentwicklung (um) der
volvimento urbano . penilaian semula pembangunan bandar . (re) penser le développment urbain . (ri) pensa
nking urban development . (re) pensando el desarrollo urbano . Stadtentwicklung (um) denken . (re) pensan
o . penilaian semula pembangunan bandar . (re) penser le développment urbain . (ri) pensare lo sviluppo urba
pment . (re) pensando el desarrollo urbano . Stadtentwicklung (um) denken . (re) pensando o desenvolvime
a pembangunan bandar . (re) penser le développment urbain . (ri) pensare lo sviluppo urbano . (re) thinking ur
ndo el desarrollo urbano . Stadtentwicklung (um) denken . (re) pensando o desenvolvimento urbano . penilai
andar . (re) penser le développment urbain . (ri) pensare lo sviluppo urbano . (re) thinking urban development . (
rbano . Stadtentwicklung (um) denken . (re) pensando o desenvolvimento urbano . penilaian semula pemb
r le développment urbain . (ri) pensare lo sviluppo urbano . (re) thinking urban development . (re) pensando
ntwicklung (um) denken . (re) pensando o desenvolvimento urbano . penilaian semula pembangunan b
oppment urbain . (ri) pensare lo sviluppo urbano . (re) thinking urban development . (re) pensando el desarrollo
m) denken . (re) pensando o desenvolvimento urbano . penilaian semula pembangunan bandar . (re) penser le
ensare lo sviluppo urbano . (re) thinking urban development . (re) pensando el desarrollo urbano . Stadtentwick
ndo o desenvolvimento urbano . penilaian semula pembangunan bandar . (re) penser le développment u
oo urbano . (re) thinking urban development . (re) pensando el desarrollo urbano . Stadtentwicklung (um) der
volvimento urbano . penilaian semula pembangunan bandar . (re) penser le développment urbain . (ri) pensa
nking urban development . (re) pensando el desarrollo urbano . Stadtentwicklung (um) denken . (re) pensan
o . penilaian semula pembangunan bandar . (re) penser le développment urbain . (ri) pensare lo sviluppo urba
pment . (re) pensando el desarrollo urbano . Stadtentwicklung (um) denken . (re) pensando o desenvolvime
a pembangunan bandar . (re) penser le développment urbain . (ri) pensare lo sviluppo urbano . (re) thinking ur
ndo el desarrollo urbano . Stadtentwicklung (um) denken . (re) pensando o desenvolvimento urbano . penilai
andar . (re) penser le développment urbain . (ri) pensare lo sviluppo urbano . (re) thinking urban development . (
rbano . Stadtentwicklung (um) denken . (re) pensando o desenvolvimento urbano . penilaian semula pemb
r le développment urbain . (ri) pensare lo sviluppo urbano . (re) thinking urban development . (re) pensando
ntwicklung (um) denken . (re) pensando o desenvolvimento urbano . penilaian semula pembangunan b
oppment urbain . (ri) pensare lo sviluppo urbano . (re) thinking urban development . (re) pensando el desarrollo
m) denken . (re) pensando o desenvolvimento urbano . penilaian semula pembangunan bandar . (re) penser le
ensare lo sviluppo urbano . (re) thinking urban development . (re) pensando el desarrollo urbano . Stadtentwick
ndo o desenvolvimento urbano . penilaian semula pembangunan bandar . (re) penser le développment u
oo urbano . (re) thinking urban development . (re) pensando el desarrollo urbano . Stadtentwicklung (um) der
volvimento urbano . penilaian semula pembangunan bandar . (re) penser le développment urbain . (ri) pensa
nking urban development . (re) pensando el desarrollo urbano . Stadtentwicklung (um) denken . (re) pensan
o . penilaian semula pembangunan bandar . (re) penser le développment urbain . (ri) pensare lo sviluppo urba
pment . (re) pensando el desarrollo urbano . Stadtentwicklung (um) denken . (re) pensando o desenvolvime
a pembangunan bandar . (re) penser le développment urbain . (ri) pensare lo sviluppo urbano . (re) thinking ur
ndo el desarrollo urbano . Stadtentwicklung (um) denken . (re) pensando o desenvolvimento urbano . penilai
andar . (re) penser le développment urbain . (ri) pensare lo sviluppo urbano . (re) thinking urban development . (
rbano . Stadtentwicklung (um) denken . (re) pensando o desenvolvimento urbano . penilaian semula pemb
r le développment urbain . (ri) pensare lo sviluppo urbano . (re) thinking urban development . (re) pensando
ntwicklung (um) denken . (re) pensando o desenvolvimento urbano . penilaian semula pembangunan b
oppment urbain . (ri) pensare lo sviluppo urbano . (re) thinking urban development . (re) pensando el desarrollo
m) denken . (re) pensando o desenvolvimento urbano . penilaian semula pembangunan bandar . (re) penser le
ensare lo sviluppo urbano . (re) thinking urban development . (re) pensando el desarrollo urbano . Stadtentwick
ndo o desenvolvimento urbano . penilaian semula pembangunan bandar . (re) penser le développment u
oo urbano . (re) thinking urban development . (re) pensando el desarrollo urbano . Stadtentwicklung (um) der
volvimento urbano . penilaian semula pembangunan bandar . (re) penser le développment urbain . (ri) pensa

CHAPTER IV

SUSTAINABLE URBAN INFRASTRUCTURE AND DISASTER RISK REDUCTION

Prof. Cor Dijkgraaf
Huynh Le Hai Chau
Rossana Poblet Alegre
José Luis Chong Chong
Alexander White

SUSTAINABLE URBAN INFRASTRUCTURE AND DISASTER RISK REDUCTION: INTRODUCTION

Prof. Dijkgraaf, Cor[1]

I write this paper in Bangkok, which is at the moment flooded. The water was coming from the North after heavy rainfall. The ancient city of Ayutaya, on the UNESCO World Heritage list, is already under two meters of water. six large industrial estates are flooded and production of Honda, Toyota etc has come to a standstill. More than 200.000 people are unemployed. Millions of people had to leave their homes. But also in the part of Bangkok, which is still dry, supermarkets and restaurants close, because the whole transport system does not work anymore. The railroad to the North is underwater and the second largest airport of Bangkok is closed. The rice fields have disappeared under water and the harvest is lost. It is not just the physical aspects of flooding, it wreaks havoc upon the socio-economic structures. This flooding really hits Thailand's Economy very hard. At the last moment the Thai Government is building dikes with sandbags and every body is trying to protect its property with sandbags, this does not help against floods of more than two meter water.

Could this have been avoided?

One of the consequences of Climate Change is heavy concentrated rainfall. We have witnessed the flooding this year in Australia, in Pakistan and now in Thailand. Like in many countries the absorption capacity in the mountains and hills has been reduced through deforestation and urbanisation, making the water run down much faster. The seawater level rising as another consequence of Climate Change (melting of the glaciers) and this makes it more difficult to release the water into the sea.

Can it happen again?

Yes it will happen again in Thailand and in other countries. Climate change is not anymore a distant future hazard but it is a hard reality. It is time to take the necessary measures to avoid the havoc upon socio-economic

---

1 *Former director (19 years) of the Institute for Housing and Urban Development (IHS)in Rotterdam, Senior Advisor to the Board and former President of the Pacific Rim Council on Urban Development (PRCUD).*

What can be done?

An integrated system of water management is necessary starting at the beginning in the mountains of the small brooks. In The Netherlands where a large part of the country is already below sea level, the struggle against flooding has a history of hundreds of years, Climate Changes are taken serious. The measures advised in the Delta report of 2008 are being implemented. Dike along the rivers and sea are strengthened and retention areas are constructed to temporarily store the water. This process starts with the small brooks and also is being implemented for the big rivers Rhine and Meuse. The Dutch have concluded that the present safety norms are not enough to deal with the consequences of climate change. We also have to see to it that the water of the rivers can release into the sea. With a rise of the level of the sea water (a fact, caused by the melting of the glaciers world wide) the rivers the water will flood the land rather streaming into the sea. In Thailand the serious flooding lasts already for more than a month, caused by spring tide in the Gulf of Bangkok. When the sea water level will be 49 cm higher than at the moment, Bangkok will be permanently flooded. Building a dam in the Gulf and controlling the water level of the new lake is one of the options. The Dutch live for hundreds of years below the sea level. When you arrive at Schiphol Amsterdam airport, you are 4 meters below sea water level, The airport is there for almost hundred years and have never been flooded. Technically there are good solutions. It needs the political will and vision to take action. If not, the economic damage will be larger than the investment costs.

URBAN PLANNING APPROACH TO URBAN FLOODING. THE HO CHI MINH CITY CASE STUDY

Huynh, Le Hai Chau[1]

Abstract

As an emerging Southeast Asian megacity, Ho Chi Minh City (HCMC) is facing numerous urban environmental challenges that remain unsolved. Among these challenges, urban flooding is the one that directly affects the daily lives of the city's inhabitants. The effects of urban flooding are threatening the whole development of the city. It is expected that the problem will be compounded by sea levels rise due to climate change. Reconsidering the fundamental causes of the urban floods in HCMC, it is revealed that unsustainable urbanisation has primarily resulted to the problem. However, the urban flooding management in HCMC is predominantly based on a conventional engineering-centric approach, which addresses the impacts of floods rather than the rooted-causes of floods and diminish the urban planning aspects. Hence, there is a missing linkage between urban planning and flooding management in HCMC. This research paper, through analysing the main causes of the floods in HCMC, reveals that there is a necessity to integrate urban planning aspects into the city's flooding management strategies throughout an urban planning approach to urban flooding.

Keywords: *Climate Change, Ho Chi Minh City, Sustainable Flood Management, Urban Flooding, Urban Planning.*

---

1 *Research Associate at Department of Urban Planning and Spatial Design, Brandenburg University of Technology Cottbus, Germany. M.Sc. International Cooperation and Urban Development; Technische Universität Darmstadt. Germany. B.A. of Architecture, Ho Chi Minh City University of Architecture, Ho Chi Minh City, Vietnam;. email: huynhlechau@gmail.com*

Introduction

After the 1980's 'Doi Moi', the economic reforms to the socialist-orientated market economy in Vietnam, HCMC has been developing steadily in both economic and spatial dimensions. In 2010, there were 7.4 million registered inhabitants in the city (GSO, 2010). It is projected that in 2025, the city will be populated by 10.2 million inhabitants, and thereby, it will be ranked as the 31st largest urban area in the world (Wendell Cox, 2009). However, as with any city facing rapid urbanisation, HCMC is facing a number of urban environmental challenges, in which urban flooding is one of the most significant. Frequent urban floods of 0.2-0.6m in both rainy and dry seasons are spoiling the living environment, affecting the population's health, causing traffic congestion and damaging buildings and infrastructure. It was estimated that the flooding costs the city up to 26.86 billion USD in 2005 (Nicholls et al., 2007) and this cost is promising to continue to rise with the effects of climate change.

Consequently, many anti-flood programmes have been established and implemented in the city with most of the strategies focused on constructing large-scale structures. These projects are expensive; however, positive results are just limited. This raises questions of whether the current approach is appropriate to the city's context; and if not, what is a more holistic approach to flooding should be taken.

Methodology

This research uses hydrologic, geographic and urbanisation data to show the correlation between urbanisation impacts and urban flooding in HCMC. Thereby, through literature reviews and international case studies, it revealed that urban planning is a more holistic approach to HCMC's urban flooding than engineering-centric approach. Based on such finding, the research puts forth both possible measures and implementation strategies.

Results and discussions

Causes of urban floods in HCMC

Theoretically, sea level rise would partly result to the severity of flooding. In fact, this is not yet the case in HCMC. From 1990 to 2008, while the mean-river-level in the city has increased by an average of 1.5cm per year, the mean-sea-level at Vung Tau sea gauge remains constant (Ho, 2010; *Figure 1*).

The causes of the significant river-level rise and the severe floods in HCMC could be explained better through the resulted impacts due to the city's rapid urbanisation. Firstly, the loss of un-paved surfaces and the expansion of paved surfaces have led to the reduction of the absorbent ability of the land and an increase in surface run-off in the city. Since 1989, built-up areas and impermeable surfaces of the city have been doubled (Tran and Ha, 2007). At the same time, upstream areas have faced deforestation. There is also the loss of agriculture lands, wetlands and other water bodies in the city (DONRE, 2009). Secondly, it is the high surface temperature during throughout the urbanisation period has resulted to the increase of city's precipitation and occurrences of heavy rainfalls (Tran and Ha, 2008; Ho, 2010). Although facing the high and increasing precipitation, the existing city's combined sewer and stormwater management network is degraded and cannot support the increased load of the run-off water. Moreover, there is a significant land subsidence problem due to dense construction and overuse of underground water, which makes the city's areas even more vulnerable to flooding (Le and Ho, 2009). Based on the above consequences of unsustainable urbanisation, urban flooding in HCMC goes beyond a climate change problem.

The rise of mean water level:
▲ Significantly
♦ Insignificantly
● Constantly

Figure 1: Changes of mean water levels from 1990 to 2008 in HCMC
Based Source: Ho, 2010.

Current approaches to urban floods in HCMC

Although unsustainable urban development impacts are the main causes of flooding in HCMC, the current flood management strategies of the city have not focused on addressing these issues. In 2010, the HCMC

Steering Committee on Flooding Control (SCFC) introduced the "Urban flooding mitigation programme from 2011 to 2015 and targeted to 2025". It is an achievement that the programme recommended interdisciplinary adaptation measures. However, the measures are focused strongly on a civil engineering approach, in particular, the city's drainage system. Most of the tasks are focused on elaborating the existing drainage network, constructing new drainage systems, upgrading drainage techniques, allocating funds for drainage constructions, and human resources recruiting for the drainage sector (Table 1).

Table 1 - Summarised of SCFC's "Urban flooding mitigation programme from 2011 to 2015 and targeted to 2025"

Objectives	Overall measures	Specific measures	Areas of the measures
Reduce number of current flooded sites & prevent emergences of new flooded sites	Upgrade existing and construct new drainage system	1) Ensure the schedule of the current drainage upgrading projects and strengthen the supervising on these projects	Drainage project management
		2) Apply urgent drainage technique, construct new and upgrade the drainage system	Drainage technology/ drainage constructions
	Reclaim water surface	4) Maintain and create more water retention spaces in the city. Enhance urban control, set up urban regulations of water reclaiming	Land use/ urban regulations
Executing & control the national daptation programmes	Land management	5) Protect agriculture lands and reserve wetlands, rivers and canals	Land use
		6) Increase green areas	Land use
		7) Building reservoirs at upstream areas	Hydrological structure
	Integrated planning	8) Develop an integrated strategy that examine the correlations of rain, tide, flood and the ecological environment	Flood management Strategies
	Funding allocating for drainage upgrading	9) Use effectively ODA funds; encourage organisational and private funds; increase the water prices	Drainage management funding

Based Source: SCFC 2010a

Mundus Urbano: (re) thinking urban development

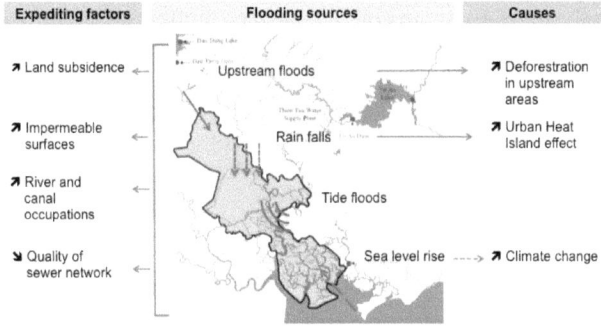

Figure 2: The causes of urban floods in HCMC, showing that most of the causes are from unsustainable urban planning impacts during urbanisation.

Objectives	Overall measures	Specific measures	Areas of the resources
Science &Tech. cooperation	Enhance the science and technology cooperation	10) Encourage science and technology cooperation among international, national experts, institutions and universities.	Cooperation
Strengthen government's control on drainage system, wastewater management and flooding control	Improve the (drainage) institutional framework	11) Centralize and restructuring the drainage management work	Drainage management administrative
	Improve (drainage) technology	12) Develop the database of city on the drainage network	Drainage management/ data-building
		13) Develop drainage management technology	Drainage technology
	Human resource recruiting for drainage sector	14) Enhance and expand water drainage college training programmes	Drainage management/ Human resourcing
		15) Adjust working policies in water drainage sector to attract more experts	
Education & communication	Raise public's awareness	16) Mainstream knowledge into primary and elementary schools; enhance the communication activities; strict policies and penalties due to offenses.	Education and public awareness
Enhance the construction		17) Fund allocating for dike construction, tide control gates, canal clearance, water drainage and wastewater treatment projects	Funding for drainage & defence structures

------- Measures which are related to the drainage system

Likewise, when analysing the on-going projects dealing with urban flooding, it has been shown that all of these projects are engineering construction projects focused on the drainage network, defensive structures or pumping stations (Table 2).

Table 2 - SCFC's on going projects

Project Name	Scope of work	Initial Budget	Funded by	Start	Finish
1 Nhieu Loc-Thi Nghe Environmental Sanitation Project – 2nd Phase	• Construct drainage network connecting the 1st phase drainage with the water treatment plant • Build one new water treatment plant	470 (million USD)	WB /ADB/ Vietnam Government (VNGov)	2011	2017
2 Ben Nghe - Tau Hu - Kenh Doi - Kenh Te Environmental Sanitation Project – 2nd Phase	• Upgrade capacity of the existing pumping stations, existing drainage network and the water treatment plants • Construct a 23,560 m3 reservoir at Me Coc 2.	(Budget of the 1st phase was 250 million USD)	JICA	2010	2014
3 Tham Luong - Ben Cat drainage system & water pollution treatment	• Upgrade drainage system and sewage system • Construct 3 new water treatment plants	250 (million USD)	VNGov	2010	2014
4 Nhieu Loc- Thi Nghe tidal controlling sewer	• Tide controlling sewer • Water pumping station	12 (million USD)	VNGov	2010	2012
5 Tidal controlling, dike controlling, canal dredging projects based on decision 1547/QĐ-TTg	• 8,200 m dike construction along Saigon river; • Tidal controlling at Kinh river, Tan Thuan, Ben Nghe, Phu Xuan, Vam Thuan • Dredging main drainage		VNGov	2010	2015

Based Source: SCFC 2010

These projects cost billions of USD and are funded with international loans, as well as with the national budget, but few positive results have been shown. There have been already the significant new emergences of flooded sites in the new urbanised areas, in parallel with the re-emergences of flooded sites in the anti-flood projects' zones (Ho, 2011). More drainage structures and flood defence have been constructed; nevertheless, the rooted causes of the problem have not been treated: the land subsidence still significantly occurs; the heavy rainfall occurrences still steadily increase; and the unpaved surfaces are still rapidly covered by built-up areas. Throughout an online survey in 2008, the city's inhabitants have officially shown their dissatisfaction on the efficiencies of the anti-flood projects (*Table 3*). These facts require a review in the city's flooding mitigation and adaptation strategies.

Table 3 - Online public survey about the flooding situations since implementing the anti-flood projects in HCMC.

Q: How do you find about the flood occurrences in HCMC?	
Less than before	2.3%
As much as before	10.1%
As much as before, but will be improved when drainage projects are completed	7.3%
Worse than before	80.3%
	Total vote: 11,826

Source: Vnexpress.net 2008

A necessity to link urban planning with urban flooding adaptation and mitigation strategies

The inefficiencies of the flooding management in HCMC can be explained under many aspects; but the primary aspect is its engineering-centric approach. Since the HCMC's engineering-centric approach addresses only the flood impacts rather than the main causes of urban floods, it hardly achieves sustainable and holistic outcomes. In fact, many other countries in the world have recognised this limitation of the engineering-centric approach. They have shifted this conventional approach to 'Integrated flood management'[2] approach, in which, in addition to the engineering solutions, the urban forms and urban structures are adjusted to enhance the natural environment, to give more spaces for water, and to reclaim more un-paved surfaces (White 2008; Johnson, Watson, and McOuat 2008). Consequently, urban planning[3] has been recognised as the most appropriate tool to apply

---

2 The term 'Integrated Flood Management' is referred to different flood management concepts, which are developed in various places in the world under different terms such as 'Natural flood management' (Scotland), 'Water sensitive urban design' (Australia), Low Impact Development (USA), Sustainable Urban Drainage System (UK), or Decentralised Stormwater Management (Germany).

3 The term 'urban planning' is used throughout in this paper is to refer to planning for the whole city as well as planning for medium and small sized urban spaces and building design.

this concept (White, 2008; Godschalk, Kaiser and Berke, 1998). Firstly, it is because urban planning has the strong influences on urban forms and urban structures and can adjust these patterns. Secondly, urban planning can integrate flooding management strategies with other economic and social development strategies through its long-term and short-term planning visions to ensure balanced development (WMO, 2008). Thirdly, it can take charge of providing new formations and alternatives to improvements and helping communities adapt to climate change and urban flooding impacts through slum upgrading and public participation projects. Moreover, rather than only mitigating the urban flooding through physical implementations, it can raise the communities' awareness and enhance public knowledge about urban flooding through its public capacity building programmes (Burby and May, 1998). In short, urban planning is taking a leading role in sustainable urban flooding mitigation and adaptation.

The important role of urban planning, however, is not recognised in HCM's flood management strategies. Urban planning and flood management are still the two separated fields. There is a need to link the HCMC's flood management with its urban planning system throughout an urban planning approach to urban flooding.

Urban planning approach to urban flooding in HCMC and its principles

Based on various 'Integrated flood management' concepts that have been developed in different places in the world, this paper identifies that there are three main principles of an urban planning approach to urban

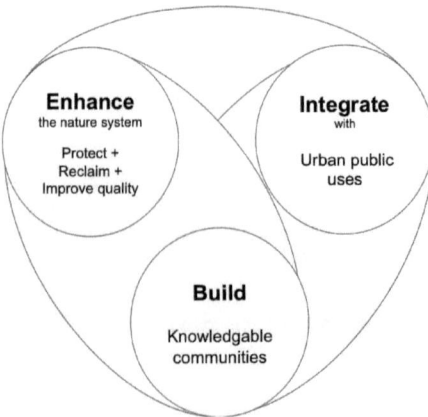

Figure 3 : The three principles of urban planning approach to urban flooding.

flooding, which are: to enhance the natural environment; to integrate urban public uses with flood management facilities; and, to build knowledgeable communities.

a. To enhance the natural environment:

The first principle is to protect, reclaim and improve the quality of the natural environment that has been destroyed and altered during urbanisation process of the city. This enhances the natural water cycle in the city, in which, stormwater is absorbed into the soil and evaporated into the air, while tide-surges are transferred into natural detention ponds, to await absorption or evaporation. Thus, this principle targets the original causes of the urban floods.

b. To integrate urban public uses with flood management facilities:

The second principle is to integrate urban public uses with flood management facilities. Through this principle, the approach does not only give solutions to sustainable flood management, but also to other public demands such as more green space, sport, recreational space and cultural space. This approach enhances the vibrancy of the urban areas while raising public awareness through their uses of the public facilities. Examples of how to integrate urban functions with flood management include:

- Integrating existing urban functions with flooding management functions such as adding retention ponds in recreational parks, adding more green to paved areas or combining water retention ponds with urban squares.

- Integrating existing flooding management functions with 'new' urban functions such as adding recreation places at water defence structures, combining wetlands with recreational parks or using floodplains as neighbourhood playgrounds during the falls of tide and floods.

c. To build knowledgeable communities:

The third principle is to build knowledgeable communities through urban planning anti-flood programmes. This is the grounding strategy of flood adaptation and mitigation in both long-term and short-term. When the communities are provided with sufficient knowledge about flood protection, mitigation and adaptation, they can protect themselves from the impacts of floods in an active manner.

Specific objectives and suggested measures

Based on the above principles, there are key measures of how an urban planning approach to urban flooding can be implied in HCMC, considering its context. Here, it is necessary that obligatory flood risk assessment data and urban data are collected.

The measures are classified into four catalogues: Regulations, Public investment, Incentives and Knowledge enhancement, following each objective and the specific targets (*Table 3*). Still, the most promising approach is to adopt multiple measures, which are applied by different tools and address different components of flood risks in HCMC. It is also necessary to note that, due to the diversity of the urban planning area, there are also other possible measures for each target; likewise, some measures can be applied

Table 4- The specific targets and related measures of urban planning approach to urban flooding in HCMC

		SPECIFIC OBJECTIVES	MEASURES	
			(R)- Regulation	(I)-Incentive
FLOOD MITIGATING	1	Restrict development in flood risk zones	Apply restriction regulations, density control, set back control and disadvantaged taxation in flood risk areas	-
	2	Protect the existing un-paved lands and water surfaces	Prohibit deforestation and occupations of wetlands, agriculture lands; rivers, canals, streams and natural retention ponds in upstream and downstream areas	Preferential taxation on agricul lands and wetlands
	3	Reclaim more green and permeable surfaces	Apply Ecological Area Factor regulations as planning and building codes	Planning bonus and subsidy
				Free or low cost techn consultancy
	4	Reclaim more capacity for water retention and detention	On-site rainwater harvesting, retention and detention regulations	Planning bonus and preferer taxation
FLOOD ADAPTING	5	Apply flood adapted building and neighbour-hood design	Apply flood proof building codes and planning codes in flood risk zones	Low interest loan for flood p building construction
				Free or low cost techn consultancy
	6	Improve the quality of stormwater	Restriction on locations of potential contamination source facilities (factories, petrol stations, landfills etc.)	-

to achieve more than one target. Additionally, there are some benchmarks of the suggested measures, which have been successfully implemented in different places in the world, are shown in *Table 4*.

Implementation strategies

The implementation of the urban planning approach to urban flooding should, firstly, involve different stakeholders including public authorities and committees, community-based organisations and institutions, practical experts and citizens. The implementation strategy should be a dual strategy between the top-down and bottom-up approaches and should take place through urban pilot projects. The pilot projects are recommended to be applied first in low-income communities which are most vulnerable to floods.

(P)-Public Investment	(K)-Knowledge enhancement
Locate public amenities and infrastructures away from flood risk zones to attract development	Raise public awareness about flood risk zones and the restriction regulations
Increase density in high-lying areas but reduce density in low-lying areas	
Provide public amenity functions to these protected land and water resources	Raise public awareness about the protection of un-sealed lands and water surfaces and the restriction regulations
Add new green and permeable surfaces in public and semi-public spaces	Promote green city and green architecture
	Workshops for architects and builders
Rainwater harvesting in public buildings as pilot projects	Public awareness campaigns and technical publications
Connect the existing water networks	
Add more stormwater retention and detention in upstream and downstream areas	Workshops and educational programmes for architects and builders
Research about flood adapted building and neighbourhood design	Public awareness campaigns and technical publications
Pilot projects of flood adapted buildings and neighbourhoods	Workshops and education programmes for architects and builders
Locate potential contamination source facilities out of flood risk zones	Raise public awareness about environment protection
Use infiltration plants in wetlands/ ponds,/ neighbourhood's open drainage or infiltration trenches and swales	

Table 5 - Benchmarks of the suggested measures

Measure codes	Focus	Project names
2-P-K	Water resource reservation	Singapore Active Beautiful Clean (ABC) waters
2-P-K	Wetland reservation	Hong Kong national wetlands park
3-R-I-K	Biotope Area Factor	Berlin Landscape Programme
3-P	Street design to reduce stormwater runoff	Portland 12th Avenue Green Street
4-R-I-P-K	Rainwater harvesting and recycling	City of Tucson - Rainwater Harvesting Ordinance
5-P	Adapted housing and neighbourhood design	Dordrecht project – BACA UK
K	Community Based Adaptation	TU Cottbus - ENDA Vietnam

One of the difficulties for implementation of this approach is the current inefficiencies of the planning system in HCMC, including overlapping duties of the planning departments, confusions within planning law, lack of an unified and sufficient planning database and lack of capacity among local authorities. Moreover, the lack of public awareness about the issue and public participation in the planning process could further hinder implementation. Therefore, in order to apply successfully the urban planning approach to urban flooding in HCMC, it also requires a strong will and strong desire to reform the existing urban management system. On the other hand, citizens are also required to be more active, knowledgeable and responsible in their contributions to building a sustainable future for the city.

Conclusions

The preceding paper has attempted to raise a discussion about the necessity to apply an urban planning approach to urban flooding in HCMC. It analyses the three key principles of this urban planning approach to urban flooding that can be applied to the city's context and outlines key measures that can be applied to the principles and objectives. However, to implement successfully the strategies, firstly, it requires strongly on the firm commitments from the government and the cooperation among different stakeholders and the society as a whole.

References

Burby, R. J., and May, P. J. (1998) 'Intergovernmental environmental planning: Addressing the commitment conundrum'. *Journal of Environmental Planning and Management*, 41(1), pp. 95–110.

General Statistic Office Vietnam (2010) *Population and population density in 2010 by province.*

Godschalk, D. R., Kaiser, E. J., & Berke, P. R. (1998) 'Integrating hazard mitigation and local land use planning' in Raymond Burby (Ed.), *Cooperating with nature: Confronting natural hazards with land use planning for sustainable communities*, Washington, DC: Joseph Henry/National Academy Press, pp. 85-118.

Ho, Long Phi (2010) 'The Need for an Integrated Strategy for Flood Management to Adapt with Climate Change in Ho Chi Minh City'. In proceedings: *Conference on Climate Change and Sustainable Urban Development in Vietnam.* Hanoi (Vietnam)

Ho, Long Phi (2011) *The challenges of urban flood management in HCMC.*

Johnson, Richard, Matt Watson, and Eleanor McOuat (2008) *The Way Forward for Natural Flood Management in Scotland.*

Le, Van Trung, and Ho, Tong Minh Dinh (2009) 'Monitoring Land Deformation Using Permanent Scatterer INSAR Techniques - case study: Ho Chi Minh City'. *7th FIG Regional Conference Spatial Data Serving People: Land Governance and the Environment – Building the Capacity* (pp. 19-22). Hanoi.

Nicholls, R.J., S. Hanson, C. Herweijer, N. Patmore, S Hallegatte, Jan Corfee-Morlot, Jean Chateau, and R. Muir Wood. (2007). *Ranking of the World's cities most exposed to coastal flooding today.*

Wendell Cox Consultancy. (2011) *Demographia World Urban Areas – World Agglomerations.*

World Meteorological Organisation (2008) *Urban flood risk management - A Tool for Integrated Flood Management.* Risk Management.

Steering Committee Flooding Control HCMC (2011) *Report about the mitigating urban flooding activities in 2010.*

Storch, H,, Schwartze, F. (2010) 'Spatial Planning as an Adaptation Strategy to Climate Change in Ho Chi Minh City, Vietnam'. In *Future megacities in balance conference.* Essen, Germany.

Tran, Thi Van, and Ha, Duong Xuan Bao. (2007) *Uban land cover change through development of imperviousness in HCMC.* Engineering.

Tran, Thi Van, and Ha, Duong Xuan Bao (2008) 'A study on urban development through land surface temperature by using remote sensing: in case of Ho Chi Minh City'. *VNU Journal of Science,* Earth Sciences, 24, 160-167.

White, Iain (2008) 'The absorbent city: urban form and flood risk management'. Proceedings of the *ICE – Urban Design and Planning 161,* no. 4, January 12th: 151-161. doi:10.1680/udap.2008.161.4.151.

World Meteorological Organisation (2008) *Urban flood risk management - A Tool for Integrated Flood Management.*

APPROACH TOWARDS SUSTAINABLE MANAGEMENT OF WATERSHED AREAS IN DRY CLIMATIC CONDITIONS. LIMA, PERU

Poblet Alegre, Rossana[1]

Abstract

According to the United Nations Environmental Programme (UNEP), water scarcity is one of the main global problems worldwide being only 3% of the water of the planet suitable for human consumption. At same time urbanisation processes are increasing being expected that by 2030, 85% of the world's population will be in developing countries creating new challenges regarding water, urbanisation and landscape. If we add to these facts the degradation of water sources and river basins, the non-integration of watershed management, water management and urban planning and the non-consideration of the hydrological cycle and alterations due to climatic phenomenon then the future scenarios for cities in dry climatic conditions are more uncertain. In this connection is Lima, Peruvian capital and second largest city in a desert. It faces water scarcity and dependency but the watershed management and the urban water cycle have not been considered yet into the urban planning process creating a critical unsustainable condition along its main catchment area. This paper is based in the author's Master thesis (Poblet 2011) which review ways to reorient unsustainable urban development through a Water Sensitive Urban Planning and Design approach.

Keywords: *Lima, Desert, Watershed, River, Urban Water Cycle, Landscape, Water Sensitive Urban Development, Ecological Infrastructure, Urban-Environmental Regeneration.*

---

1 *Institut für Landschaftsplanung und Ökologie / Universität Stuttgart. M.Sc. International Cooperation and Urban Development; specialisation in Sustainable Emergency Architecture. Technische Universität Darmstadt, Germany/ Universitat Internacional de Catalunya, Barcelona, Spain. MS in Urban Renewal, Lima, Peru. B.A. in Architecture, Universidad Ricardo Palma, Lima, Peru. email: rossana.poblet@ilpoe.uni-stuttgart.de*

Introduction

Lima, located in the South American Pacific desert coast, is the second largest megacity located in a desert after Cairo in Egypt. Similar conditions due to its desert natural environment and informal urban expansion characterise both cities however from the hydrological perspective the comparison is minimum because Cairo, with approximately 15 million inhabitants, has an average of 25mm of annual precipitation and an average river flow of 2830 m3/s in the Nile River, while Lima with around 9 million inhabitants, has an average of 9mm of annual precipitation and 10 m3/s of river flow in Rimac River (Sedapal, 2011). Consequently, the Nile River carries greater volumes of water that helps to irrigate valleys while providing water related services for most of the population in Egypt. Contrarily, the Rimac River, which is mainly a seasonal torrent of water due to its high pending and short length, depends on the seasonal rain, the melt of the Andean glaciers and the transfer of water from other basin in order to fulfil the water demands of those within its watershed. But in the last 60 years the population has grown in Lima from 645 000 in 1949 to 7 536 000 inhabitants in 2000, multiplying its population by 11 fold and increasing its surface area from 5000 Ha to 78000 Ha, almost 16 times more. This immense growth, which currently reaches around 9 million has consequently dramatically increased its water needs and dependency on Rimac River watershed, reason and witness of Lima's origin and development as main city in the country (*Figure 1*).

Figure 1: *Rimac River on its way through Lima to the Pacific Ocean.*
Source: Rossana Poblet

Located between the provinces of Huarochiri, Lima and Callao, Rimac River watershed is one of the most important territorial hydrological units in the country. It originates on the western side of the Andes Mountains over 5100 meters above sea level (masl), accumulates water through the rainfall of the highlands and runoff from melting glaciers and terminates at the Pacific Ocean in the province of Callao. The Rimac River is its main source of water and Lima depends on its water for human consumption, agricultural irrigation, industrial and mining activities and energy production. In spite its importance, Lima's urban expansion developed neglecting the Rimac River watershed and exhausting its resources; losing its historical memory, cultural landscape, open spaces and its relation with natural ecosystems. Additionally global pressures and the pursuit for economic development have postponed the integration of fundamental components of spatial planning, watershed management and water management in the city. This has created as consequence in the urban and rural watershed, rapid urbanisation processes, changes of land use, massive informal constructions, social exclusion, physical fragmentation, landscape degradation and over use of natural resources in a disconnected watershed. Throughout the time the previously fertile valleys of Lima have reduced dramatically; the Rimac River watershed and the natural connection between the city and its natural water sources has almost disappeared; the Rimac River itself has been transformed into a waste and wastewater channel and the poverty has increased for those inhabitants living along these neglected areas. Therefore in order to prevent and reverse unsustainable urban development processes for cities in dry climatic conditions and uncontrolled urban development like Lima, urban water paradigm shifts are needed in order to introduce a water sensitive urban development approach which considers a watershed holistic approach.

Watershed: an integral landscape vision

According to the Human Development's UN Programme, Inform Peru 2009, there are two main factors that hinder the development of the country: (1) social and economic gaps in the territory and the density of the State in relation with social welfare distribution and (2) the lack of consideration of watersheds as potential spatial areas for a sustainable human development.

The chapter, "A vision from the watersheds" (*Una vision desde las cuencas*) analyses the current conditions of the watersheds in Peru and emphasises the importance of watersheds from a political-administrative, socio-economic, environmental and physical point of view as part of a natural system.

Furthermore it proposes ways to integrate future spatial planning and land use with watersheds as organics and systemic territorial units organised around the hydrological cycle, with the ultimate aim of a sustainable human development (PNUD, 2010). But how to implement these sorts of approaches if, throughout history, humanity has been characterised by a multitude of predatory practices, and have tended to consider themselves apart from nature and ecosystems? And how do we suddenly pursue development focused on the hydrological cycle in a country that always neglected this aspect during the spatial planning of the territory?

In the case of Peru, occupation modes of the last century have been characterised by the "littoralisation of the country and concentration of activities in coastal areas resulting in a coastal hegemony, a loss of importance of the mountain areas and a predatory, colonial occupation of the jungle" (HDI 2009, 2010: 23). Such practices extended until the end of the 20th century and had decisive consequences in the occupation of the remaining urban areas, which were mainly reckless and informal resulting in the overuse of natural resources. Therefore, the population along the coast has increased from 1.8 million in 1940 to almost 15 million in 2007, passing from 28% to 55% of the national total. Due to this pervasive process of concentration which characterised the country during this time, the majority of these inhabitants are located in the metropolitan areas of Lima and Callao. But was the arid coastal land able to satisfy even the basic needs of the new residents? Analysis of the hydrologic composition of the country shows that there are three main hydrologic basins: the *Pacific* basin, which covers 21.7% of the territory; the *Amazon* basin, representing 74.5% of the territory; and the *Titicaca Lake* basin, covering 3.9% of the territory and located in the South East of the country. The average annual mass of surface water produced in the 3 basins is 780 000 MCM (million cubic meters) but 90% of the water goes to the Atlantic via the Amazon River and the remaining 10% has restricted use due to the seasonal regime of the waterways. Thus less than 2% of the country's water is located in the Pacific basin yet it supplies the needs of more than 60% of the total population; meanwhile, inefficient practices waste large amounts of drinkable water in a thirsty region.

Moreover, concerns arise due to frequent extreme meteorological events and unpredictable climate change effects over non-resilient cities. In fact, according to the Tyndall Centre for Climate Change Research, Peru is considered the third-most sensitive country when it comes to impacts of climate change on precipitation and water availability therefore one of the countries most strongly affected by climate change worldwide (Rosenberger,

2006). Considering that, and how Andean countries are already seriously affected by the melt of glaciers (Sedapal, 2011) is urgent to define new strategies of spatial planning which consider sustainable watershed and water management, and their interrelation (PNUD, 2010: 12). Therefore, there are strong reasons to take into consideration the hydrological reality in the urban planning contexts. Thus, the real challenges are related to an integral spatial planning and watershed and water management approach.

The importance of watershed-based spatial planning for sustainable urban development

Nowadays, there is a clear understanding that urban spatial planning developments influence natural system dynamics and that ecosystems influence the urban structures, as well too (Folch, 2003: 14). From a spatial planning point of view, a new approach towards sustainable development can be seen if we accept territorial functions as part of a system where socio-economic, cultural, geographic, environmental factors can develop in a holistic way. In this context, watershed scale is the most appropriate level for sustainable development. According to the UN Human Development's Inform Peru (HDIP), watersheds are "territorial units of geographical divisions defined by the nature around the water cycle" (PNUD, 2010: 7). The watershed coherence allows its consideration as an option for social, economic, cultural and physical integration. If the territory is organised around the water cycles "water collection, distribution and diverse applications becomes a source of life for people" (PNUD, 2010:7).

In spatial terms, a watershed is a topographically defined area of land where the water within flows to a common point. Within a watershed, surface and groundwater are generally connected as water flows across the landscape through waterways or vertically through the various layers of soil and substrate. This movement of water across and through the landscape connects an area hydrologically (UNEP, 2004). That understanding would help society to have a sustainable watershed-based spatial planning approach, adapting and organising the space with a less impact on natural systems, promoting holistic development and longer life of the watershed and the ecosystems they contains. According to PNUD (2010), watersheds fulfil four main functions: hydrologic, ecosystemic, environmental and socio-economic.

- *Hydrologic* because it is a natural water manager, catching, storing and running off water;
- *ecosystemic* because it sustains all the species that inhabit it;

- *environmental* because they are integral in maintenance of the soil, regulation of the water cycle and preservation of biodiversity, helping also to absorb the CO_2;
- and *socio-economic* because they provides water needed for life and for producing energy, various forms of production and economic activities (Agua para la vida, 2010:12).

But unfortunately, even though recognised in theory, in practice such value has not been reflected into practice, being ignored the important role watersheds serve, provoking exhaustion of resources in pursuit of "development" and dramatic levels of landscape degradation. Apart from the water quantity problems, the water quality shows that Rimac River is one of the most polluted in the country. According to the *Dirección General de Salud Ambiental* - DIGESA (General Direction of Environmental Health), there are pollutant agents all along water bodies. For instance, in the upper section, mainly rural, they are represented mainly by the mining industry (active and passive mining wastes), other industries and dumpsites and in the lower section, mainly urban, pollutants are represented by all kind of discharges water upstream plus domestic sewage, which combines all kind wastewaters. Therefore in order to reach an average standard for drinkable water, before the entrance to the city, the Rimac River is kept in the Atarjea water treatment plant (WTP) to pass through a very long and expensive process conducted by the water company, in order to produce drinking water for most of the population in Lima. Additionally, during the dry season (8 months) the river water is storaged in the Atarjea WTP for future drinking water production and supply for the city; thus removing the river and its water from the city's landscape and converting it into an open space used mainly as dumpsite and waste and wastewater channel.

Water sensitive urban planning and design approach for an integrated watershed-based spatial planning

During the last decade different concepts have appear focusing on watershed management and water management. In this context appears Integrated Watershed Management (IWM), which is the process of managing human activities and natural resources on a watershed basis. This approach allows protecting important water resources, while at the same time addressing critical issues such as the current and future impacts of rapid growth and climate change (UNEP, 2010). In this respect the most famous experience about watershed reclamation has been the International Building Exhibition (IBA) EM.Sc.her Park in the EM.Sc.her region (catchment area), Ruhr area in Germany. The EM.Sc.her was in the 80's a region passing a transitional process from an economy based on coal mining and heavy industry to a modern service-oriented economy. The site consisted of abandoned coal-mining and steel manufacturing sites, with a population of and around 2.4 million inhabitants and a density of 2.775 persons/km^2 - being Europe's most densely populated area, and fragmented by railway bodies and other infrastructural elements. Therefore IBA had the overall goal to promote urban development from a watershed perspective (Shaw, 2002). In this context a new approach to understand the watershed, the river and the landscape was needed in order to revitalise the highly urbanised area formerly called "*the sewage of the Ruhr*" (Salian and Anton, 2011). Hence, with the closure of the mining activities in the 80's started the opportunity for a regional transformation including the chance for a sustainable long-term restoration in the EM.Sc.her catchment area through the IBA EM.Sc.her Park. It focused mainly in an Integrated Regional Development (IRD) and the aim was the regeneration of the EM.Sc.her River in order to improve the ecology and the environment of the region showing possibilities to return lost habitats to nature rebuild ecological and scenic qualities through the EM.Sc.her landscape park and link the territory. Considering it we can see that this approach see watersheds as geographical units where entire watershed area can be part of an overall reclamation process through the water element. It also has shown that if well planned and articulated then it can have very positive results for upgrading areas, replacing former economies but preserving the urban memory. Additionally it implies a long term process and therefore need to have well defined strategies for short, medium and long term but also strong political, technological and planning approach. The success of the programme depend on the continuation of the strategy therefore it should be respected over the time and the policies should continue although governments change in order to make it sustainable. In the Lima context that would be difficult to achieve considering the socio-economic and physical fragmentation of the entire watershed, improvisation at political level and the lack of spatial planning at watershed level. At the same time we should consider that while in the EM.Sc.her watershed the mining activity was closing, in the Rimac watershed the mining activity is very active and productive and core of the Peruvian economy therefore it is important to consider the different context and momentums.

Another interesting concept is the Water Sensitive Urban Design (WSUD). It embraces the concept of integrated land and water management in a particular integrated urban water cycle management. The concept was developed as an Australian approach to water management, urban planning and urban design and was first referred to in various publications in the early

1990's (as summarised in Lloyd 2001) in the need to explore concepts and possible structural and non-structural practices in relation to urban water resource management. This has been paralleled by a wider international movement towards the concept of integrated land and water planning and management however the concept is mainly focusing on urban areas in temperate climates and related to sustainable storm water management. Therefore the concept as it is now for wet cities can't be applied in dry cities like Lima although some solutions can be implemented in the settlements in the wet watershed. The key WSUD principles includes: protect natural systems; protect water quality; integrate stormwater treatment into the landscape; reduce runoff peak flows from developments by minimizing impervious areas; add long-term value while minimising development costs and reduce potable water demand by using stormwater as a resource through capture and reuse for non-potable purposes (Hoyer et al, 2011). However there is a need to develop options for cities in dry climatic conditions, which can focus on watersheds considering the different water cycles that happen in these regions. Thus the concept could be considered for other climatic conditions where rainwater doesn't exist. According to Wong the WSUD concept has evolved from its early association with sustainable stormwater management to include a broader framework for integrating the holistic management of all urban water streams with the urban planning and urban design framework, resulting in a more sustainable management of urban water. Thus the main philosophy of the concept can be applied in any context although, in the case of Lima, the principles should be defined for arid climatic conditions for arid climatic conditions and considering existing urban water streams.

Possibilities and limitations for Rimac River watershed

After reviewing the different water sensitive approaches it is important to mention that in the case of Lima there are currently negative factors that difficult the integration and multidisciplinary approach. *Table 1* describes the main problems identified at different levels. It includes no political will mainly due to conflicts of interest at different levels where central and local governments have different political agendas and instead to work in a joint way exist a competition at different levels. Besides Lima has not a city vision that can help to orient the city. Moreover it doesn't exist yet a valid Master or Strategic plan because the last one ended in 2010 and the previous metropolitan administration didn't prioritise the future urban planning of the city, therefore now an important capital as Lima, almost megacity, has not yet any urban planning instrument that can guide its urban development from a watershed perspective and in a sustainable

Table 1- *Current negative conditions to recover Rimac River Watershed at Regional and Metropolitan level*

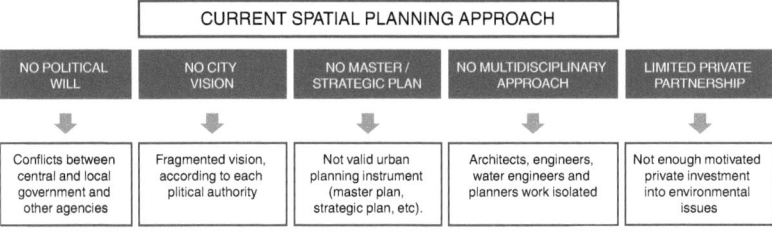

Source: Poblet, Rossana, 2011

way. Additionally there is not tradition of a multidisciplinary approach where professionals from different water and urban planning institutions get along together in a practical work. Finally economic investment in the environmental aspect is minimum. Local authorities invest mainly in partial solutions against flooding during rainy season, without to consider that most of these infrastructural man-made solutions worsen the natural flow of the river transferring problems to the lower part *(Figure 2)*. Therefore there is a need to create strategies in order to promote a more sustainable urban development considering the Rimac River as part of a geographical territorial unit called watershed and it should be the base for the future integrated watershed planning approach. That will allow taking into consideration that any kind of partial intervention will have an impact over the entire watershed.

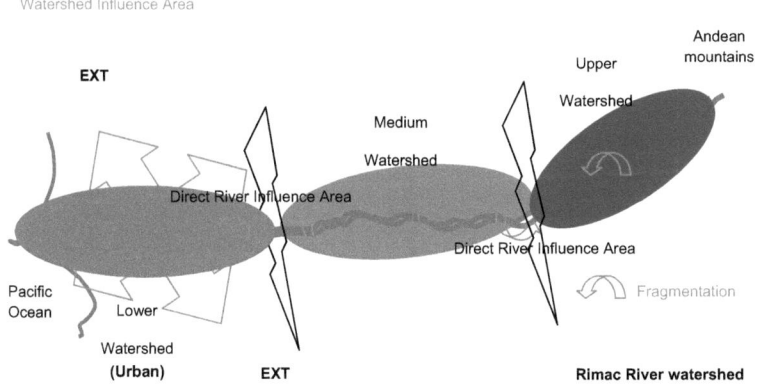

Figure 2. *Rimac River Watershed Fragmentation*
Source: Poblet, Rossana, 2011

A river reclamation process would allow in the upper part to protect ecosystems, mitigate climate change effects over catchments areas due to fast melting of glaciers, prevent losing fresh water defining solutions to catch the water for future uses, eliminate discharges of toxic materials by mining industry over the river, eradicate mining tailing from river banks in order to protect the river from toxic leaks, replace inefficient farm irrigation systems towards more effective and sustainable ones and promote the application of water sensitive urban design proposals applying the principles for sustainable stormwater management improving the water quantity and quality along the river. And in the mainly urban lower part a reclamation process would allow to recover natural and cultural heritage as part of the UNESCO world heritage site, facing the city to the river as part of the urban tissue, recognizing the river as main axis of the future ecological infrastructure network in Metropolitan Lima, sewing the urban tissue and integrating the river as open connector component of the system. Thus the city will gain open space and green areas reducing reckless occupation over this buffer zone in order to avoid disaster effects caused by seasonal events. Moreover new flora and fauna would develop and water quantity and quality would improve recovering the urban river during the entire year allowing its natural flow to the ocean giving possibilities for a change of perception from a sick river into a new "way of life".

Table 2 - *Future actions needed to recover Rimac River Watershed at Regional and Metropolitan level*

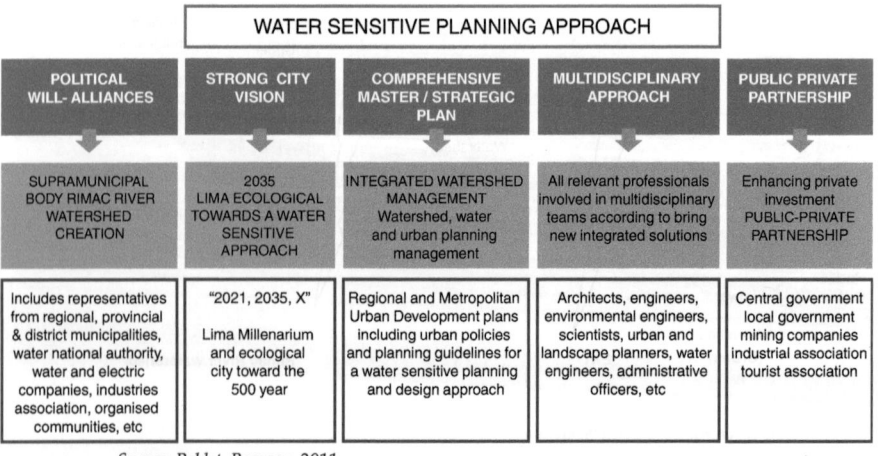

WATER SENSITIVE PLANNING APPROACH					
POLITICAL WILL- ALLIANCES	STRONG CITY VISION	COMPREHENSIVE MASTER / STRATEGIC PLAN	MULTIDISCIPLINARY APPROACH	PUBLIC PRIVATE PARTNERSHIP	
SUPRAMUNICIPAL BODY RIMAC RIVER WATERSHED CREATION	2035 LIMA ECOLOGICAL TOWARDS A WATER SENSITIVE APPROACH	INTEGRATED WATERSHED MANAGEMENT Watershed, water and urban planning management	All relevant professionals involved in multidisciplinary teams according to bring new integrated solutions	Enhancing private investment PUBLIC-PRIVATE PARTNERSHIP	
Includes representatives from regional, provincial & district municipalities, water national authority, water and electric companies, industries association, organised communities, etc	"2021, 2035, X" Lima Millenarium and ecological city toward the 500 year	Regional and Metropolitan Urban Development plans including urban policies and planning guidelines for a water sensitive planning and design approach	Architects, engineers, environmental engineers, scientists, urban and landscape planners, water engineers, administrative officers, etc	Central government local government mining companies industrial association tourist association	

Source: Poblet, Rossana, 2011

Further strategies at watershed level

Considering the different approaches studied previously, *Table 2* describes possible actions that should be taken into consideration for an integrated watershed management approach. It includes: *Political Will Alliances-Creation of a Supramunicipal body*, formed by the main political bodies influenced by the Rimac River watershed; *Strong City Vision* definition that consider Lima millennial origin and ecological indigenous principles and its multicultural development; *comprehensive Master/Strategic Plan* elaboration, which include water sensitive urban planning principles for an arid city like Lima; *Multidisciplinary approach* and inter-institutional alliances to work in a coordinated direction and *Public-Private Partnership* in order to get financial means for the process. Thus private industry, represented mainly by the mining, industrial and tourism activity, should be active part of the process.

In this respect, the current metropolitan administration is starting the development of the *Plan Regional de Desarrollo Concertado* (Regional Development Plan), which intends to include an integrated watershed management and water management approach *(Figure 3)* connected with the urban planning towards a future water sensitive urban development.

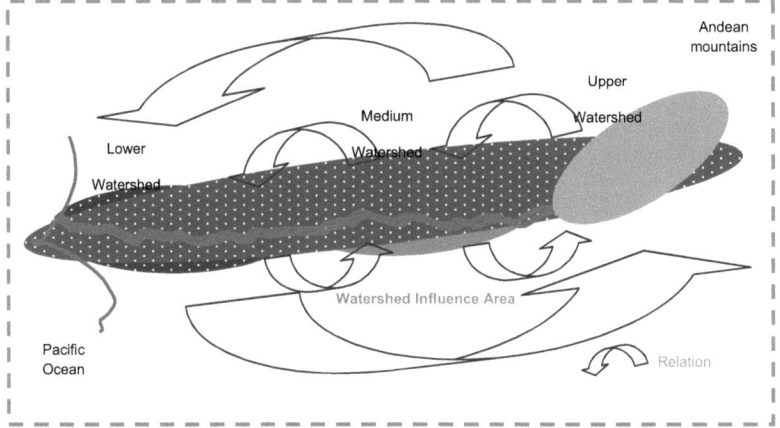

Figure 3. *New Integrated Rimac River Watershed Management. Source: Poblet, Rossana, 2011*

Conclusions

Watershed-based spatial planning and sustainable urban development are related and interconnected. However the lack of identification with the hydrological conditions has led to the unsustainable situation a megacity like Lima faces now. PNUD studies state that in a context like Peru, with so many gaps and unsustainable processes, there is a need to identify the importance of watersheds and the strong interrelation that exist between urban planning, watershed management and water management, especially considering the desert conditions. In this respect, the reclamation of the Rimac River watershed is urgent in order to reduce physical, economic and social fragmentation consolidated through years of inequalities along the entire watershed. Therefore there is a need to sew the rural/urban tissue along the Rimac River watershed bringing a new approach recognizing the river watershed as a territorial and hydrological unit and the river as connector element along the watershed that creates a physical link between the upper and lower watershed sections but also creates identity and a sense of belonging, being this element fundamental in order to preserve the landscape. Any future urban development should consider a water sensitive approach considering all the possible ways to incorporate and integrate the urban water cycle.

References

De Souza, J. (2011) 'Futuro del Agua en Lima y Callao', [Electronic], *First Roundtable Water and Climate change in Lima and Callao - LIWA* (Lima Water): Sustainable Water and Wastewater management in urban growth centres coping with climate change - Concepts for Metropolitan Lima (Perú) -. Lima: Available: http://www.limawater.de/en/documents.html?Menu=5 ' [12 Jul 2011]

Folch, R. C. (2003) *El Territorio como Sistema - Conceptos y herramientas de ordenación*. Barcelona, España: Diputación de Barcelona.

Hoyer, J., Dickhaut, W., Kronawritter, L., & Weber, B. (2011) *Water Sensitive Urban Design. Principles and Inspiration for Sustainable Stormwater Management in the City of the Future*. Hamburg: Jovis Verlag BmbH und hafenCity Universität Hamburg.

Poblet, R. (2011) *Approach towards Sustainable Management of Watershed areas in dry climate conditions*. Master Thesis Dissertation. Universitat International de Catalunya, Barcelona: UIC.

Programa de las Naciones Unidas para el Desarrollo - PNUD (2010) *Informe sobre Desarrollo Humano Perú 2009 - Por una densidad del Estado al servicio de la gente*. Lima: PNUD.

Programa de las Naciones Unidas para el Desarrollo - PNUD (2010) *Agua para Beber, Agua para Vivir*. Informe sobre Desarrollo Humano - Peru 2009 Cartilla II : 'Una visión desde las cuencas' Lima: PNUD.

Rosenberger, M. (2006) *Klimawandel in Peru - alle zwei Minuten ein Fußballfeld weniger*. Dokument 10909, Bonn: Konrad-Adenauer-Stiftung.

Salian, P, Anton, B. (2011) *The EM.Sc.her Region - the opportunities of economic transition for leapfrogging urban water management- A case study investigating the background of and the drivers for sustainable urban water management in the EM.Sc.her Region*. SWITCH - Managing Water for the City of the Future/WP 6.1.5/6 - WP 6.1.5/6 – Comparative analysis of enabling factors of sustainable urban water management. Bonn: ICLEI. [Online], Available: http://www.switchtraining.eu/fileadmin/template/projects/switch_training/files/Resources/Salian_2011_Leapfrogging_urban_water_management_for_economic_transition_-_Achievements_in_the_EM.Sc.her_Region.pdf [15 Nov 2011].

Shaw R. (2002) 'The International Building Exhibition (IBA) EM.Sc.her Park, *Germany: A Model for Sustainable Restructuring?* European Planning Studies, Routledge 10: 1, pp. 77 – 97.

United Nations Development Programme- UNDP (2010) *Regional Human Development Report for Latin America and the Caribbean 2010 - Acting on the future: breaking the intergenerational transmission of inequality*. Costa Rica: United Nations Development Programme Publications.

United Nations Environment Programme (2004) *Integrated Watershed Management - Ecohydrology & Phytotechnology - Manual*. Osaka: United Nations Publication.

Wong, T. (2007) *Water Sensitive Urban Design – the Journey Thus Far*. Australia. Australian Journal of Water Resources

STRATEGIC APPROACH TO PREVENT FUTURE DISASTERS IN RISK PRONE AREAS. CASE STUDY: LIMA'S HILLSIDES

Chong Chong, José Luis[1]

Abstract

The paper analyses the main effects of unplanned urban growth, in particular in risk-prone areas, and explores some possible strategies to tackle this critical problem. The research uses the slopes of the mountain chain surrounding the Lima metropolitan area as a case study, in order to extract lessons applicable to many cities in the global south. Despite the existing regulations which attempt to prevent informal occupation over vacant and public property, the problem of land grabbing persists. This situation can be explained by a number of factors, such as the lack of affordable housing for the poor, weak control mechanisms from public institutions, lack of community awareness, and land speculation. The problem is severe, particularly in light of Lima's seismic location. During its urban history the city has suffered several earthquakes, endangering informal settlements located in steep slopes. Current regulations have not prevented informal occupation, thus, it is necessary to develop more innovative solutions to avoid urban settlements in these areas. A strategic plan is needed in order to define long, middle and short term objectives that are responsive to current realities. In the short term, Urban Agriculture is proposed as an immediate strategy for avoiding informal occupation that also features additional benefits. However, it is essential to implement more integrated activities that ensure the sustainable development of the whole city, while reducing unnecessary risks.

Keywords: Disaster Risk Reduction, Informal Growth, Strategic Urban Planning, Sustainable Development, Urban Agriculture, Lima

---

[1] M.Sc. International Cooperation and Urban Development; specialisation in Sustainable Emergency Architecture. Technische Universität Darmstadt, Germany/ Universitat Internacional de Catalunya, Barcelona, Spain. M.Sc. in Renewable Energies, Sustainable Architecture and Urbanism, Universidad Internacional de Andalucía, Spain. Lic. in Architecture and Urbanism, Universidad Ricardo Palma, Lima, Peru. Urban Planning and Design Consultant. United Nations Human Settlements Programme (UN-Habitat). Nairobi, Kenya. email: jose.chong@unhabitat.org

Introduction

How does one avoid informal occupation of risk prone areas? This a pressing question in cities such, as Lima where a seismic movement can occur at any moment, with a large proportion of the population living in informal settlements without access to basic urban services and in poorly constructed buildings. This is also an important question for many cities facing similar challenges. Is it possible to avoid the grabbing of public land through legislation? Numerous experiences have demonstrated that control mechanisms are very weak at enforcing urban regulations.

With approximately nine million inhabitants, Lima has almost reached is geographic limits for expansion. This condition is exacerbated by population growth, and the difficulties poor populations face in accessing affordable housing. Without any other choice, these groups have settled in risky areas such as the steep slopes. The general hypothesis of this paper is that productive occupation of the risk-prone land can avoid informal growth. In this context, the paper presents an overview of the major challenges and proposes possible strategies that can help to prevent disasters in the future.

Disaster risk reduction

Disaster Risk Reduction (DRR) is an important topic for Urban Planning. Where and how to grow are the key questions of urban planning, and it is important for planners to develop mechanisms to steer the urban settlement process. Another important consideration relates to which urban planning instruments one can apply to address new informal settlements. The intensity and frequency of "natural" disasters have increased due to climate change and this is a factor of growing importance which must be taken into account (UN-HABITAT, 2011:1). Risk management has become an indispensable consideration that cities must incorporate into the urban planning process to account for issues such as rapid climate change, and adapting to survive in the face of increasing threats from disasters.

Disaster risks are related to existing conditions of the community or society and can lead to future losses. To minimise the consequences of a disaster it is important to assess the current situation and implement measures to mitigate its effects. Disaster Risk Management is used to deploy the different activities to prevent and reduce the consequences that the disaster risk has identified. To sum up, DRR is a comprehensive and systematic approach that takes into consideration disaster risk in order to identify the current situation, and uses Disaster Risk Management strategies to implement the necessary measures to lessen or avoid the effects of a disaster.

Non-formal occupation

> "Urban growth in the poorest countries would be synonymous with slum growth" (UN-HABITAT, 2008:30)

Informal settlements are growing very quickly, predominantly in the so-called least-developed and developing countries around the world. Generally, urban land is too expensive for new immigrants from rural areas to acquire legally so, in order to access employment opportunities, they create informal settlements in unoccupied land within the city or peri-urban areas. Many countries have regulations preventing the occupation of risk prone areas but squatters often settle in risk-prone areas despite urban regulations and safety considerations. Cities need to explore how to provide housing to recently arrived and low income populations, which poses a significant challenge for urban planners and municipal authorities. Urban growth is a very complex issue and there are many factors to consider, with each city having to explore possible solutions relevant to their own context to face this challenge.

A difficulty which arises for influencing the development of cities is that only a small percentage of the built environment is constructed by professionals such as architects and urban planners. In many countries, only the elite can afford to pay for the services of an architect and self-help housing emerges as the answer, particularly for low-income populations. They have managed to create their own communities and, over time, improve their living conditions. However, in seismic countries such as Peru, these practices are very dangerous. There is an urgent need for the local government to find ways to regulate and control the quality of the constructions in informal settlements in order to avoid future disasters.

Lima: living with risks

Peru is located in a seismic area. The country is on the South American plate opposite to the Nazca plate in the Pacific Ocean, which runs along the whole coast of South America from Chile to Panama in Central America. These plates are in constant collision, which generates seismic movements in Peru, and throughout Peruvian urban history city dwellers have suffered the consequences of natural disasters. One of the most destructive events took place in the coastal and mountain areas of North Central Peru in May

Figure 1: Informal settlements on the hillsides. Aerial View.
Source: Google Earth

1970, where an earthquake, measuring 7.7 on the Richter scale claimed approximately 70,000 lives and damaged or destroyed an estimated 186,000 buildings (Oliver-Smith, 1977:107). The entire town of Yungay was buried in the span of a few minutes. In August 2007, a large earthquake struck south of Lima (in the city of Pisco, 7.9 on the Ritchter scale) killing approximately 500 people and destroying approximately 76,000 houses. Although the epicentre of the earthquake was around 150 kilometres away from Lima, it nonetheless damaged buildings in the city centre.

Lima city is the Peruvian capital located on the central coast of the Pacific Ocean (Latitude: 12º2' S and Longitude: 77º1' O). It reaches an altitude of 101 meters above sea level and has a surface of approximately 2,670 km². The Peruvian Coast, including the region where the city of Lima is located, is predominately a desert region traversed by rivers flowing from the Andes to the Pacific Ocean, which laps its shores. In fact, Lima is the second biggest city in the world settled in a desert region, after Cairo. The arid landscape of the city is interrupted by the vegetative cover generated by the three river basins: Chillón (north), Rimac (middle) and Lurin (south).

Lima has suffered earthquakes throughout its urban history and each one of them has changed the physical morphology of the city. The last large earthquake in Lima was in 1974 when the city had approximately three million inhabitants. Since then the population has grown and the city has increased its surface over some risk-prone areas. According to the *Instituto Nacional de Defensa Civil* (INDECI), approximately 50,000 people would lose their life in an eight on the Richter scale earthquake in Lima with the majority of the casualties being among those populations living in vulnerable, informal areas.

The poor population has chosen to settle in dangerous areas – such as hillsides with steep slopes, river banks, flooding areas, and on soil with poor resistance (sand dunes) - due to the lack of other land for affordable housing. Self-help constructions increase the vulnerability of these populations, as housing and neighbourhoods are built without technical support to ensure the quality of the building (Miyashiro, 2009). Additionally, new informal settlements continue to grow over the slopes of the surrounding mountain chain of Lima. These populations are settled on high risk areas with landslides posing a genuine threat to these populations. For these reasons, it is imperative to recognise the importance of urban planning instruments to guide urban growth. That is why it is important to find innovative and creative mechanisms in order to accommodate population growth while avoiding major disasters.

Defining the problem(s)

"Sprawl happens when population growth and the physical expansion of a city are misaligned" (UN-HABITAT, 2008:10)

The target problem of this paper is non-formal occupation over risk prone areas in Lima (see *Table 1*). The focus of the research is the vacant public land over the slopes of the surrounding mountain chain. This occupation pattern has two relevant aspects, the first are the threats which exist for the people living on the slopes and the second is the informal occupation of public property. It has affected the living conditions of these populations for a long time because the national government does not legalise the tenure of the land in these risky areas. This is one of the reasons why the dwellers fail to invest in upgrading their houses. In addition, if an earthquake occurs, there will likely be a large number of casualties due to the poor construction conditions.

The national government has made efforts to provide social housing over the last few years through different programmes. Yet, they generally do not reach the poorest among the population. The housing deficit remains very high, with the population in Lima growing and the available urban land reducing. Lima is reaching its geographic limits to growth with the Pacific Ocean to the west and the Andes Mountains to the east serving as natural borders.

The last social housing project built by the national government was in the eighties. The following decade, the government stopped social housing programmes and the housing supply was then totally provided by the

Table 1 - Problem analysis diagram: informal occupation over risk prone areas.

Source: Chong, 2011

private sector, which focused on the middle and high-income population. As a consequence, there was/has been a deficit of housing, especially for low income groups, and by the end of the nineties the government launched programmes such as *MiVivienda*[2] and *Techo propio*[3] in an effort to reduce that deficit. For instance, *MiVivienda* is a public-private partnership where the national government subsidises a part of the total cost of the building, private banks manage the debt and private investors and constructors promote and build the housing.

However, the housing deficit continues, particularly for the poorest part of the population. The criticism of governmental housing programmes, such as *MiVivienda*, is that they reach only the middle-income population because the amount of money required to apply to this finance scheme is too high relative to the monthly income of the poor. As a consequence, the

---

2 The "Fondo hipotecario de Promoción a la vivienda- Fondo Mi vivienda" (FMV) was created in 1998 to face the housing deficit in Peru. It was a national government initiate with the private sector as a partner. The role of the state is only as a facilitator while the private sector is in charge of the construction. The banks and financial institutions qualify those who are creditworthy.

3 The National Government through the Ministry of Housing created the programme "Mi Lote" (2009) with the aim to provide plots for housing in state-owned land on behalf of disadvantaged families and to encourage the production of low-cost and quality housing, both in urban and rural areas. (Fondo Mi vivienda, 2011)

national government created new programmes such as *MiLote* in an effort to focus on the poorer populations; however, the number of houses built with this programme has been insufficient to solve the housing problems.

In this context, illegal constructions still continue to meet the housing demand, in spite of the regulations determining those areas which are not for residential purposes, such as those located on steep slopes. However, no mechanisms exist to enforce the law. The local governments have too few resources to maintain permanent control over these areas and they do not work in coordination with national institutions at speeds sufficient to deal with urbanisation rates.

Informal occupations are a very complex topic. There are many stakeholders involved, with many private interests relating to the high value of urban land. The majority who are affected by the policies are the poorest part of the population, and those who could lose their life if an earthquake occurs due to their poor living conditions. There are other factors that generate urban occupation over risk prone areas such as weak control mechanisms from public institutions, lack of a proper identification of the risks, community awareness, land speculation and availability of vacant land. Informal urban growth is a very difficult problem that requires structural and institutional changes and participation by all stakeholders to be solved. A multidimensional approach is necessary to solve the problem, requiring the implementation of long, middle and short term strategies. It is not only a physical problem, but is connected with social and economic issues, as well.

Exploring possible strategies

"The solution lies not so much in prescribing the relative density of urban areas as in good local governance that can guide urban development, and yield appropriate densities" (UNFPA, 2007:53)

The distribution of urban populations among cities is a crucial issue. Lima's urban settlement pattern has produced a segregated city where the poor population is located in the peri-urban and the vulnerable areas of the territory. Hence, is it feasible to stop urban expansion over risk prone areas? Are there other reasonable options for where the poorest populations can live? Most of the time, people settled in vulnerable areas are aware of the dangers of living in the river banks (flooding) or on the steep slopes (landslides); nevertheless it is the most affordable land available to live on. Living in these areas is not free or inexpensive, as the majority of the people think, due to the extra costs paid for settling there, which may be higher than for land offered in the consolidated urban area. One example is the provision of water, for which access in informal areas is often much expensive and less clean or reliable than in formal areas. For these reasons, the city administration should propose projects that can generate a better social balance and avoid segregation.

Table 2 - Long, middle and short term strategies

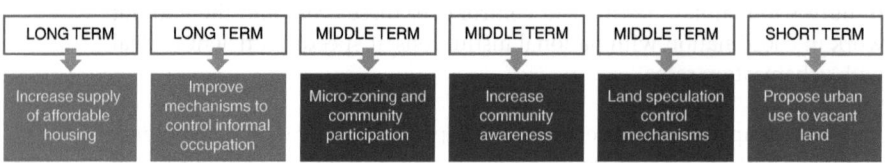

Source: Chong, 2011

It is fundamental to plan in advance to prevent future urban problems derived from rapid population growth. A good strategic plan allocates the limited resources in key urban projects related to the vision of the city and prepares its new developments. Lima needs a strategic plan to define its future urban image and to generate projects that manage its on-going construction. A strategic plan for Lima needs to have long, middle and short-term objectives (see *Table 2*) relating to priorities defined for the city in a participatory way. It is important to invite all stakeholders to assist in developing these priorities; public institutions, civil society and the private sector need to work together. One must account for the municipality's availability of resources in order to develop a strategic plan in accordance with the available budget; it is better to be realistic in the objectives and expected results of the plan, rather than create false expectations.

The best way to avoid disasters is to stay away from risky zones, however sometimes it is difficult to impede new settlements in these parts of the city. A possible strategy is to occupy the vacant land with productive activities that can generate income for the families, thereby avoiding its occupation in the short and middle term. It will prevent permanent occupation for housing purposes which is dangerous due to poor construction techniques employed. In addition, it is important to build capacity regarding the dangers of living in vulnerable areas. Community engagement would protect the land from future incursions. Nevertheless, in parallel, at the city level, it is important to increase opportunities to access social housing for the poorest part of the population. If not, the informal occupation process will continue.

Main strategy: Urban Agriculture

"In addition to providing crops and animals for consumption or income, urban farming contributes to environmental enhancement and disaster management" (Smit, Nasr, & Ratta, 2001:3).

Table 3 - Strategy: land occupation for productive purposes

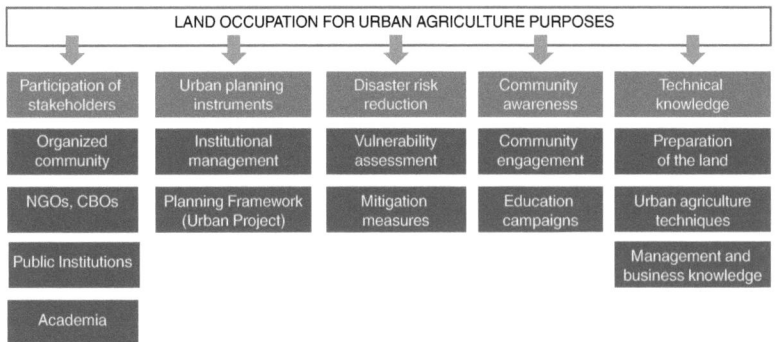

Source: Chong, 2011

Urban agriculture[4] can be seen as a short term solution (see *Table 3*) to the current informal urbanisation trend in the pilot project area. It is an economic activity that can solve many problems at the same time. It can provide food security, generate jobs, engage the community, stabilise the soil, improve the urban image, and mitigate effects of climate change. Yet, the construction of the terraces for urban agriculture requires technical specifications and techniques and particular technologies are necessary for the construction of retaining walls, irrigation and drainage systems, and paths. Pre-Hispanic cultural techniques were used traditionally to shape the land and examples of these *"andenes"* (agricultural terraces) can still be seen in the high mountains of Peru (*Figure 2*).

It is necessary to consider that agriculture in the city is different than that in rural areas. It has to be more efficient because water and soil is limited and there are waste-streams than can be incorporated in urban agriculture practices. Organic waste can be used as compost to fertilise the soil, and grey water, with the appropriate measures in place, can be used for irrigation.

---
4   *Urban Agriculture needs to be integrated with other strategies. The pilot project uses it as an immediate entry point.*

Figure 2: "Andenes", traditional terraced agricultural technique. Source: Jose Chong

The aim of the supplies produced has two main purposes: food security and as a source of income. Organic food has an added value that can generate revenue for the population. It is essential to build capacity in business and management, fortunately there are civil organisations existing in Lima South that have active urban agriculture programmes. With the support of Resource centres on Urban Agriculture and Food Security (RUAF), these groups have implemented successful models that can be replicated. The majority of participants in these programmes are women, for which urban agriculture is a way to generate a much-needed source of income.

The community can be the guardian of the vacant land; however they would need to feel they gain some benefits from it. The local government can help with the provision of basic infrastructure, and municipal tax reductions could be offered. These initiatives have to be implemented with social programmes that improve the economic situation of the dwellers. Community participation is a key component for the success of an urban project. It helps to discover the real necessities of a neighbourhood and can assure its sustainability in the long term. In sum, civil society needs to be engaged in the all the steps of the design of the proposed urban agriculture projects.

Conclusions

The paper above started with a very ambitious question: how to avoid informal growth in Lima's risk prone areas? This is a very complex topic that has multiple components and dimensions. Informal growth is a trend that is changing the landscape of our built environment, with each city having its own particular necessities. There is no unique answer. Proper urban density, for example, is an important factor in finding the solution of how the city may grow.

The hypothesis for this research was based on the idea that the barring off of land is the appropriate solution to avoid invasion of risk prone areas. During its development, the research found that this approach only addresses a small part of the multifaceted problem, including the deficit of affordable housing, weak mechanisms to control the occupation, and lack of community awareness. National Government programmes have reduced the housing deficit, but they have not reached the lowest part of the social pyramid. There are other structural problems in the public administration that need to be solved, such as the lack of coordination between state agencies.

To sum up, the paper broadly overviews the problem of informal occupation in Lima and describes a possible solution in the short term: utilise vacant land for productive purposes to avoid occupation by informal settlements. It will benefit inhabitants and prevent further expansion into these areas. However, it is necessary to combine this approach with long and middle term strategies that can solve other structural problems such as the lack of strategic urban planning or the housing deficit. If these problems are not solved, the occupation over the slopes will continue.

Lima is facing a big challenge: where and how to grow? This is the key question for the future. The answer should be to build with the participation of citizens and local authorities, based on a deep understanding of the territory and its urban history. This case study can be applied to other cities facing similar problems. To conclude, society needs to envision the kind of city it wants to live in and work towards realising this vision, with both feet on safe ground for all citizens.

References

Anyamba, T. (2011) 'Informal Urbanism in Nairobi'. *Built Environment*, 37 (1), p.57.

Fondo Mivivienda. (2011) *Mivivienda*. Retrieved June 13, 2011, [Online], Available: http://www.*mivivienda*.com.pe/portal/ [15 Nov 2011]

Miyashiro, J. (2009) *Vulnerabilidad físico territorial. Tarea de todos. ¿Responsabilidad de alguien?* DESCO.

Oliver-Smith, A. (1977, February) 'Traditional Agriculture, Central Places, and Postdisaster Urban Relocation in Peru'. *American Ethnologist*, 4 (1), pp.102-116.

Smit, J., Nasr, J., & Ratta, A. (2001) 'Urban Agriculture, Food Jobs and sustainable cities'. *Washington: the urban agriculture network*.

UNFPA (2007) *State of the world population 2007. Unleashing the potential of urban growth*. New York: UNFPA.

UN-HABITAT (2008) *State of the World's Cities 2010/2011. Bridging the Urban Divide*. Nairobi: Earthscan.

UN-HABITAT (2011) *Global Report on Human settlements 2011. Cities and Climate Change*. London: Earthscan.

INFRASTRUCTURE FOR DEVELOPMENT: URBAN INFRASTRUCTURE, *SHARI'AH*-COMPLIANT INVESTMENTS AND DEVELOPMENT BANK MEMBERSHIP

White, Alexander[1]

Abstract

This study addresses African, Asian and Islamic Development Bank (AfDB, AsDB and IDB) member countries with the question: does IDB membership - a possible proxy for Shari'ah-compliancy and collection of Islamic investments by the society - have an effect on private investment in urban infrastructure and the overall quality of infrastructure in the country? The paper investigates the link between infrastructure and urban development and the financing of infrastructure, with a focus on the growing participation of private and Islamic sources and the involvement of Multilateral Development Banks (MDBs).

A composite index of 11 components was developed for 67 members of the AfDB, AsDB and IDB to quantify and rank their attractiveness to private infrastructure investors. The factors of the index were those generally deemed important by private infrastructure investment funds. The results show the top 10 most attractive countries to be China, Botswana, Azerbaijan, India, Vanuatu, Algeria, Angola, Malaysia, Rwanda and the Solomon Islands. No link was found between IDB membership and the countries' attractiveness to private infrastructure investment or overall infrastructure quality. Instead, political stability and pro-business regulations were found to be the dominant factors influencing these outcomes.

Keywords: Islamic, Shari'ah, Finance, Urban, Infrastructure, Investment, Economics, Multilateral, African, Asian, Development Bank, Growth.

---

1 M.Sc. International Cooperation and Urban Development; specialisation in Development Economics. Technische Universität Darmstadt. Darmstadt, Germany/ Università degli Studi di Roma Tor Vergata, Rome, Italy. Bachelor of Science in Biological and Environmental Engineering. Cornell University, United States of America. Project Engineer. Toronto Terminals Railway Co. Ltd. Toronto, Ontario. Canada. email: alexander. white@ttrly.com

Introduction

Infrastructure acts as the arteries and veins of society and is necessary for a strong economy. This is true for nations and particularly so for the world's rapidly growing cities where the majority of people and highest concentrations of infrastructure exist. This paper investigates how urban infrastructure investment affects economic growth and may be affected by the growth in private and *Shari'ah*-compliant financing, particularly in AfDB, AsDB and IDB member countries. Eleven important factors are identified – measuring market size, financial health, government stability and the business environment – to determine the relative attractiveness of member countries to private infrastructure investors. Infrastructure fund managers are targeted for the large amounts of capital they wield and the factors are those that they refer to when specifying country selection strategies. Ultimately, the factors are combined to develop a multi-dimensional index which is used to rank and analyse the 67 AfDB, AsDB and/or IDB member countries in the study.

Infrastructure investment and urban development

Infrastructure constitutes the basic physical and organisational structures and facilities needed for the operation of society. The physical infrastructure most important to society includes those for energy, information transfer and communication, transport, water supply and sanitation. Many forms of infrastructure are described as non-rival public goods or natural monopolies (i.e. electrical distribution systems) which results in much of their provision coming from the public sector.

Infrastructure and economic growth

The role Infrastructure has in enabling people, goods, commodities, water, waste, energy and information to move efficiently results in infrastructure investment being a necessary factor for economic development. It influences individuals' activities, increases competitiveness and yields high social and economic returns (Economist, 2011). Infrastructure investment contributes to economic growth in a number of ways. Most fundamentally, infrastructure services - such as transport, water and electricity - are intermediate inputs to production and any reduction in their input costs raises the profitability of production and promotes increased output, income and employment. Other important ways in which infrastructure services increase labour productivity include: reduced commuting time, travel costs and travel stress and increased economies of scale through expanded market access.

Infrastructure and increased quality of life

Infrastructure investment can have many positive effects on society. For example, it includes the provision of: (i) electricity and gas to use electrical appliances, heat homes and cook food more cleanly and efficiently; (ii) roads, rail and urban mass transit to ease access to employment, markets, health and education services, *et cetera*; and (iii) clean water and sanitation. All these effects can lead to improved health outcomes and are only a few of the ways in which infrastructure investment can result in improved quality of life (Canning and Bennathan, 2000: 3).

Negative effects and alternative investments

Infrastructure analyses must account for negative effects of new infrastructure development as well as investigating alternative investments such as maintenance of existing infrastructure or investment in other sectors. So called crowding-out effects, whereby investment in infrastructure displaces private investment, could be direct (i.e. municipal rail transport displacing private taxi services) or indirect (i.e. increased taxes causing a reduction in the expected net rate of return to private capital).

Though less politically valuable, maintenance expenditures often prove to be more cost-effective investments than constructing new infrastructure. This results from increased efficiency and durability of public and private capital; for example, in Latin America, studies show a $3 (US dollar) increase in vehicle operating costs for each dollar not spent on road maintenance due to poor road conditions (Agénor and Moreno-Dodson, 2007: 412-413).

Spending must be distributed across sectors; for example, pro-health policies cannot rely entirely on infrastructure alone. To function properly, hospitals need access to roads, electricity, water, sanitation and waste disposal facilities as well as doctors, nurses, drugs and other supplies.

Urban infrastructure

With a world population near seven billion people, population growth is compounded by the even greater phenomenon of rural to urban migration resulting in rapid growth of cities around the globe. The world's urban population exceeded that of its rural population in approximately 2008 and this trend shows no signs of subsiding (UNPD, 2009: 2). Most of the world's cities lack the infrastructure necessary to achieve adequate economic opportunities and quality of life for their residents, new or old. Therefore the majority of future infrastructure investment must be in these areas.

Financing urban infrastructure development supply and demand

The global demand for infrastructure investment is enormous. The stated needs by MDBs, such as the World Bank, include estimates from $130 billion to $600 billion annually with much of this needed investment in Africa and Asia. For example, Pakistan's underperformance in the transport sector is stated to cost its economy $5 billion a year and the deficit in irrigation and other water infrastructure costs the economy around $70 billion annually. Estimates for the total annual infrastructure investment needed in Pakistan are stated to be $13.3 billion (AsDB, 2009: 2).

The existing supply of infrastructure finance falls far short of the demand described above. Both public and private equity and long-term debt are needed to finance new infrastructure and maintain existing stocks; however, the availability of neither debt nor equity is expected to meet the projected demand.

Approximately $280 billion was invested in infrastructure projects in the Asia and Pacific region between 1992 and 2003. Though a substantial sum, spent over 12 years it is around the projected expenditure needed *annually* in the region in the coming years. The $280 billion was composed of funding from the public sector (70%), private sector (22%) and Official Development Assistance (ODA) sources (8%) (AsDB, 2009: 3).

Private-sector participation

Infrastructure deficits globally have resulted in increased interest in private sector participation. Net private sector flows to emerging Asian markets increased from $259 billion in 2006 to $315 billion in 2007. These flows, however, are notoriously erratic and contracted sharply in response to the 2008 global financial crisis to $96 billion the following year (AsDB, 2009: 3).

Many countries have difficulty accessing private equity funding and few global funds have investment strategies that target poor regions. Therefore, although private investment may lead to higher overall capitalisation, the investment is often not drawn to those areas most in need.

Investments for infrastructure used by rich users are typically more attractive as user-fees are the typical means to recover project costs. These prices can generally only capture private benefits to those who directly use the service. If an infrastructure project has large positive effects on society as a whole, public sector intervention (i.e. through subsidies) may be needed to promote its development by the private sector.

Islamic finance

The Islamic financial sector is growing globally and many of the 67 countries included in this study are integral to that trend. Islamic finance is based on the relevant tenets of the Islamic legal system, *Shari'ah*, including: (i) interest (*riba*) is forbidden (*haram*) and may not be included in any transaction; (ii) uncertainty (*gharar*) is forbidden, though risk taking may be allowed if all terms and conditions are clear to all parties; (iii) transactions involving industries deemed unlawful by *Shari'ah* are forbidden (i.e. weapons, pornography); (iv) all parties in a transaction must share in the risks and rewards; and (v) a tangible asset must back each transaction (S&P, 2010: 61).

A particular area of growth for *Shari'ah*-compliant banking is infrastructure project finance and *sukuk* due to the requirement that transactions be backed by physical assets. *Sukuk* are analogous to bonds but do not yield a fixed rate of return. Instead, holders own a portion of the underlying assets with their returns tied to those generated by the assets.

Islamic capital for infrastructure

Oil and gas revenues, in particular, have resulted in great wealth for those in many Middle Eastern countries. Sovereign wealth funds in Gulf Cooperation Council (GCC) countries had an estimated value of $1.2 trillion in 2008, which represented a decrease of approximately $100 billion from 2007 due to investment losses but included an annual inflow of $300 billion from oil proceeds.

The high demand for infrastructure investment globally, including many of the countries studied, has led governments and firms to court Gulf investors to provide the necessary funds. Investors are increasingly interested in *Shari'ah*-compliant investment opportunities with estimates for their demand growing by up to 15% a year. More suitable investment products must exist to attract that capital to infrastructure investment in the region (AsDB, 2009: 4).

Islamic, African and Asian Development Banks' infrastructure investments

Since their inception, the AfDB, AsDB and IDB (see overview in *Table 1*, below) – along with the World Bank and its International Bank for Reconstruction and Development – have invested heavily in infrastructure. They continue to invest, betting on the critical link, described earlier in this paper, which infrastructure has with economic growth and poverty reduction.

The IDB provides financing and technical assistance for projects and enterprises among its members. It is authorised to accept and provide funds only in accordance with the principles of *Shari'ah* and proclaims itself at the forefront of promoting and supporting Islamic banking institutions. The largest contributors to the Bank in 2010 were Saudi Arabia, Libya, Iran, Egypt, Kuwait, Turkey, Qatar and the United Arab Emirates (IDB, 2011). The IDB's 2010 report *36 Years in the Service of Development* points out how poor infrastructure in many countries acts as an impediment to sustained economic growth and development, preventing them from reaping the benefits and opportunities brought by globalisation. Of all IDB project financing, as of the end of 2009, 15% went to water and sanitation projects alone (IDB, 2010: 12).

The IDB has worked in parallel with the AfDB and AsDB in many of the countries of study since the IDB's formation in 1975. All institutions have placed a particular emphasis on infrastructure investment yet only

Table 1: AfDB, AsDB & IDB Overview

	African Development Bank (AfDB)	Asian Development Bank (AsDB)	Islamic Development Bank (IDB)
Founding Year	1964	1966	1975
Headquarters	Abidjan, Cote d'Ivoire Relocated temporarily to Tunis, Tunisia in 2003	Manila, Philippines	Jeddah, Saudi Arabia
# Member Countries	53 Regional Member Countries (RMCs)	48 RMCs	56 Member Countries
	24 Non-RMCs	19 Non-RMCs	27 in AfDB, 13 in AsDB, 16 in neither*

* IDB countries in neither AsDB nor AfDB: Albania, Bahrain, Iran, Iraq, Jordan, Kuwait, Lebanon, Oman, Palestine, Qatar, Saudi Arabia, Suriname, Syria, Turkey, United Arab Emirates, Yemen

Sources: AfDB, AsDB, IDB, 2011

recently have they emphasised closer cooperation. In 2009 the AsDB and IDB created the $260 million Islamic Infrastructure Fund, L.P., a *Shari'ah*-compliant private equity fund for infrastructure projects in the thirteen member countries common to both institutions. Then in December 2010, the AfDB and IDB signed a memorandum of understanding to contribute equal parts into a $1 billion cooperative fund investing in projects located in the 27 countries belonging to both MDBs (Parker, 2010).

Analysis of Islamic Development Bank membership, attractiveness for private infrastructure investment and infrastructure quality

Given the preceding background, let us investigate the primary question of this paper: whether IDB membership of a country – a possible proxy for the importance of *Shari'ah*-compliancy within the society and the country's role as collector of Islamic investments from other IDB member countries – has an effect on the attractiveness of private investment in urban infrastructure and/or the overall quality of infrastructure in the country.

Index development methodology

All 117 AfDB, AsDB and IDB member countries were investigated yet only 67 countries had sufficient data for inclusion in the creation of the Z-score index. The methodology of a similar index outlined in Harischandra and Orr (2009: 5-8) – who used country-selection strategies of infrastructure funds and input from private infrastructure investors at pension and sovereign funds – was consulted to isolate eleven country-level factors, with widespread data availability, to represent the criteria important to private investors. The individual factors (outlined in *Table 2*, next page) were combined into a composite index using the Z-score method[2] to create a

---

2 *The Z-score index is a composite index used to measure economic and social well-being by organisations such as the World Bank and United Nations (UN). The Z-score is useful when combining variables with different distribution means and/or standard deviations. It indicates how far and in what direction a variable deviates from its distribution mean in units of the distribution's standard deviation.*

The Z-score for each variable is calculated using the following formula:

Z-score = (Variable – Mean) / Standard deviation

The Debt and Ease of doing business variables differ from the others in that lower values are considered better, therefore in the Z-score calculation the variable value was subtracted from the mean to account for this.

Table 2 - Overview of Criteria, Private Infrastructure Investment Attractiveness Index

Factor	Rational	Source
Population (total)	Total population, combined with GDP per capita, indicate overall market size and, roughly, the current demand for infrastructure	WDI, 2010
GDP per capita (current $)		WDI, Average 2007-2009
Population growth (annual %)	Growth in population and GDP indicate future demands for infrastructure services	WDI, 2010
GDP growth (annual %)		WDI, Average 2007-2009
Urban population growth (annual %)	Urbanisation creates demand for new and better infrastructure in and around cities	WDI, 2010
Present value of external debt (% of GNI)	Highly indebted countries face risks from high debt repayment costs and weakening of currency	WDI, Average 2007-2009
Current account balance (% of GDP)	Foreign trading positions and the extent of reserves indicate the availability of funds to meet investment needs and to fulfill government guarantees	WDI, Average 2007-2009
Total reserves (% of external debt)		WDI, Average 2007-2009
Foreign direct investment, net inflow (% of GDP)	FDI inflows indicate the relative attractiveness of countries to foreign investors and implicitly signal the strength of a country's economic and political fundamentals	WDI, Average 2007-2009
Ease of doing business rank (scale 1 to 181, best rank=1)	The attractiveness of regulatory environments to business. Sub-indicators: ease of starting a business, protecting investors, obtaining construction permits, paying taxes, employing workers, trading across borders, registering property, enforcing contracts, obtaining credit and closing a business	WDI, 2010
Political Stability & Absence of Violence/Terrorism Estimate (scale ~-2.5 to 2.5, higher=better)	Regime stability impacts economic fundamentals of a country and business risks of private investors	WGI, 2009
Additional Data Used in Analysis		
Total private sector infrastructure investment (total $)	Past level of private involvement in infrastructure projects; telecommunications, energy, transport, water and sanitation sectors.	WDI, Total 2007-2009
Quality of overall infrastructure index (scale 1 to 7, best score=7)	The Global Competitiveness Report 2011-2012 includes a measure of overall infrastructure quality; roads, rail, ports, air transport, electrical supply, telephony and available seat kilometers.	WEF, 2011

The Z-score index is constructed by aggregating the variables; weights are assigned as deemed appropriate. In this case the economic growth and Ease of doing business variables were multiplied by 1.5. (Harischandra, 2009)

Z-score index = Pop. + Pop. Growth + Urbanisation + (Gross Domestic Product) per capita + (1.5 × GDP growth) + Public debt to GDP + CAB (Current Account Balance) + Reserves + FDI (Foreign Direct Investment) + (1.5 × Ease of doing business) + Political Stability multidimensional ranking. All components were weighted equally with the exception of economic growth and the World Bank's *Ease of Doing Business* indicator. Seen to have greater significance to potential investors they were weighted more heavily (x1.5).

Results and analysis

The computed Z-scores, and the values of their underlying criteria, are listed in *Table 3*. The results show the 10 most attractive countries to private urban infrastructure investment are China, Botswana, Azerbaijan, India, Vanuatu, Algeria, Angola, Malaysia, Rwanda and the Solomon Islands.

Upon its creation the Z-score index was compared to actual World Bank data of total private infrastructure investment data from 2007-2009 and the World Economic Forum's quality of overall infrastructure index. A positive and statistically significant correlation was found between the Z-score index and actual private infrastructure investment. No correlation was found between the Z-score and overall infrastructure quality, as measured by the World Economic Forum (WEF) index.

No statistically significant correlation was found to exist between the computed Z-score index and: (i) IDB membership among AfDB members, (ii) IDB membership among AsDB members or (iii) IDB membership among all countries. The relationship between recorded private infrastructure investment from 2007-2009 and overall infrastructure quality in 2011 were also tested against IDB membership but neither were found to have a statistically significant correlation.

In addition, linear regression models were created comparing past recorded private infrastructure investment (2007-09) and current infrastructure quality with all the individual criteria used in developing the Z-score index (total population was excluded in the private infrastructure investment model). Private infrastructure investment was found to be most dependent on the factor related to political stability and violence but interestingly the correlation turned out to be negative. This result means that higher political stability related to lower rates of private investment in infrastructure during the period. Further investigation is needed but possible explanations could be that more politically stable countries have higher public-sector investment in infrastructure as well as greater longevity for the stock of infrastructure due to better maintenance and/or less harsh conditions. These factors would likely result in lower real, or perceived, need by the private sector to invest in infrastructure.

Table 3 - Relative attractiveness of countries to private urban infrastructure investment

Country	Overall Z-score Index	Rank	MDB Membership Year AfDB	z	IDB	Suttary Data Private Infrastructure Investment, Avg 2007-09 (million $)	Infrastructure Quality Score, 2011
China, People's Rep.	11.63	1	.	1986	.	16,804.80	4.21
Botswana	6.24	2	1972	.	.	165.86	4.56
Azerbaijan	4.94	3	.	1999	1992	869.90	4.35
India	4.86	4	.	1966	.	85,703.09	3.79
Vanuatu	4.71	5	.	1981	.	35.00	
Algeria	4.34	6	1964	.	1969	3,064.00	3.67
Angola	3.18	7	1981	.	.	932.00	2.09
Malaysia	3.13	8	.	1966	1969	2,242.50	5.67
Rwanda	3.12	9	1965	.	.	341.00	4.65
Solomon Islands	3.11	10	.	1973	.	-	
Kazakhstan	2.22	11	.	1994	1995	2,566.00	3.81
Zambia	1.83	12	1966	.	.	386.00	3.65
Mozambique	1.81	13	1976	.	1994	140.60	3.11
Nigeria	1.75	14	1964	.	1986	9,475.00	3.03
Mongolia	1.71	15	.	1991	.	-	2.48
Viet Nam	1.70	16	.	1966	.	2,040.98	3.08
Mauritius	1.60	17	1974	.	.	102.10	4.56
Uganda	1.59	18	1964	.	1974	2,451.80	3.57
Tanzania	1.41	19	1964	.	.	1,434.50	3.12
Gambia, The	1.34	20	1973	.	1974	35.00	4.57
Jordan	0.85	21	.	.	1969	2,900.00	5.04
Egypt, Arab Rep.	0.59	22	1964	.	1969	6,952.00	3.9
South Africa	0.28	23	1995	.	.	6,357.00	4.51
Ethiopia	0.21	24	1964	.	.	4.00	3.62
Cape Verde	-0.06	25	1976	.	.	27.70	3.64
Papua New Guinea	-0.33	26	.	1971	.	150.00	
Tunisia	-0.40	27	1964	.	1969	1,302.00	5
Djibouti	-0.54	28	1978	.	1978	396.00	
Mali	-0.55	29	1964	.	1969	583.00	3.59
Benin	-0.58	30	1964	.	1983	382.70	3.13
Indonesia	-0.67	31	.	1966	1969	12,599.70	3.86
Kyrgyz Republic	-0.76	32	.	1994	1992	80.00	3.66

Country							
Syria	-0.81	33	.	.	1972	307.70	4.06
Lao PDR	-0.88	34	.	1966	.	790.00	
Thailand	-0.97	35	.	1966	.	4,317.00	4.74
Burkina Faso	-1.06	36	1964	.	1974	390.60	2.73
Georgia	-1.09	37	.	2007	.	1,667.40	4.61
Albania	-1.46	38	.	.	1992	1,303.00	4.2
Kenya	-1.64	39	1964	.	.	2,570.80	3.89
Bangladesh	-1.90	40	.	1973	1974	2,842.53	2.82
Samoa	-1.91	41	.	1966	.	-	
Yemen	-1.95	42	.	.	1969	341.40	2.96
Sierra Leone	-2.02	43	1964	.	1972	72.38	
Maldives	-2.06	44	.	1978	1976	-	
Niger	-2.14	45	1964	.	1969	251.70	
Swaziland	-2.18	46	1971	.	.	48.30	4.2
Cambodia	-2.28	47	.	1966	.	1,129.60	4.05
Senegal	-2.53	48	1964	.	1969	1,519.00	3.63
Sao Tome and Principe	-2.54	49	1976	.	.	-	
Morocco	-2.63	50	1964	.	1969	1,999.00	4.29
Cameroon	-2.63	51	1964	.	1974	638.40	3.11
Armenia	-2.70	52	.	2005	.	1,310.80	4.04
Fiji	-2.84	53	.	1970	.	90.25	
Lebanon	-2.89	54	.	.	1969	-	2.49
Congo, Rep.	-3.06	55	1965	.	.	1,055.70	
Tonga	-3.07	56	.	1972	.	-	
Turkey	-3.10	57	.	.	1969	22,614.10	5.31
Pakistan	-3.61	58	.	1966	1996	10,877.80	3.47
Philippines	-3.76	59	.	1966	.	12,866.48	3.38
Liberia	-3.77	60	1964	.	.	63.30	
Togo	-3.89	61	1964	.	1997	234.00	
Sudan	-4.17	62	1994	.	1969	1,162.70	
Burundi	-4.33	63	1968	.	.	-	2.61
Sri Lanka	-4.56	64	.	1966	.	1,107.90	4.72
Seychelles	-5.15	65	1977	.	.	-	
Cote d'Ivoire	-5.41	66	1964	.	2001	872.40	3.57
Guinea-Bissau	-8.63	67	1975	.	1974	96.40	
Max	11.63	67.00	1995	2007	2001	85,703.09	5.67
Min	-8.63	1.00	1964	1966	1969	-	2.09
Average						3,478.58	3.81

Infrastructure quality correlated most significantly with the countries' Ease of Doing Business ranks. This implies that the more efficient and business-friendly countries' policies are relates to better infrastructure in the countries. It is not unsurprising that this relation exists but it is notable that it is the only significant factor in the model.

Conclusion

The analysis conducted shows that IDB membership, as a proxy for *Shari'ah*-compliancy of the investment, has no effect on the attractiveness of private investment in infrastructure, urban or otherwise, nor overall quality of infrastructure. Instead, political stability and business and investment friendly regulations, which promote competitiveness and efficiency, were found to correlate with private infrastructure investment and better quality infrastructure.

According to the World Bank, "governments are selected, monitored and replaced ... to effectively formulate and implement sound policies ... for the institutions that govern economic and social interactions" (World Bank, 2011). The evidence shows that policy-makers must account for the variety of channels, direct and indirect, through which their policies affect the development of infrastructure. Though spending on infrastructure directly has its merits, life is not so simple for policy-makers as to allow only that. Instead, this study found that creating an environment which enforces laws and protects property rights – where regulations are effective and efficient – will help develop a strong private sector and, in turn, promote infrastructure development, as well.

Acknowledgements

Thanks to my family and the assistance of my advisor: CATTELAN, Valentino – PhD. Post-Doctoral Research Fellow, Università degli Studi di Roma Tor Vergata. valentino.cattelan@uniroma2.it

References

Agénor, P.-R. and Moreno-Dodson, B. (2007) 'Public Infrastructure and Growth: New channels and policy implications', in Francese, M., Franco, D. and Giordano, R. (ed) *Public Expenditure*, Rome: Banca d'Italia, pp. 403 - 447.

African Development Bank (AfDB) (2011) *About us*, [Online], Available: http://www.afdb.org/en/about-us/ [15 Jun 2011].

Asian Development Bank (AsDB) (2009) *Report and Recommendation of the President to the Board of Directors: Proposed Equity Investment Islamic Infrastructure Fund*, L.P., April, Regional: Internal.

Asian Development Bank (AsDB) (2011) *About ADB*: Key Facts, [Online], Available: http://beta.adb.org/about/key-facts [15 Jun 2011].

Canning, D. and Bennathan. B. (2000) *Policy Research Working Paper 2390: The Social Rate of Return on Infrastructure Investments*, July, The World Bank: Policy Research Dissemination Centre.

Economist (2011) *Economics A–Z: Infrastructure*, [Online], Available: http://www.economist.com/research/economics/alphabetic.cfm?letter=I#infrastructure [15 Jun 2011].

Harischandra, K. and Orr, R.J. (2009) 'Private Infrastructure Investment Opportunities in *Islamic Countries'*, Stanford University, Working Paper #54, April, Stanford: Collaboratory for Research on Global Projects.

Islamic Development Bank (IDB), (2010) *36 Years in the Service of Development*, June, Jeddah: IDB, Economic Research and Policy Department.

Islamic Development Bank (IDB), (2011) *About IDB*, [Online], Available: http://www.isdb.org [15 Jun 2011].

Parker, M. (2010) 'IDB joins hands with AfDB to boost development' [online], *Arab News,* December, 26. Available from: http://arabnews.com/economy/islamicfinance/article223978.ece [15 June 2011]

Standard & Poor's (S&P), (2010) *Islamic Finance Outlook 2010: The Five Pillars of Islamic Finance*, [Online], Available: http://www.standardandpoors.com/about-sp/gcc/en/eu [30 Nov 2011].

United Nations, Population Division (UNPD), (2010) *World Urbanisation Prospects, the 2009 Revision: Highlights,* March, New York: Department of Economic and Social Affairs.

World Bank (2011) *What is Governance?,* [Online]. Available: info.worldbank.org/governance/wgi/ [15 Jun 2011].

World Development Indicators (WDI), (2007-2010) *World databank: World Development Indicators (WDI) & Global Development Finance (GDF)*, [Online], Available: databank.worldbank.org/ddp/home.do?Step=12&id=4&CNO=2 [15 Jun 2011].

World Governance Indicators (WGI), (2009) *The Worldwide Governance Indicators, 2010 Update: Political Stability and Absence of Violence/Terrorism*, [Online], World Bank, Available from: http://info.worldbank.org/governance/wgi/pdf/wgidataset.xls [15 Jun 2011].

World Economic Forum (WEF), (2011) *The Global Competitiveness Report 2011-2012: Rankings: 2.01 Quality of overall infrastructure*, [Online], Available: http://gcr.weforum.org/gcr2011/ [15 Jun 2011].

About The Authors

Britto Pólvora, Jacqueline; Ph.D- Brazil. Brazilian urban anthropologist working on poverty and urban exclusion. She obtained her university education in Porto Alegre (PUCRS, UFRGS), Brazil, and her Ph.D. in the U.S. from the University of Texas at Austin, where she specialised in African Diaspora Studies. Ms. Pólvora's research focuses on the disputes between "formal" and "informal" city in countries of the South hemisphere. Currently, she collaborates with the Graduate Programme in Social Sciences of the University of Cape Verde, teaching and researching

Chong Chong, José Luis- Peru. M.Sc. International Cooperation and Urban Development; specialisation in Sustainable Emergency Architecture. Technische Universität Darmstadt, Germany/ Universitat Internacional de Catalunya, Barcelona, Spain. M.Sc. in Renewable Energies, Sustainable Architecture and Urbanism, Universidad Internacional de Andalucía, Spain. Lic. in Architecture and Urbanism, Universidad Ricardo Palma, Lima, Peru. Urban Planning and Design Consultant. United Nations Human Settlements Programme (UN-Habitat). Nairobi, Kenya. email: jose.chong@unhabitat.org

Dijkgraaf, Cor- The Netherlands. Former director for 19 years of the Institute for Housing and Urban Development (IHS) in Rotterdam, Senior Advisor to the Board and former President of the Pacific Rim Council on Urban Development (PRCUD)

Guimaraes, Carolina- Brazil. M.Sc. International Cooperation and Urban Development, Technische Universität Darmstadt. Darmstadt, Germany. B.A. in Economics and Political Sciences, University of British Columbia, Vancouver, Canada. email: carguima@yahoo.com.br

Huynh, Le Hai Chau- Vietnam. M.Sc. International Cooperation and Urban Development; Technische Universität Darmstadt. Germany. B.A. of Architecture, Ho Chi Minh City University of Architecture, Ho Chi Minh City, Vietnam. email: huynhlechau@gmail.com

Lim, Hui Ling- Malaysia. M.Sc. International Cooperation and Urban Development; specialisation in Development Economics. Technische Universität Darmstadt, Darmstadt, Germany/ Università degli studi di Roma Tor Vergata, Rome, Italy (Hons) in European Studies, National University of Singapore, Singapore. International Programme Diploma, Sciences-Po, Paris, France. email: limhuiling.lim@gmail.com

Melgaço, Lorena- Brazil. M.Sc. International Cooperation and Urban Development; specialisation in Urbanism, Habitat and International Cooperation. Technische Universität Darmstadt, Germany/ Université Pierre-Mendès-France, Grenoble, France. M.arch Escola de Arquitetura, Universidade Federal de Minas Gerais, Brazil. email: melgaco.lorena@gmail.com

Orvañanos Murguía, Regina- Mexico. M.Sc. International Cooperation and Urban Development; specialisation in Urbanism, Habitat and International Cooperation. Technische Universität Darmstadt, Germany/ Université Pierre-Mendès-France, Grenoble, France. Lic. in Architecture, Instituto Tecnológico y de Estudios Superiores de Occidente, Guadalajara, Mexico. Consultant, Share the Road Programme: Non-Motorised Transport for East Africa. United Nations Environment Programme. Nairobi, Kenya. email: regina.orvananos@unep.org

Poblet Alegre, Rossana- Peru. Institute of Landscape Planning and Ecology (ILPOE), Stuttgart University, Germany. M.Sc. International Cooperation and Urban Development; specialisation in Sustainable Emergency Architecture, Technische Universität Darmstadt, Germany/ Universitat Internacional de Catalunya, Barcelona, Spain. M.Sc. Urban Renewal, Universidad Nacional de Ingeniería, Lima, Peru. B.A. in Architecture, Universidad Ricardo Palma, Lima, Peru. e-mail: rossana.poblet@ilpoe.uni-stuttgart.de; contact: http://www.ilpoe.uni-stuttgart.de/mitarbeiter/rp

Rahman, AKM Fazlur- Bangladesh. Planner, IMC Worldwide Ltd., M.Sc. International Cooperation and Urban Development; specialisation in Development Economics. Technische Universität Darmstadt, Darmstadt, Germany and Università degli studi di Roma Tor Vergata, Rome, Italy. Bachelor of Urban and Rural Planning, Khulna University, Pakistan. email: russel82@gmail.com

Rajasekharan, Rajesh- India M.Sc. International Cooperation and Urban Development; specialisation in Housing. Technische Universität Darmstadt/ Universitat Internacional de Catalunya. B.A. in Architecture, India.

Rapoport, Amos- United States of America. Distinguished Professor in the School of Architecture and Urban Planning at University of Wisconsin–Milwaukee, USA. Author of many books and articles, among them the book House, Form & Culture. One of the founders of the field of Environment-Behaviour Studies (EBS).

Saharan, Tara- India. PhD student, Amsterdam Institute of Social Science Research, University of Amsterdam, Amsterdam, The Netherlands. M.Sc. International Cooperation and Urban Development; specialisation in Urbanism, Habitat and International Cooperation. Technische Universität Darmstadt, Germany/ Université Pierre-Mendès-France, Grenoble, France. M.U.R.P. Masters in Urban and Rural Planning, Indian Institute of Technology, Roorkee, India. B.A. in Architecture, Manipal Academy of Higher Education, Manipal, India. email: tsaharan@gmail.com

Sanches Correa, Greta- Brazil. M.Sc. International Cooperation and Urban Development; specialisation in Sustainable Emergency Architecture. Technische Universität Darmstadt, Germany/ Universitat Internacional de Catalunya, Barcelona, Spain. B.A. in Architecture and Urban Planning, Universidade Estadual de Campinas, Campinas, Sao Paulo, Brazil.

Smith, Kari- United States of America. PhD student, University of Wisconsin, United States of America; research interests in human resilience in the context of urban interventions and public policy. M.Sc. International Cooperation and Urban Development; specialisation in Urbanism, Habitat and International Cooperation. Technische Universität Darmstadt, Germany/ Université Pierre-Mendès-France, Grenoble, France. Bachelor of Science in Business Administration, Northern Arizona University, United States of America. Professional experience in NGO administration. email: kari.smith@yahoo.com

Ugur, Lauren- South Africa. Lauren Ugur is a South African born urban development planner. She is currently undertaking doctoral research within the field of urban violence prevention and is employed as the programme manager for the Master of Science programme in International Cooperation and Urban Development at the TU Darmstadt. Lauren holds postgraduate degrees in both Tourism Management and Business Administration from Wits University in Johannesburg.

Ureña Chaves, Ana Eugenia- Costa Rica. M.Sc. International Cooperation and Urban Development; Technische Universität Darmstadt. Germany. Architecture and Urbanism, Instituto Tecnológico de Costa Rica, San José, Costa Rica

Varatanovic-Guso, Alma- Bosnia and Herzegovina M.Sc. International Cooperation and Urban Development; specialisation in Sustainable Emergency Architecture. Technische Universität Darmstadt, Germany/ Universitat Internacional de Catalunya, Barcelona, Spain. Architecture, Sarajevo University School of Architecture, Sarajevo, Bosnia and Serjegovina. email: varialma@gmail.com

White, Alexander- Canada. M.Sc. International Cooperation and Urban Development; specialisation in Development Economics. Technische Universität Darmstadt. Darmstadt, Germany/ Università degli Studi di Roma Tor Vergata, Rome, Italy. Bachelor of Science in Biological and Environmental Engineering. Cornell University, United States of America. Project Engineer. Toronto Terminals Railway Co. Ltd. Toronto, Ontario. Canada. email: alexander.white@ttrly.com

Xavier Pinto Coelho, Luana- Brazil. M.Sc. International Cooperation and Urban Development; specialisation in Urbanism, Habitat and International Cooperation. Technische Universität Darmstadt, Darmstadt, Germany/ Université Pierre-Mendès-France, Grenoble, France. Graduated in Law. Professor and researcher in Urbanism and Law, Belo Horizonte, Brazil. email: luanaop@yahoo.com.br

Yang, Guiqing- China. Professor in urban planning, deputy head of Urban Planning Department, Tongji University. Urban Planning Department, College of Architecture & Urban Planning. Tongji University, 1234 Siping Road, Shanghai, 200092. P.R.China